PIERRE GASSENDI

# SYNTHESE HISTORICAL LIBRARY

## TEXTS AND STUDIES IN THE HISTORY OF LOGIC AND PHILOSOPHY

VOLUME 30

BARRY BRUNDELL

*Saint Paul's National Seminary, Sydney, Australia*

# PIERRE GASSENDI

## *From Aristotelianism to a New Natural Philosophy*

D. REIDEL PUBLISHING COMPANY

A MEMBER OF THE KLUWER  ACADEMIC PUBLISHERS GROUP

DORDRECHT / BOSTON / LANCASTER / TOKYO

**Library of Congress Cataloging in Publication Data**

Brundell, Barry, 1939–
    Pierre Gassendi:From Aristotelianism to a new natural philosophy.

    (Synthese historical library; v. 30)
    Bibliography: p.
    Includes index.
    1.  Gassendi, Pierre, 1592–1655.  2.  Aristotle–Influence.  3.  Epicurus–
Influence.  I.  Title.  II.  Series.
B1887.B84    1987        194        86–31348
ISBN 90–277–2428–8

---

Published by D. Reidel Publishing Company,
P.O. Box 17, 3300 AA Dordrecht, Holland.

Sold and distributed in the U.S.A. and Canada
by Kluwer Academic Publishers,
101 Philip Drive, Assinippi Park, Norwell, MA 02061, U.S.A.

In all other countries, sold and distributed
by Kluwer Academic Publishers Group,
P.O. Box 322, 3300 AH Dordrecht, Holland.

Printed in The Netherlands

*To the memory of Nellie and Rupe, our parents.*

# CONTENTS

# PREFACE

Pierre Gassendi (1592-1655) lived in three civilizations in the span of one life-time: medieval ecclesiastic, Renaissance humanist and modern scientific; and he never cut himself loose from any of them. It is probably because he managed to be at home in all three that history has allocated to him a position somewhere on the fringe of the inner circle of genius in the seventeenth-century scientific revolution. While he was not a front-runner, Gassendi was nevertheless a pioneer of modern corpuscularianism and his influence on the development of empirical science was truly international.

It is precisely because Gassendi was a figure of the second rank - a significant but lesser luminary - that we need to examine his work closely, for the less famous contemporaries help us to explain what the great ones do. It might seem that Gassendi has received his share of attention from scholars, even though it is sometimes suggested otherwise. Several full-length monographs have been published in the past three decades, and there have been a number of articles in scholarly journals. Yet, despite the indisputable worth of these studies, the picture of Gassendi that has emerged from them has been partial and at times wide of the mark, so that the true story remains to be told. The reason for offering this study, therefore, is that it aims to present, if not the definitively true account, at least a "truer" account than has hitherto been given of the work of this well-known but inadequately understood architect of the mechanical philosophy. Philosopher of the more probable that he was, Gassendi would entirely approve of the aim; one hopes that he would also approve of the conclusions.

This book should be of interest to scholars and students of the history and philosophy of science, and to anyone who has an interest in the intellectual history of the seventeenth century. The focus of the study is Gassendi's design to bring about what amounted to a revolution in natural philosophy, and the cultural background of the late Renaissance and early modern era are presented as the context which goes far towards making his radical ambitions intelligible.

The aim has been to study Gassendi's work in the light of his own avowed goals. To achieve that aim a new effort has been made to interpret his almost completely neglected early manuscripts. Particular attention has been paid to some of the more significant developments and modifications of his philosophical positions that are to be discerned by comparing the

ix

contents of the manuscripts with the later, published version of his philosophy. The conclusions reached by these efforts amount to a new interpretation of Gassendi and his philosophy: Gassendi was not a philosopher who made Epicureanism respectable; nor was he a materialist *malgré lui*; nor was he a collaborator with Marin Mersenne in resisting a sceptical crisis. He was essentially an anti-Aristotelian promoter of Epicureanism, the philosophy which he deemed more suitable for the needs of the seventeenth century, both for supporting the Christian faith and for enabling philosophers to participate in and contribute to the progress of the new experimental and observational sciences.

I owe a debt of gratitude to many people. Many scholars have given generously of their time, advice and support; in particular I wish to thank Dr D.R. Oldroyd, Dr O.R. Bloch, Dr A.C. Crombie and Dr J.A. Schuster for their assistance, and my friends and former teachers in the School of History and Philosophy of Science in the University of New South Wales for providing a community of scholarship. I acknowledge with heartfelt thanks the help that I have received from library staffs in a number of places: at the University of New South Wales, the Bibliothèque Nationale, Paris, the Bibliothèque Municipale, Tours, the Bodleian Library, the University Library and Whipple Library, Cambridge. Finally, I thank my fellow-staff members and the students of St Paul's National Seminary, Sydney, who have given me the space to bring this project to its completion.

# INTRODUCTION

## Pierre Gassendi

Pierre Gassendi was born in a hill-top village named Champtercier, a few kilometres from Digne in Provence, on the 22nd January, 1592. His father Antoine and mother Françoise were worthy but undistinguished village folk. Gassendi received his early education in the humanities in Digne and Riez, and at the age of twelve years he received tonsure from the Bishop, a rite which signified admission to the clerical state. Thereafter, the rest of his formal education formed part of his training for ordination to the Catholic priesthood and was supervised by the Church authorities. He studied Aristotelian philosophy and Catholic theology for the next eight years (1604-1611) at the college of Aix-en-Provence.

Gassendi was a very gifted student. He held the chair of rhetoric at Digne from the age of sixteen, while still completing his own studies. In 1614 he received his doctorate in theology at Avignon, and was thereupon made *théologal*, or official diocesan teacher of theology and superintendent of theological education. When the chairs of theology and philosophy at Aix fell vacant in the year 1616 Gassendi became a candidate and won both chairs. He chose philosophy. In the same year he was ordained a priest.

For the next six years Gassendi occupied the chair of Aristotelian philosophy at Aix. But then his teaching came to an abrupt halt, for the Bishop elected at that time to bring in the Jesuits and to assign the college to their care. This change evidently constituted a tardy implementation of the reform of seminaries decreed by the Council of Trent.[1] As a consequence, Gassendi, along with the rest of the academic staff, found himself without a teaching post. The change was effected with some measure of inconvenience according to one account:

> The Jesuit fathers just came into the town and took over the school. He [Gassendi] was obliged to complete his course ... in the St Ivan quarter [where] his friend M. Bergamon, at that time a Canon of Aix, gave him a large room in his own house for the purpose. [2]

Thereafter, Gassendi had no further involvement in the scholastic system of education. Instead he devoted himself to what he termed "genuine" philosophy - of the kind that is cultivated by very few, in obscurity and silence.[3] His home base continued to be the Chapter of the Cathedral

1

ofDigne, of which he had been a member Canon since his student days. He was finally appointed provost of the Cathedral in 1634, after ten years of litigation, and this was to be his official ecclesiastical position throughout the remainder of his life.

Gassendi did not need much money: he lived a frugal, possibly even vegetarian[4] life-style, and could always depend on the devoted support of wealthy friends. Consequently, he was able to devote himself to a life of study and writing that was relatively free of interruptions.

In 1645 Gassendi reluctantly accepted the chair of mathematics at the Collège Royal upon the insistence of the patron of the Collège, the Cardinal of Lyons. Ill-health forced Gassendi to leave his chair and the city of Paris after the first academic year.

Gassendi died, fortified by the last rites of the Church, in the year 1655, at the age of sixty-three. He was carried off by a pulmonary infection, rendered fatal by a total of fourteen bleedings.

Gassendi was much acclaimed during his life, and his influence was considerable in the seventeenth century. Though his star faded thereafter, the town of Digne, with its 'boulevard Gassendi' and a statue of the philosopher in the main square, and the village of Champtercier, with its 'rue Gassendi', keep his memory alive to this day.[5]

### Manuscripts and published works

Gassendi's first publication was the *Exercitationes paradoxicae adversus Aristoteleos* Bk. 1 (1624).[6] A second book of the same work was ready for publication in 1624, but was withheld from publication until it appeared posthumously in the *Opera omnia* which was published in 1658.[7] After 1624 Gassendi's working life was predominantly devoted to the task of restoring the philosophy of Epicurus. He first mentioned his studies on Epicurean philosophy in his correspondence in a letter to his patron and friend Peiresc, written in 1626,[8] and the fruits of these studies began to appear as manuscript writings on the philosophy of Epicurus a couple of years later,[9] though none of these very early manuscripts seems to have been preserved.

In 1629 Gassendi made a new translation of Book X of the *Vitae philosophorum* of Diogenes Laertius, and this translation was published with notes at the head of a work entitled *Animadversiones in decimum librum Diogenis Laertii* (1649).[10] In 1631 Gassendi described in a letter to Peiresc[11] a first version of his Epicurean philosophy which was already more than half finished. It contained an apologia for Epicurus, the *De vita et moribus Epicuri*, an expanded version of which was published in 1647,[12] one book on Epicurean canonic (or logic), and more than two books of a projected four books of *physica*. The actual manuscripts of this 1631 version have not been preserved. Consequently Gassendi's first version of the *Pars logica* and the *Pars physica* of his Epicurean philosophy has entirely disappeared.

A copy of a second version of Gassendi's logic, composed in 1634 and written in several different hands, has been preserved as MS Carpentras 1832. This manuscript is held in the Bibliothèque Inguimbertine, in Carpentras, France; it contains three books of logic, and the first two chapters of the first book of the *Pars physica*. Most probably the manuscript belonged to the collection of Peiresc, Gassendi's patron, which collection is also held in the Bibliothèque Inguimbertine. Gassendi wrote more logic in 1636 and then began to write the *Pars physica*. The first manuscript of this latter section of his philosophy to be completed was what is now referred to as MS Tours 709, which contained an exposition in ten books of his basic Epicurean system of natural philosophy. There followed: MS Tours 710, which dealt with the Earth, atmospheric phenomena, stones, metals and plants; MS Tours 708, which treated living things - brute animals and human beings. The whole of the *Pars physica* was completed by the end of 1645.

All the "Tours" manuscripts are preserved in the Municipal Library of Tours. In the year 1716 they were bought by the Abbey of Marmoutier, which is close to Tours, in a sale held at Toulouse of manuscripts that belonged to the collection of a certain Constable of Lesdiguieres. During the French Revolution they were confiscated from the library of the Abbey and became the property of the municipality. They were preserved through the special efforts of the librarian during the German bombardment of Tours in 1940, when the Municipal Library and many very precious manuscripts of its collection were destroyed. Of the ten books that originally made up MS Tours 709, the last is conserved in the collection of Lord Ashburnham in the Biblioteca Laurentiana, Florence, where it is catalogued as MS Ashburnham 1239. This manuscript was among the twenty-three items that were stolen from the Municipal Library of Tours between 1842 and 1847, and were sold to Lord Ashburnham in 1847 by Libri.[13]

After completing the four "Tours" manuscripts, Gassendi published them in a very different form in the *Animadversiones* (1649), mentioned above. By that date Gassendi had also written a *Pars ethica*, which constituted the third volume of the *Animadversiones*. At an undeterminable date he also wrote a *Philosophiae Epicuri syntagma*, a small work which is a *précis* of the philosophy of Epicurus.[14]

Between 1649 and his death in 1655, Gassendi prepared a new series of manuscripts: MS Tours 706, from which MS Ashburnham 1237 has been detached (also by Libri, it is believed), and which constitutes a new version of all the manuscripts listed above, except MS Tours 707 and 708. MS Tours 706, 707 and 708 were published posthumously in the *Opera omnia* of 1658 under the title which is to be found at the head of MS Tours 706 in Gassendi's own handwriting: *"Syntagma philosophicum"*.[15] So far, mention has been made only of the anti-Aristotelian *Exercitationes* and the manuscript versions of Gassendi's Epicurean philosophy. However, Gassendi also published a variety of more occasional and non-systematic treatises. The relationship of these writings to the *Exercitationes* and the Epicurean project has been variously interpreted. On the one hand they have been considered as purely incidental and something of a distraction. On the other hand they have been seen as documents reflecting discussions and controversies that fundamentally determined the subsequent development of Gassendi's philosophy. In my judgment the relationship was usually a more symbiotic one, and I shall attempt to make that clear in the course of my analysis of Gassendi's manuscripts and published works.

The following, presented in chronological order, were the more occasional writings of Gassendi. In some ways the most striking is the record of Gassendi's astronomical observations, the *Commentarii de rebus caelestibus*, that was compiled during the period 1618 - 1655 and which bears witness to his constant and enthusiastic involvement in practical astronomy.[16] In 1629 Gassendi completed a treatise against Robert Fludd and the Rosicrucians entitled *Examen philosophiae Roberti Fluddi*, and written in response to a request from Gassendi's friend Marin Mersenne.[17] In the same year he wrote an epistolary treatise entitled *Parhelia sive soles quatuor spurii* in which he gave an explanation in terms of the corpuscular theory of light of a celestial phenomenon described by the Jesuit Father Scheiner.[18] In the year 1631 Gassendi wrote an account addressed to William Schickard of his observation of the transit of Mercury across the Sun predicted by Kepler. Gassendi's was the only accurately recorded observation of the event. The letter describing his observation is entitled *Mercurius in sole visus*.[19] In 1634, at the request of the author, Gassendi wrote a critique of the *De veritate* of Herbert of Cherbury who has often been called "the father of deism";[20] again Gassendi chose the epistolary form, and the letter was entitled *Ad librum Dedoardi Herberti Angli, de veritate*.[21] In his critique Gassendi employed the same sceptical techniques which he had previously used against the Aristotelians in the *Exercitationes*. In 1636 Gassendi wrote a letter to his friend and Pyrrhonist Gabriel Naudé, librarian of Cardinal Mazzarin, concerning the optical question of the differing apparent sizes of the Sun according to its position in the sky. This letter was followed by another in 1640 written to the Aristotelian Fortunato Liceti, and by two further letters in 1641, one to the Pyrrhonist Ismael Bouillard and the other to a young friend of Gassendi named John Capella. The series of letters was entitled *De apparente magnitudine solis humilis et sublimis*.[22] In 1639 Gassendi wrote a locally much-acclaimed biography of his friend and patron Peiresc who had died in 1637.[23] Gassendi wrote this biography at the urging of Gabriel Naudé.[24]

In 1640 Gassendi wrote a treatise in the form of two letters to a learned Parisian friend, Pierre du Puy, concerning the causes of projectile motion. It was a treatise on the mechanics of Galileo, as expounded in the *Discorsi e dimostrazioni* ... (1638). It included Gassendi's theory on the causes of motion, descriptions of his own experiments, and the implications for the Copernican debate. The treatise was published in 1642 under the title *De motu impresso a motore translato epistolae duae*.[25] In 1643 Gassendi wrote a third letter on these subjects to Joseph Galtier, an eminent and learned friend and former teacher, in which Gassendi replied to the criticism of Galtier's other pupil, Jean-Baptist Morin, directed against the two earlier letters of Gassendi. All three letters were published together in the *Opera omnia* under the title *De motu impresso a motore translato*.[26]

In 1642 and 1645, Gassendi wrote another series of three letters on Galileo's mechanics, this time to the Jesuit Father Pierre de Cazrée, rector of the College of Metz. In these letters Gassendi replied to Cazrée's Aristotelian objections against Galileo's analysis of the acceleration of falling bodies as presented in the *Discorsi*. Gassendi's letters are entitled *De proportione qua gravia decidentia accelerantur*.[27]

In 1641 Gassendi became embroiled, at the request of Mersenne as in the controversy with Fludd, in a dispute with Descartes. Mersenne sent a copy of Descartes' *Meditations* to Gassendi and asked him "on account of their friendship"[28] to write to Descartes giving an account of his objections. Gassendi's Pyrrhonist objections and Descartes' replies were published by Descartes as the "Fifth objections" and by Gassendi's friend, Samuel Sorbière, with Gassendi's authorisation, under the title *Disquisitio metaphysica*.[29]

Gassendi published the *Oratio inauguralis* or inaugural lecture which he delivered when he took up the Chair of mathematics at the Collège Royal in 1645. He called the lecture a "hymn to the Creator of the world", and presented himself as a Christian Plato explaining the reasons why he considered that the Creator was a geometer.[30] Gassendi also published his *Institutio astronomica*, or notes for the course of lectures on astronomy which he gave at the Collège Royal.[31] In addition, he wrote a life of Tycho Brahe in 1653, which he followed with a much briefer life of Copernicus, written at the request of his friend John Capella. Again at the request of Capella, he wrote brief lives of Peurbach and his pupil Johann Müller or Regiomontanus in order to provide "a reasonably good account of the beginnings of the restoration of astronomy from Peurbach to Tycho."[32] All these biographies were published in 1654 in one volume which was given the short title *Tychonis Brahei vita*.[33]

### Bibliographical survey

It is only since the 1950s that it has been generally accepted as the golden rule of historiography of science that the past is to be understood in the terms of its own historical context. It is not surprising, then, that in studies of Pierre Gassendi which were published in the nineteenth and early twentieth centuries scholars often paid scant attention to the network of beliefs, presuppositions and goals which determined the course of the intellectual development of their subject, so that generally speaking these earlier studies did not measure up to our standards of contextual and social history of science.

Scholars have already pointed out the limitations of a number of the earlier studies, judged according to our contemporary historiographical canons. For instance, in the opening pages of his study on Gassendi entitled *Scetticismo ed empirismo* which was published in 1961,[34] Tullio Gregory has stressed the fact that it is common for authors to be preoccupied with the task of reconstructing a complete philosophical system from Gassendi's writings. Olivier Bloch, in his *La philosophie de Gassendi* published in 1971,[35] re-echoed the criticism, stating that a number of works have been "vitiated" by a "systematic postulate".[36] According to this systematic postulate, the most significant feature of Gassendi's work was his alleged attempt to provide a thoroughly ordered treatment of all philosophical disciplines. The criticism is justified, for the principal defect of a number of studies of the late nineteenth and early twentieth centuries is that their authors attempted to provide a synthesis of Gassendi's philosophical doctrine or some part thereof, and in so doing, concentrated exclusively on the *Syntagma philosophicum*,[37] or the first two volumes of the six-volume *Opera omnia*. They neglected the non-systematic and more occasional writings including the *Exercitationes*, the writings against the contemporary authors, Fludd, Descartes and Herbert of Cherbury, also Gassendi's scientific writings and voluminous correspondence. Consequently, these authors attempted to study Gassendi in isolation from the people with whom he was in continual dialogue, the developments to which he responded and the problems to which he offered solutions. Furthermore, they largely neglected his work as polemicist, historian, classicist, astronomer and experimenter.

A prime early example of such a non-contextualist study such as has just been described is *La philosophie de Gassendi* of P.-Félix Thomas, published in 1889.[38] Not only did Thomas fail to study Gassendi's philosophy in relation to his times but, more remarkably, showed a tendency to interpret it as an early expression of nineteenth-century idealism. Furthermore, he referred to Gassendi's occasional writings as *"accidents"* and *"hors-d'oeuvre"* which (fortunately) "did not distract" their author from his grand design of compiling the *Syntagma*. Thus, while it is true that the *Syntagma philosophicum* was Gassendi's *magnum opus* (a fact which, it should be said, Gregory did not stress sufficiently in his criticism of Thomas),[39] nevertheless, by underrating the significance of the occasional writings, Thomas precluded serious consideration of any possible evidence contained in them of development in Gassendi's thought and expression which might have been stimulated by his discussions with other scholars.

Other studies published since the close of the nineteenth century which often examine Gassendi's philosophy in isolation from its context, and consequently may be judged unsatisfactory by modern historiographical standards, are the lengthy sections which are devoted to Gassendi by G. Sortais in his history of modern philosophy;[40] *The philosophy of Gassendi* of G.S. Brett published in 1908;[41] the *Pierre Gassendis Metaphysik* by P. Pendzig also published in 1908;[42] the papers published on the occasion of the tricentenary of Gassendi's death in the *Synthèse* collection,[43] and in the Acts of the congress for the tricentenary.[44]

A number of studies have been devoted to Gassendi's scepticism. In 1893 F.X. Kiefl published *Pierre Gassendis Erkenntnisstheorie* a predominantly analytical study of Gassendi's "theory of knowledge".[45] This was followed by a short monograph in 1898 written in Latin by Henri Berr and entitled *An jure inter scepticos Gassendus numeratus fuerit*[46] in which the character of Gassendi's scepticism was discussed. The *Pierre Gassendi* of G. Hess, published in 1930,[47] examined Gassendi's scepticism against the background of the humanist movement. Then, in 1943, René Pintard published his *Le libertinage érudit* a study of Gassendi's scepticism which was composed in the form of history writing described by the author himself as "moral history".[48]

In this work, Gassendi's writings were examined in their alleged 'moral context', and it was claimed that the dominant influences on Gassendi's philosophy were moral. Following the publication of Pintard's work, much discussion arose on the question of Gassendi's sincerity, and on whether he was a libertine philosopher posing as a devout Churchman or an honest liberal philosopher who allowed his freedom to be suffocated in his later writings by a philosophy of concession, conciliation and calculation. Pintard took the unpopular view that Gassendi was, to some degree, a two-timer, and he further defended his thesis against its critics in an article entitled "Modernisme, humanisme, libertinage" which was published in 1948.[49] One finds echoes of this controversy in studies of Gassendi's work years after the argument surrounding Pintard's thesis had died down; this is particularly true of the work of B. Rochot. I believe, however, that a closer examination of Gassendi's goals in relation to his intellectual and cultural context reveals that much of the discussion was based on a series of misinterpretations. This should become apparent in the arguments that I develop in the following pages.

The most significant treatment of the subject of Gassendi's scepticism, at least for this thesis, is that which has been given by R.H. Popkin in articles and in his history of scepticism, all of which appeared during the 1960s.[50] Popkin presented a new version of what has been called "the 'general crisis of the seventeenth century' thesis",[51] claiming that the alleged crisis was essentially epistemological; a "sceptical crisis". Accordingly, Popkin maintained, Gassendi advocated a mitigated scepticism which was specifically intended to be a response to the supposed sceptical crisis. In a later chapter[52] I give reasons why I consider that Popkin's interpretation of Gassendi's scepticism cannot be upheld.

In terms of literary output B. Rochot has been the most important specialist in Gassendi studies. Rochot traced the development of Gassendi's interests in Epicureanism in an historical account of Gassendi's labours entitled *Les travaux de Gassendi sur Epicure et sur l'atomisme*, published in 1944.[53] But he is best known for his work in editing some of Gassendi's occasional writings, *viz*, some of Gassendi's letters,[54] the *Exercitationes*,[55] and Gassendi's critique of Descartes' *Meditations*.[56] Rochot also wrote a number of articles that are replete with biographical details, the most noteworthy being the portrait of Gassendi, his life and his work, which was published in the *Synthèse* collection.[57] In other articles, Rochot dealt with Gassendi's views on mathematics;[58] his anti-Cartesianism;[59] his formulation of the principle of inertia;[60] his writings on experiments with the barometer;[61] and on space and time.[62] Rochot's historiographical approach now makes a somewhat dated impression, as he tended to evaluate Gassendi's work anachronistically by the standard of subsequently accepted theories, thereby presenting Gassendi as a precursor of later developments.

Gassendi emphasised the need for the natural philosopher to be an experimenter, warning that it was not enough to contemplate nature in a lazy, superficial manner, but that one must actively search out the truth, probing and exploring the natural world.[63] On his part, Gassendi probed and explored nature in a great variety of ways, but especially by astronomical observation.

Gassendi's astronomical work has been described in a number of publications written by Pierre Humbert between the years 1931 and 1953.[64] In Humbert's assessment, Gassendi was one of the most accomplished astronomers in the period between 1610, when Galileo first turned the telescope on the heavens, and 1667, when Azout discovered the micrometer. Gassendi also did experiments with bodies in motion, and his writings on them have received a measure of attention from A.G. Debus,[65] P.E. Ariotti,[66] P.A. Pav[67] and J.T. Clark.[68] The article of J.T. Clark might well be considered the most illuminating of the latter articles, for the author argued that there was a link between the following aspects of and events in Gassendi's intellectual development: his anti-Aristotelianism, his Epicureanism, his meeting with Isaac Beeckman in 1629, his interest in Galileo's writings, and his debate with Pierre de Cazrée. Clark concentrated in his discussion on the alleged development of Gassendi's exposition of the principle of inertia. I have come to similar conclusions from a more wide-ranging consideration of Gassendi's work, and I shall be presenting my conclusions at length in the chapters that follow.

Articles such as those that have been referred to in the foregoing paragraphs can offer only limited insights into a philosopher's mentality and activities. More systematic and comprehensive studies are required in order to 'situate' the subject and his concerns and projects in their intellectual and social context. Two particularly noteworthy studies of this kind have been published in the last thirty years. Both have already been referred to: the first is Tullio Gregory's *Scetticismo ed empirismo. Studio su Gassendi* (1961), and the second is Olivier René Bloch's *La philosophie de Gassendi. Nominalisme, matérialisme et métaphysique* (1971).

Gregory was one of the scholars who reacted strongly to the influence of the "systematic postulate" in studies of Gassendi's philosophy and to the consequent lack of reference in such studies to the historical context in which Gassendi worked. At the same time he offered an analysis of what he considered to be the "fundamental structures" of Gassendi's thought in relation to the problems and discussions of his age.

Gregory described Gassendi's philosophy as a humanist re-discovery of an ancient philosophical tradition that is not to be reduced to a simple continuation of scholastic Aristotelianism. Gassendi made experience the way to knowledge and progress in knowledge. He rejected the metaphysical pretentions of rationalism in favour of a more limited but more 'useful' and more 'human' way of philosophising: the phenomenological description of 'what is', together with a recognition of the provisional nature of the solutions arrived at by human reasoning.

In the light of these "fundamental structures" of Gassendi's philosophy - empiricism and scepticism or the hypothetical philosophy - Gregory examined the reasons for Gassendi's opposition to the Aristotelians, to Robert Fludd's neo-Platonist and magical philosophy of nature, Herbert of Cherbury's neo-Platonism, and to the metaphysics of Descartes. In all cases, Gregory maintained, the reason was essentially the same: Gassendi worked to achieve the separation of "physics" and (religious) metaphysics. He considered that science and faith were concerned with two distinct kinds of truth, one human and hypothetical, the other divine and absolute, and that confusion could be avoided only by the clear separation of the two. Matters of faith were not to be treated as matters of the natural world: they belonged to a different order of knowledge based on different principles and required a different methodology.

Thus Gregory saw Gassendi's philosophy as a break from the medieval, 'pyramid' concept of knowledge in which each science or branch of science was co-ordinated with every other and subordinated to higher sciences. At the apex of the pyramid was metaphysics, the *"scientia scientiarum"*, the most noble science because the most distant from the world of becoming. In place of the 'pyramid' concept, Gassendi, according to Gregory, worked with a non-unitary, non-subordinationist concept which allowed autonomy to each sphere of knowledge and did not attribute a minority status to the empirical sciences.

Gregory considered that the aforesaid distinction of "orders" - of nature and supernature, reason and faith, free philosophical research and unconditional allegiance to religious authority - was the most significant aspect of Gassendi's philosophy. It permitted the co-existence of mechanistic physics and finalist metaphysics; of a theory of life as local motion of atoms and a theory of the soul as the form of the body; of a natural ethics based on the pleasure principle and a Christian ethics of salvation and grace. Gregory wrote:

> Anyone who wants to place these solutions in opposition, as though each must necessarily exclude the other, forgets one of the principal characteristics of the author and of the period: the awareness of the limits of all human knowledge, and hence the possibility of the co-existence of diverse solutions.[69]

Never was there such a conviction as in the seventeenth century, Gregory further asserted, that truth is not of one order or type alone, but that there are many orders or types of truth just as there are many orders of reality. Consequently, in the opinion of Gregory, one can glimpse already in Gassendi's work in the first half of the seventeenth century the coming crisis of the European mind.

I believe that Gregory's interpretation might be found useful as a description of the relationships of Gassendi's work to medieval scholasticism and later modern philosophy. Gassendi might be suitably described, following Gregory, as an example of a post-scholastic and early modern philosopher. One might also agree with Gregory in his presentation to the extent of affirming that certain basic structures of Gassendi's philosophy and certain ends which Gassendi deliberately aimed to foster were related to the resurgence of empiricism and the emancipation of the lower-order disciplines on the medieval pyramid of knowledge.

But I consider that Gregory's conclusions are too general in character. He has located Gassendi as a philosopher within a generally accepted scheme of historical interpretation which embraces practically the whole of the second millennium of European intellectual history. While it might be found illuminating in some ways for him to have done this, I believe that Gregory's account of Gassendi's philosophy is markedly *a prioristic*, and that his account of Gassendi's aims and purposes is inadequate: for while Gassendi may be considered to have been influenced by the general philosophical trends that Gregory has described, his conscious goals were, I consider, more specific than those which Gregory has presented.

Bloch was the first scholar to examine closely the early versions of Gassendi's *Syntagma philosophicum*. Like Gregory, he reacted to the presupposition that a complete and coherent philosophical system is to be discovered in Gassendi's writings. Bloch contended that Gassendi never constructed such a system. Indeed, he failed in his efforts to do so. Bloch made this failure the object of his study, which he described as "the anatomy of an abortive system".[70] He argued that Gassendi's philosophy was a compromise, marked by a conscious refusal to systematise.

First, Bloch gave an account of what he termed the "constants" of Gassendi's philosophy. These, Bloch maintained, were Gassendi's theory that vision is the model of knowledge; his views concerning philosophical liberty and its limits (which views Bloch described as "mitigated modern");[71] his scepticism and agnosticism; and his nominalism. Bloch concluded that although Gassendi managed to give an impression of unity in his philosophy, this impression was superficial and masked a diversity of mutually exclusive orientations which were all held together by the deeper current of nominalism that runs through all his writings.

Next, Bloch turned to Gassendi's "scientific philosophy" and again discovered a diversity of orientations which Gassendi did not systematise. There was an orientation towards materialism: Bloch explained that he meant by this that Gassendi presented a natural philosophy in which the basic explanatory principles were formulated solely in terms of matter, its properties, structures and processes.[72] Gassendi's nominalism was the source of an orientation towards a positive science of nature founded on observation and experiment. He developed a concept of space that was adapted to the mechanics of Galileo, and a materialist concept of dynamic matter that was suitable for the new physical science. His biology also moved towards materialism, though definite elements of vitalism and animism were discernible. And his atomistic chemistry contained contradictory orientations towards materialism and hylozoism. Bloch maintained that Gassendi did not tidy up all these contradictions into a synthesis because he held back from following the direction that his philosophy was pointing. Gassendi chose, Bloch considered, not to develop his philosophy to its logical conclusion; consequently he presented an abortive system rather than a fully coherent synthesis.

Bloch explained that Gassendi strove throughout his work to maintain an accord between his scientifically inspired materialism and the demands of his Christian faith, and that the achievement of his goal took precedence for Gassendi over philosophical coherence. Bloch considered that there was a rupture between Gassendi the man with his sentiments and Gassendi the philosopher; or, if the word "rupture" is too strong, at least a wedge had been driven between the two. Gassendi was consequently concerned to prevent the materialist themes of his scientific philosophy and epistemology from harming the faith. Throughout, he strove to make it possible for physical materialism to co-exist with religious metaphysics. According to Bloch's account, Gassendi's efforts were of two kinds. First, he was satisfied simply to juxtapose his philosophy of nature and the various orthodox affirmations that were intended to render this philosophy acceptable. Then, after 1641, Gassendi attempted to integrate his materialist philosophy into an all-embracing religious and metaphysical world-view, with the intention of arresting the trend towards materialism in his own philosophy. Gassendi was thus, in Bloch's view, a link person between the nominalist prematerialism of the middle ages and the materialism of the classical era. As Bloch wrote in an article which he published two years after the appearance of his major study,[73] he considered that an historical interpretation made by Karl Marx is verified in Gassendi's philosophy, *viz.* that nominalism was the first expression of modern materialism.

Bloch's analysis is illuminating in many different ways. It is the most thorough examination of Gassendi's writings that has yet been produced. However, I do not agree with his general interpretation of Gassendi's philosophy, and in the course of this study I explain why. Principally, I do not agree that Gassendi was concerned about an alleged drift towards materialism. Consequently, while I find Bloch's study informative and valuable for many reasons, I believe that we must not be satisfied with his interpretation of Gassendi's work.

Three further book-length studies have been published since that of Bloch. The first, by Reiner Tack,[74] is a comprehensive study of two hundred and forty three pages which deals with Gassendi's scepticism, the principles of his Epicurean physical theory and his application of these principles to Galilean mechanics, his doctrine of the soul and the mental faculties, and his Epicurean ethics. The second work is that of Wolfgang Detel,[75] who has compared the empiricism of Gassendi with that of Epicurus. Each of these works in its own way, helps to fill out the picture of Gassendi and his philosophical concerns, due allowance being made for the need to complement them with the findings of more recent scholarship. The third and the most recent study written by Howard Jones,[76] is of greater interest. This is a full-length study of Gassendi's life and work, the sole such study in English apart from that of G.S. Brett (1908). Howard Jones is skilled in the art of criticism of seventeenth-century philosophical texts and brings his learning to bear upon Gassendi's philosophical *corpus*. Jones introduces us to Gassendi's philosophy by way of a section of more general biography. He then proceeds to pay special attention to Gassendi's anti-Aristotelian writings, his critique of the *De veritate* of Herbert of Cherbury, his acrimonious disputes with Descartes, his efforts to restore Epicureanism and his eventual presentation of his own philosophy in the *Syntagma philosophicum.* The result is an informative and interesting exposition of Gassendi's philosophy from the original texts which will spare the non-specialist much heavy, plodding labour. But it will not adequately satisfy the historian of science who will be looking for a sharper focus on the central themes of Gassendi's life-work rather than a biographical and chronological account, and more critical assessment of accepted interpretations.

The most recent contributions of all to the literature on Gassendi have been articles which have appeared since 1982. In two articles,[77] Louise Sarasohn has studied Gassendi's ethical and political theory. Noting in her first article (Sarasohn, 1982) that Epicureanism was widely reputed to sanction anti-social morality and political passivity, Sarasohn has argued that Gassendi's attempt to rehabilitate Epicurus not only transformed

Epicureanism into a theory of social and political involvement, but issued in one of the first, if not *the* first, modern defenses of individual liberty and natural rights within society and the political state. In her second article (Sarasohn, 1985) she has explored the interaction between Gassendi and Hobbes. She has claimed that the two philosophers stimulated each other in the development of their political and ethical theories: Hobbes adopted some themes from Gassendi's Epicureanism but developed them in overtly materialistic and deterministic ways; Gassendi was greatly disturbed and reacted by incorporating more theology into his physics and by developing further his doctrine on human liberty.

Margaret Osler (1983) has argued that Gassendi's voluntarist theology played a formative role on his empiricist approach to natural philosophy.[78] Her discussion of Gassendi forms part of a more general examination that she is undertaking concerning the influence of theological notions of God, Creation and Providence on the development of science.

Thus scholars from the late nineteenth century to the present have laboured to explain the work of Pierre Gassendi. He was a significant figure in the most crucial period of transition to the modern era: in the seventeenth century at least, Gassendi's philosophy was read and discussed widely, especially after the publication of Walter Charleton's *Physiologia Epicuro-Gassendo-Charltoniana* in 1654[79] and François Bernier's *Abregé* in 1678.[80] His Epicurean system was taken as the rival to Descartes' vortices, the *Syntagma philosophicum* was read widely and Gassendi himself was highly respected as a philosopher.[81] Consequently the aspirations that drove him on and the stratagems he adopted throw considerable light on the moods and activities of learned Europe in the first half of the seventeenth century and beyond. It is important that he and his philosophy should be correctly understood.

Yet I am convinced that we still have not adequately understood Gassendi or his life-work. It is true that the more immediately striking aspects have been presented at some length in the literature: that Gassendi was anti-Aristotelian and a sceptic, and that he laboured to restore Epicurean philosophy in the seventeenth century, these truisms constitute the mainstays of any interpretative reconstruction of his philosophy. But what has not been clearly understood or agreed upon is the trajectory of Gassendi's life-work: what he did - opposed Aristotelianism, adopted a sceptical approach and promoted Epicureanism - in the light of what he *aimed* to do. Or, to make the same point in more technical language: the structure of Gassendi's philosophy has been identified, but we have not reached the same clarity about its function.

It will be my purpose, therefore, to explain what I consider to have been the function of Gassendi's philosophy. This task will take us over some ground that will be familiar to anyone who has already studied the subject, but I hope that even readers already well-informed on the matters dealt with will frequently be seeing the familiar in an unfamiliar light, for that should be the effect of a more correct interpretation of our philosopher and his purposes. But we shall be exploring some less familiar tracks and by-ways as well; in particular we shall be examining the sources of Gassendi's scepticism, his Copernicanism, his ideological relationship with Marin Mersenne, and his wide-ranging hostility to occult philosophies, among other more incidental features of his work, and we will often be sifting through Gassendi's much-neglected early manuscripts. What comes into view when we begin looking in these directions will be found significant for an over-all understanding of our subject. In brief, I am presenting a new interpretation of Pierre Gassendi's philosophical work with the aim of clarifying the goals and the tactics of this pioneer architect of a mechanistic system, thereby hoping to throw some further light on the origins of mechanicism in the seventeenth century.

# CHAPTER 1

## SCEPTICAL ANTI-ARISTOTELIANISM

According to Gassendi's own account he conceived a dislike for Aristotelian philosophy during his student days in the college of Aix-en-Provence. His complaints at that time concerned an alleged ethical inadequacy in Aristotelianism, for the Peripatetic philosophy, in his view, did not measure up to the Stoic philosophical ideal to which Cicero had alluded in his praise of philosophy: "Philosophy can never be praised as she merits; the man who obeys her precepts may live all the days of his life without trouble".[1]

By his second last year as a lecturer in Aristotelian philosophy Gassendi had read all the authors that were most popular with the humanists. At that time (1621) he gave his list of favourite authors as follows: Charron, Montaigne, Lipsius, Seneca, Plutarch, Cicero, Lucretius, Horace, Juvenal, Lucian and Erasmus.[2] It would seem that these authors provided him with some relief from what he judged to be the aridity of the Aristotelian texts. At the same time they would have fuelled his discontent with Aristotelianism.

Gassendi would have us believe that his distaste for Aristotelianism was aroused in his own soul first, and that he found support for his feelings in the writings of the humanists subsequently.[3] It seems unlikely that such should have been the case, and Gassendi appears to be guilty here of a certain amount of oversimplification. In any case, Gassendi acknowledged that his anti-Aristotelianism was greatly influenced by humanist authors, specifically by Vives, Charron, Ramus and Mirandola (evidently Gianfrancesco Pico della Mirandola, the nephew). These writers, Gassendi explained, helped him overcome his fear of opposing the Aristotelians:

> When I read Vives and my own Charron my spirits rose and all my fears left me. I saw that there was nothing wrong in suspecting that the Aristotelians were not always correct just because most people approved of them. But my boldness rose as I read Ramus especially, and also Mirandola. I mention these authors because I have always made a point of naming those from whom I have drawn profit.[4]

Gassendi's criticism of the Aristotelians did become surprisingly strong for someone who had the reputation of being a mild-mannered man.[5] He

15

attacked the whole scholastic system of education - its teaching methods, course content and the teachers themselves. The methods, in his view, were purely theatrical, the philosophy was empty, useless, unworthy of the title Aristotelian and of the name philosophy, while the teachers were credulous, arrogant, supercilious and presumptuous fools.[6] The Aristotelians, he claimed, had perverted philosophy, the study of truth, into a great mishmash of useless disputations designed to produce disputants rather than philosophers.[7] Instead of concerning themselves with true and legitimate knowledge of things, he accused, the Aristotelians ran after absurdities, argued about chimerical questions and indulged in frivolous conjectures.[8]

More specifically, Gassendi criticised the Aristotelian pedagogues for neglecting the genuine sources of wisdom and knowledge. First, they neglected serious authors such as Plato, Cicero, Seneca, Pliny, Plutarch and others - authors who would be able to contribute much wisdom. Second, they deliberately neglected the mathematical disciplines, the part of philosophy which was not open to dispute: "It is through mathematics that we have knowledge, if we ever have it".[9] Third, they neglected the parts of physical philosophy that were open to observation and experiment, or, if they treated them, they did not take the trouble actually to make observations and do experiments. Thus, in physical philosophy they treated only the chimeras such as substantial forms, and neglected the subjects that might be treated in an historical manner. For example, they neglected the history of stones, metals, plants and animals, believing such things to be appropriate for lapidarians, goldsmiths, botanists and hunters, but not for philosophers.[10] They also neglected the questions concerning the elements, their number and kinds, and concentrated on inept and frivolous combinations of qualities. They indulged in idle discussions about heavenly bodies, and the solidity and reality of the heavenly spheres, without ever looking into the skies. Nothing of what they taught could be corroborated by observation and experiment. Gassendi wrote:

> In a word, they examine nothing in this world. When they enter their Schools they enter into another nature which has nothing in common with this nature outside.[11]

The general tenor of these criticisms is clear: the Aristotelians do not study nature but lose their time and spend their energies on irrelevant and unprofitable disputations. As a consequence, the Aristotelians do not teach their students how to study nature.

It is significant that Gassendi appears not to have made any real contact with Jesuit Aristotelians before their arrival at Aix to replace him and his colleagues in the year 1622. Had he been more familiar with the Jesuit model of education he might have realised that his criticisms were less than just when applied to the Jesuits; and it was the Jesuits who dominated Catholic education in Europe at that time.[12] In their system, education was achieved through a whole curriculum of humane and useful subjects of which philosophy was only one, albeit one of the more important.[13] In philosophy, by official Jesuit regulation, Aristotle was to be followed except where his doctrine detracted from or was repugnant to the faith,[14] and the widely used Jesuit text-books of philosophy remained faithful to that injunction.[15] At the same time, however, the Jesuit system placed considerable emphasis on the study of the authors of antiquity, both pagan and Christian. Likewise the need for training in mathematics was emphasised, and the adequacy of the teaching of the subject was assured through the efforts of Peter Clavius in creating a mathematical school within the Collegio Romano.[16] Finally, as Gassendi was himself eventually to realise, the Jesuits took a practical interest in the natural sciences: Gassendi corresponded on scientific subjects with a number of them, including Christopher Scheiner, Athanasius Kircher and Pierre Cazrée, and he was to become acquainted with Honoré Fabri, the prefect of the college of Aix 1638-1639, who is reported to have spent some time in a Roman prison for his views on the relations between Sacred Scripture and science.[17]

Nevertheless, Gassendi's criticism was that the Aristotelians did not avail themselves of the wisdom of the ancients and did not use mathematics or make observations in their *philosophy*, and that was a correct assertion as applied to at least a great many Aristotelian philosophers including the Jesuits.[18]

It is apparent from the *Exercitationes* that Gassendi's teaching of Aristotelian philosophy at the college of Aix was somewhat atypical of Aristotelian philosophers generally, for he had endeavoured to teach philosophy in a way that reflected the intellectual movements of the early seventeenth century. Most especially, Gassendi's teaching incorporated discussions of developments in the field of astronomy, physiology and alchemy. We learn this fact from the preface to Book 1 of the *Exercitationes* in which Gassendi outlined the contents of all projected seven books of the work. As it turned out, only two of these books were completed; hence we have to rely on the summary in this preface for our information on the intended contents of the other five. The whole work, as Gassendi stated in the same preface, was a publication of a newly edited version of part of his course of lectures on Aristotelian philosophy, the *anti*-Aristotelian part.[19]

According to the summary in the preface to Book 1, then, we learn that Gassendi would be arguing in Book 4 that the fixed stars and the Sun are stationary while the earth moves in the way that the planets move. In Book 5 he would trace the paths of comets through the aethereal spaces and he would establish it as a fact that these paths are no less unbroken than the paths of the visible stars. According to the same summary, Gassendi would enter into the physiological question of the circulation of the chyle, and in Book 5 he would propose a different account of the passage of chyle from the stomach to the liver from the one proposed in the accepted theory.[20] In Book 4 he would treat alchemical questions. Specifically, he would attack Aristotle's elements in respect of their number and the qualities produced by change and alteration; he would also attack the theory of transmutation of elements.[21]

It is fairly clear that we need look no further afield than Gassendi's local area to discover the influences that stimulated his initial interest in the practical sciences. It seems that local scholars and teachers first aroused and channelled his enthusiasm in that direction. According to Gassendi's own testimony, his interest in astronomy was first awakened by Joseph Galtier, mathematician, astronomer, Doctor of Arts and Theology, Prior of la Valette and Vicar General of the diocese of Aix,[22] while his interest in physiology was influenced by a surgeon at Aix, Jean Payan, whose dissections he had witnessed.[23]

Thus the men who aroused Gassendi's interest in the practical sciences were in the main, at least, local personalities. They helped him in his teaching of philosophy by encouraging him not to ignore the practical sciences. Yet it is noteworthy that Gassendi did not cite these local scholars among those whom he mentioned as having helped him to take his stand against the Aristotelians, though they did do that in fact, for, by introducing him to the methods and fruits of the sciences they put into his hands a whole range of weapons to use in his polemic against Aristotelian natural philosophy. However, at the time of publication of the *Exercitationes* (1624), Gassendi did not see their contribution to his anti-Aristotelian polemic as particularly noteworthy, and he more readily and spontaneously gave to the four humanist authors, Vives, Charron, Ramus and Mirandola, the credit for lending him the needed strength to dare to oppose the Aristotelians.

It can be seen from the *Exercitationes* that Gassendi saw things in the way just outlined. The *Exercitationes* was intended to be a work that would present objections to the whole range of doctrines contained in the Aristotelian *corpus* - the logical writings, the *De caelo* and *De generatione et corruptione*, the *Meteorologica*, *Historia animalium*, *De anima*, *Parva naturalia*, *Metaphysica* and works on ethics as well as the Aristotelian writings on natural philosophy. The summary of the projected work already referred to makes this fact clear. Consequently, when Gassendi accorded credit to the people who had assisted him in opposing the Aristotelians, he was thinking of the Aristotelians as those philosophers who were engaged in teaching the whole *corpus* of Aristotelian doctrine, and he considered those authors as his anti-Aristotelian allies who had shown him how to oppose the Aristotelians who were so engaged. It was a different kind of support from that which he received from his friends and mentors who had inducted him into the practical sciences, and whose support was of a comparatively peripheral kind, since it related only to his polemic against the Aristotelian writings on natural philosophy.

The same preface to Book 1 of the *Exercitationes* shows that, not only did Gassendi look for little support from his mentors who had inducted him into the practical sciences, but he considered that it was they themselves who were in need of support from general philosophy: he was attacking Aristotelianism for the sake of the advancement of the new sciences. He wrote:

> After I had come to see how great a gulf there is between the human mind and Nature's genius, what else could I conclude than that the intimate causes of natural phenomena totally escape the power of human discernment? Therefore I became upset and ashamed at the foolishness and arrogance of the dogmatic philosophers who boast that they have attained a knowledge of nature and propound it with such rigour.[24]

Gassendi's concern was that the enquiry into the secret causes of natural effects should be freed from the presuppositions of the (Aristotelian) dogmatic philosophers. As he wrote a little later in the same preface, he believed the Aristotelians would have made much progress in the discovery of truth if they had not been so sure that they already possessed it.

Thus Gassendi considered that a general attack needed to be mounted against Aristotelianism, one which would strike at the very foundations of their reputation for infallibility, and he decided to respond to that need in the *Exercitationes*. He recorded:

> I considered that I should strive with might and main to blunt the spearhead of all this credulity [in favour of the Aristotelians] and try to do something at the same time to lessen the arrogant presumption of the Aristotelians themselves.[25]

It was as a Renaissance philosopher rather than as a specialist in the experimental approach to nature that Gassendi confronted Aristotelianism. Accordingly, he embarked upon the ambitious project of the *Exercitationes*, a point-by-point refutation of the whole *corpus* of Aristotelian doctrine, and he looked for support in his efforts to undermine the authority of the Aristotelians particularly in the works of the sixteenth-century humanists, Vives, Charron, Ramus and Mirandola. In his own statement already quoted[26] he attributed more significance to the influence of Charron - "my own Charron" - and Ramus - "Ramus especially" - than to the significance of Vives and Mirandola. Further, he linked the four names into two pairs, Vives and Charron, Ramus and Mirandola. Gassendi had reasons for the different emphases and for pairing the names in that manner.

First, by coupling Vives and Charron, Gassendi indicated the stress that he placed on ethics as the supreme part of philosophy, and especially the conviction of the value of Stoic ethics, as alluded to in the passage from Cicero's *De senectute* quoted in the preface to Book 1 of the *Exercitationes*, because it makes it possible for a man to reach *ataraxia* or peace of mind.[27] As Gassendi said in that passage of the preface, it was the uselessness of Aristotelianism in assisting one to reach that (Stoic) goal that had caused him to turn against Aristotelianism in the first place.

Renaissance admiration for the ancients had led Vives, Charron, and now Gassendi onto contentious ground as they advocated pagan morality in a Christian world. Vives and Charron had both extolled the virtue of the Stoic sage and linked it closely with Christian virtue. Vives was somewhat ambiguous, or perhaps circumspect, but he did stress a similarity between the natural ethical way of life of the pagan sage and the ideal Christian way of life. He wrote, for instance: "In my estimation, no man has been a truer Christian than this [Stoic] sage".[28] Charron, on the other hand, was more emphatic concerning the relationship between Stoic and Christian ethics, and raised a storm of protest which has reverberated down the centuries.[29] After the publication of his work *De la sagesse* (1601)[30] Charron found himself accused of heresy and much else besides[31] and became caught up, in spite of himself, in the controversies concerning grace and freedom that were occupying theologians in the sixteenth and seventeenth centuries. Charron responded to his critics in the preface to the second and subsequent editions of the *Sagesse*, and more at length in a new work especially written for the purpose which appeared posthumously under the title *Traicté de sagesse* (1606).[32] In this work he presented human wisdom as the *way* to divine wisdom, the law of nature as the *way* to the law of grace, philosophical virtue as the *way* to theological virtue, the fulfilment of human duties as the *way* to obtaining divine favour, and concluded with an exhortation to follow nature and the natural light of reason given to us by God.[33] To an immoderate critic like Fr Garasse S.J., such doctrine made Charron a "brutal" writer;[34] to more moderate critics Charron placed too little stress on grace and the supernatural when treating of human nature, hence the accusation that he advocated a secular morality, and that he was a Pelagian.[35]

Also, by coupling Vives and Charron on his list of four names, Gassendi indicated that he was influenced by the scepticism of the two authors. Once again, Charron was acknowledged by Gassendi as the more important influence, in keeping with the fact that Charron's scepticism was more explicit and pronounced than that of Vives. Scepticism was an essential feature of Stoic ethics, for it was the only way to attain *isosthenia* or the state of mental suspense[36] which deepens into *epoché* or an habitual state of suspension of judgment,[37] which is ultimately accompanied by the *ataraxia* or peace of mind which was the supreme goal of Stoic ethics.[38]

The sceptical tendencies of Vives were moderate and unostentatious. He criticised the extreme sceptics, those who search for objections even when there are none, claiming that in undermining the false knowledge of the ignorant they also tear down the true knowledge of the learned and the experts.[39] At the same time Vives emphasised the limitations of human knowledge when he was discussing Aristotelian science, and concluded that "the whole of philosophy rests upon opinions and conjectures that are verisimilar".[40]

Charron, on the other hand advocated Pyrrhonism, or the most radical form of scepticism, and presented it as the ideal for the Christian wise man, always exempting from sceptical doubt the truths of religion and morality.[41] He claimed that Jesus "the Teacher of Truth" advocated a form of scepticism; he claimed that Pyrrhonism offered a way for a man to prepare his soul for God and his operations. It was a means of "emptying" oneself - divesting oneself of all opinion, belief and affection, becoming dead to oneself and to the world so that God might come and dwell and act within one's soul. Further, he claimed that the *Sagesse* was a manual that could be used as an instrument for the step-by-step conversion of the pagan Chinese, for instance, to wisdom and ultimately to the Christian faith. Furthermore, Charron claimed, in an obvious allusion to the theological controversies of the age, Pyrrhonists could never become heretics - Pyrrhonists and heretics were opposities.[42]

Much of the foregoing defence written by Charron of his Stoic doctrine was by way of afterthought, and should probably not be taken too seriously. Out of a need to defend his doctrine in the *Sagesse* against the critics and the *"esprits faibles"* Charron was pushed into avenues of discussion which, possibly, he was not otherwise inclined to follow. However, by emphasising emphatically the relationship between Stoic and Christian ethics, the *Traicté de sagesse* does bear witness to Charron's conviction of his own orthodoxy and shows clearly how he felt it should be defended.

Gassendi took Charron's *Sagesse* as his philosophical and ethical *vade mecum*, most probably from his student days. For a young cleric such as Gassendi, who was training to become a Canon of the diocese of Digne, Pierre Charron was in many ways a natural model and highly recommendable author, all the more so since Charron had been *théologal*, or official teacher of theology of several dioceses in the south-west of France; also *écolâtre*, or master of the Cathedral school and supervisor of all diocesan schools in the diocese of Bordeaux. As well as that, Charron's works were enjoying enormous popularity: first published in 1601, by the year 1621 the *Sagesse* had appeared in four editions and had been reprinted numerous times. Thus, when Gassendi was teaching in the school of Aix, a leading citizen of the town, Henri du Faur de Pibrac, recommended that he read Charron, and Gassendi responded with enthusiasm in a way that shows that he had already done so. Gassendi wrote:

It is most apt that you advise me to take this author with me
as I retire to solitude ... what wiser judge can be found than
Charron?[43]

Thus Vives and Charron stimulated Gassendi by their advocacy of Stoic
ethics and Pyrrhonism. But Gassendi also paired Gianfrancesco Pico della
Mirandola and Pierre de la Ramée, or Ramus, as another two authors whom
he recognised as having fortified him in his revolt against Aristotelianism.
Of the two he gave special emphasis to Ramus by the words "especially
Ramus". In naming these sixteenth-century humanists, Gassendi
acknowledged further sources for his Pyrrhonism, in this instance
Pyrrhonism as a specifically anti-Aristotelian weapon. Vives and Charron
had used scepticism and Pyrrhonism in a more general way against
dogmatists and dogmatism and made only rare mention of Aristotelian
dogmatism; Pico and Ramus, however, were more explicitly anti-
Aristotelian sceptics. Hence the particular contributions made by both Pico
and Ramus to Gassendi's philosophical development, though they were
significant, were rather directly related to his anti-Aristotelian polemic, in
contrast to the more generally humanist formative influences of Vives and
Charron.

Pico's sceptical contribution was especially limited. Gassendi did not
sympathise, at least not in any lasting fashion, with Pico's ultimate aim to
undermine all philosophy by means of a destructive scepticism, which aim
was well expressed in the title of Pico's best-known work, the *Examen
vanitatis*(1520): *A consideration of the vanity of the doctrine of the pagans
and of the truth of Christian teaching in six books: three of these books
attack all the philosophers in general, while the other three attack the
Aristotelians in particular, and with the arms of Aristotle; throughout
Christian teaching is propounded and extolled.*[44] In a deliberate reversal of
the attempts of his uncle Giovanni to demonstrate the concord among the
pagan philosophers,[45] Pico aimed to demonstrate that the whole
philosophical enterprise was in vain because of the manifold discord
reigning among philosophers, and he concluded with the words, "what is
there to be said except that the doctrine of the pagans is vain and totally
untrustworthy?"[46] However, Pico continued, while all discord comes from
the philosophers, theologians are in marvellous concord, entirely in
agreement concerning the one body of dogma that comes from the writings
of Moses, the prophets, the evangelists and the apostles. What discord has
arisen among the theologians comes entirely from the sources of the
philosophers. Hence, Pico maintained, philosophy was the source of all
heresy, and he set out to tear up every last root and branch of this vanity
which was pullulating unchecked. In propounding this view Pico was
expressing an attitude that was similar to the Protestant Reformers, *viz.* that
what was needed was a return to pure theology founded on Sacred Scripture
without any admixture of Greek philosophy.[47] One seems to detect the

influence of the preaching of Savonarola, for whom Pico wrote an *apologia*. In fact, Gassendi's acknowledgment of the influence of Gianfrancesco Pico is a little surprising, since he was not nearly as popular an author as the other three.[48] Gassendi used Pico's *Examen vanitatis* extensively as a source-book for anti-Aristotelian criticism, especially concerning the textual tradition of the Aristotelian *corpus* as Charles B. Schmitt has suggested.[49] But perhaps the chief contribution that Pico made to Gassendi's philosophy was not so much in presenting him with a series of anti-Aristotelian arguments, as in supplying something that was lacking in the scepticism of Ramus, *viz.* an example of the way to use the writings of Sextus Empiricus against Aristotelianism.

It would seem that it was through the influence of Ramus rather than Pico that Gassendi was first stimulated to deploy the weapons of scepticism against the Aristotelians. Although Ramus (1515-1572) belonged to a later generation than Gianfrancesco Pico (1469-1533), it is Ramus who has been identified as an originator, along with his colleague Omer Talon (1510-1562), of the link between scepticism and anti-Aristotelianism.[50] Ramus directed his sceptical attack especially against the Aristotelian commentators who, he claimed, had distorted Aristotle's teaching. His task, as he saw it, was one of purification and restoration of the true Aristotle, and of healing the wounds inflicted by the commentators on Aristotle's original work. He seemed to accept as an indisputable fact the philosophical supremacy of Aristotelianism in the statement: "the philosophy of Aristotle is practically the whole of philosophy and the only philosophy in the whole wide world".[51] Thus Ramus and Talon started a tradition of reformed Aristotelianism, the "Ramist" tradition. In their writings scepticism was used as a tool and a stick with which to attack the dogmatism of the Aristotelians.[52] Gassendi's description of his task as that of blunting the spearhead of the popular authority of the Aristotelians and of undermining the arrogant presumption of the Aristotelians themselves by using the techniques of scepticism shows that he had reason to recognise that he had drawn profit from the work of Ramus: in his use of scepticism against the Aristotelians he was following a tradition begun by Ramus.

However, since the time of Ramus and Talon an important development had occurred in Renaissance scepticism. The main source of information concerning ancient scepticism for Ramus and Talon had been Cicero's *Academica*.[53] Then in 1562 and 1569, too late to be of use to Ramus and Talon, Latin translations of all the works of Sextus Empiricus were printed and thereafter these works largely supplanted the *Academica*. These translations were the work of Henri Estienne, a Parisian printer, and Gentian Hervet, a Catholic scholar who promoted Pyrrhonism as a "new machine of war" to be deployed against Calvinist rationalism.[54]

Pico had used the scepticism of Sextus Empiricus against Aristotle before Ramus had begun the tradition of using the scepticism of the *Academica* against the Aristotelians. In the preface to his translation of the *Adversus mathematicos* of Sextus Empiricus, Hervet made reference to Pico, and his words were such as would catch the attention of anyone seeking to use the works of Sextus Empiricus against the dogmatists of the Renaissance - the Aristotelians, for instance. They were as follows:

> Francesco Pico della Mirandola has given a fine example of how great a use can be made of the commentary of Sextus Empiricus for safeguarding the dogma of the Christian religion against the pagan philosophers. See his book in which he defends Christian philosophy against the dogmas of the pagans.[55]

It seems highly likely that Gassendi was directed to the *Examen vanitatis* of Gianfrancesco Pico either directly through his own reading of that preface, or indirectly through the suggestion of other Catholic readers of it - the Jesuits of Coimbra, for example.[56] Through Hervet, Gassendi learned that he could find in the writings of Pico what he could not find in the writings of Ramus, namely a model for applying the arguments of Sextus Empiricus against Aristotelianism.

Thus Gassendi accepted Pico's anti-Aristotelian techniques and arguments and left aside his destructive scepticism, while it was Ramus, it appears, who influenced him to be a sceptic in the first place. The net result of these influences can be gauged from Gassendi's preface to the *Exercitationes* where he explained his reasons for adopting Pyrrhonism. The reasons, as Gassendi related them, were wholly anti-Aristotelian, largely pedagogical, and significantly, in relation to Gassendi's future philosophical development after the *Exercitationes*, only fleetingly if at all were his reasons linked to a personal philosophical commitment to Pyrrhonism.

Gassendi told his story in the *Exercitationes* as follows.[57] The first part has already been noted: Gassendi related that he had originally become a Pyrrhonist as a reaction to the aridity of Aristotelian philosophy as an ethical philosophy. For Aristotelianism did not teach one how to arrive at that Stoic tranquillity which Cicero proclaimed to be the fruit of good philosophy. At first Gassendi was afraid to oppose the Aristotelians, but he was heartened and strengthened by Vives, Charron, Ramus and Mirandola. Then, Gassendi's narration continued, he began to explore other philosophical traditions to see whether any of them could offer something more satisfactory. One might safely presume that he explored these other philosophies with the help of Pico's *Examen vanitatis*, especially as Gassendi went on to state that he encountered difficulties with all of them. As a consequence, he came to the conclusion that the only thing for him to do was to accept the *akatalepsia*, or doubt, of the Academicians and Pyrrhonists.[58] Then, after coming to realise for himself "how great was the gulf that separated Nature's genius from the human mind",[59] he came to believe that the intimate causes of natural effects totally escape the powers of penetration of the human mind. He was repelled by the levity and arrogance of the dogmatic philosophers who boasted that they had attained to true knowledge of natural things, and came to the conclusion that the Academicians and Pyrrhonists showed greater wisdom, for, in order to demonstrate the vanity and uncertainty of human knowledge, they equipped themselves to be able to argue both for and against, on any subject.

Although Gassendi was a Pyrrhonist, with special emphasis on the application of Pyrrhonism to the philosophy of nature, according to his own account as I have summarised it in the preceding paragraph, he was still officially a teacher of Aristotelian philosophy. Gassendi endeavoured to surmount the difficulties involved in such an anomalous position by training his students to defend Aristotle well in the main body of his course, while presenting them with arguments in the appendices that, he claimed, completely overturned the Aristotelian doctrines. In this way he aimed to train his students in Pyrrhonism by professing to show them that there was no proposition or opinion, be it ever so generally accepted or attractive in itself, that its opposite could not be shown to be equally probable or even more probable. Gassendi claimed that his pedagogical method resembled the original method of Aristotle himself. He wrote:

> Aristotle did not train his young students to dispute theses in the dry way of the philosophers, but with all the fulness of the rhetoricians, arguing both for and against, so that they would be able to speak with more elegance and more articulately.[60]

Thus, the *Exercitationes* is the product of Gassendi's teaching, specifically the anti-Aristotelian part of his teaching which was to be found in the sections containing objections to the Aristotelian doctrines. Yet, contrary to what one might expect, the *Exercitationes* is not a rational Pyrrhonist series of objections to Aristotelian philosophy. There is little evidence of *isosthenia*, or a state of mental suspense depending upon a balance between *pro* and *contra*. Nor is the balance between *pro* and *contra* significantly ameliorated even when one takes into account that the *Exercitationes* reproduced only one side of the argument, since Gassendi did not publish his pro-Aristotelian philosophy. Gassendi frankly considered the Aristotelian texts to be "unworthy" works,[61] meaning that the commentaries were unworthy of being called Aristotelian. Also in Book 1, *Exercitatio* 7, Gassendi gave a long list of all the things he considered to be wrong with Aristotle's philosophy, while in the next *exercitatio* he gave a similarly long list of all the things which he found to be contradictory in it. But Gassendi himself implied in the preface that he was no longer, or not always, a Pyrrhonist. For example, he used various hypothetical clauses to describe the various types of assertions to be found in the *Exercitationes*, saying:

> If I sometimes defend a doctrine like a dogmatist, or if I test something after the manner of a sceptic, if I propose something as true, or claim something to be probable ...[62]

Gassendi's "Pyrrhonism", it would appear, was a flexible state of mind that allowed him to adopt according to need or whim every position from dogmatism to agnosticism. Consequently it is not correct to use the term "Pyrrhonism" to describe his position, since Pyrrhonism, especially as portrayed in the writings of Sextus Empiricus,[63] was a radical, consistent and comprehensive scepticism. Gassendi's position is better described as a specifically anti-Aristotelian scepticism.

In this chapter, attention has been focussed on the story of Gassendi's withdrawal from Aristotelianism. But so far only part of the story has been told, for Gassendi also underwent a process of conversion to an alternative philosophy that corresponded to his movement away from Aristotelianism. That alternative philosophy was Epicureanism, a form of which was soon to become his new natural philosophy. This side of the story - the adoption of Epicureanism by Gassendi - will be explored in Chapter 3. To conclude this chapter, however, a number of features of the story of Gassendi's withdrawal from Aristotelianism should be underscored, since they are important for a better understanding of his intellectual journey away from Aristotelianism.

First, Gassendi's anti-Aristotelianism was clearly in harmony with a popular, perhaps one might say 'fashionable', movement in Provence in the first quarter of the seventeenth century. His contribution to the reaction against Aristotelianism was very favourably accepted by the people who counted for most in the region of Aix. Local notables such as Peiresc, a councillor of the Parlement of Provence, Galtier, the second highest ecclesiastical dignitary of the diocese, and Pibrac, a King's councillor and member of a very prominent family, paid special attention to Gassendi's work. According to Gassendi "the most renowned assemblies of the whole of Provence" attended his public disputations against the Aristotelians.[64] Clearly, by being so closely associated with the powers of the land, Gassendi had little to fear from the opposition of the Aristotelians. In particular, by being well received by Galtier he was thereby well received by the Church establishment. In fact, by reason of his own position he was a part of that Church establishment himself.

A similar picture of Gassendi as a popular and fashionable philosopher is obtained from a consideration of the list of intellectual influences that Gassendi recognised. Apart from Pico, whose presence on the list, nevertheless, seems to be easily explained, all the authors whom Gassendi acknowledged as having been important for him were writers who had been important for humanists generally - either classical authors like Seneca, Plutarch, Cicero, Lucretius, Horace, Juvenal and Lucian; seminal Renaissance authors like Erasmus, Vives and Ramus; or popular and fashionable writers of the sixteenth and early seventeenth century like Lipsius, Montaigne and Charron. Against such a background of cultural influences there seems to be a high degree of predictability about the philosophical positions Gassendi adopted in the *Exercitationes*, especially his so-called Pyrrhonism, his anti-Aristotelianism, and even his emphasis on the practical sciences. At the same time, Gassendi's *Exercitationes* express the mood of the dominant section of the educated public of Provence in the first quarter of the seventeenth century: humanist, anti-Aristotelian, interested in practical sciences, especially astronomy and anatomy.

Second, Gassendi's scepticism was, at least originally, a limited weapon taken up for a specific purpose, namely for his polemic against Aristotelianism. It was largely a fruit of his reading of the humanist authors, especially Charron, and according to Gassendi's own account it was originally adopted out of a dissatisfaction with Aristotelianism because it did not promote the Stoic *ethical* goal of *ataraxia*, or peace of mind. Sextus Empiricus represented Aristotelianism as a dogmatic philosophy;[65] Charron had attacked dogmatism in a general way without mentioning the Aristotelians by name; Ramus and Pico had attacked Aristotelianism in overt fashion; finally, Gassendi was able to profit by the writings of the humanists to attack Aristotelianism with the weapons of scepticism, and thereby disturb the popular myth of the infallibility of the Aristotelians.

It would seem fairly clear, then, that any sense of an impending "sceptical crisis" was far from Gassendi's consciousness as he delivered his anti-Aristotelian lectures and composed the *Exercitationes*. He did not show signs of being concerned about the epistemological vacuum that would result once Aristotelian rationalism was undermined. His principal concern was to undermine the dogmatism of the Aristotelians as a means of promoting moderate Renaissance wisdom and for the sake of the free advancement of the practical sciences. He gave no evidence of experiencing epistemological discomfort: the foundations of knowledge had not been disrupted as far as he was concerned; only the pretentions of the Aristotelians had been overthrown. Such a conclusion does not agree with the interpretations of many previous commentators as refined more recently by R.H. Popkin. However, it does fit well with the interpretation of O.R. Bloch, and it will be further corroborated in the next and later chapters.

Third, Gassendi's anti-Aristotelianism differed from that of Vives and Ramus in one important way: while Vives and Ramus criticised Aristotelianism, they retained a basic loyalty to the Aristotelian tradition and especially to the philosophy of Aristotle himself. Gassendi, on the other hand, accepted the view that it was time to abandon Aristotelianism and look for something to take its place. Vives wrote, for instance:

Aristotle the Stagyrite was the prince of our philosophers
and easily the wisest of all philosophers.[66]

And, again:

There seems to have been no greater genius than Aristotle.[67]

Ramus also accepted the pre-eminence of Aristotle as being beyond
question, and he attacked the commentators who, he claimed, had distorted
Aristotle's teaching. For instance, he considered that Porphyry's account of
the Aristotelian concept of 'difference' was:

a trifling and preposterously inept doctrine, in no way true
to Aristotle.[68]

Also, he wrote, if Aristotle was at times obscure, the Aristotelian
commentators:

rob [Aristotle's] text of all the clarity achieved by his
definitions and divisions: in place of his elegant examples
they put their puerile figments.[69]

All the effort of Ramus was directed towards purifying Aristotelian
doctrine to make it more closely accord with the original doctrine of
Aristotle: he claimed to be healing the wounds inflicted by the
commentators.[70]

But Gassendi was of a different frame of mind. While he also professed
that he had the greatest esteem for Aristotle and that his intention was to
attack the Aristotelians rather than Aristotle himself,[71] he did not set out to
renew, reform or restore Aristotle's doctrine. For Gassendi, it was time to
abandon both Aristotle and the Aristotelians. After a cursory glance
through the other ancient philosophies, probably with the assistance of Pico
through his *Examen vanitatis*, Gassendi settled for Pyrrhonism, seemingly
as a result of his youthful enthusiasm for Charron, and as a preliminary to
the development of his interest in Epicureanism.

Now the point has been reached at which an examination of Gassendi's
Epicureanism may be opened. However, before passing to Gassendi's life-
long effort to resuscitate Epicurean philosophy, it will be valuable to
examine another life-long concern, Gassendi's astronomical work which in
fact pre-dated his Epicureanism. It is particularly appropriate to study
Gassendi's astronomy before his Epicureanism because it was especially in
his astronomical writings that his Pyrrhonism lingered on. In fact it did
much better than linger: Gassendi's Pyrrhonism, as has been seen, tended to
wax and wane, but in his astronomical writings it most definitely "waxed".

It was his Pyrrhonism that enabled Gassendi to live with the demands of ecclesiastical authority and even helped him to thrive in contented Stoic peace of mind within the confines of the guidelines for orthodoxy handed down by that authority.

# CHAPTER 2

## COPERNICAN ANTI-ARISTOTELIANISM

Scepticism was Gassendi's chief weapon against Aristotelianism because it enabled him to cast doubt on *all* that the Aristotelians asserted. But there were other weapons, more limited in range than scepticism, in Gassendi's arsenal, and chief among these was astronomy. Aristotelianism was losing ground in astronomy in the late sixteenth and early seventeenth centuries as a number of discoveries were made which refuted particular doctrines of Aristotelian cosmology. Galileo Galilei became a leader in the field during this period, and especially under his influence the anti-Aristotelian potential of the new developments in astronomy were exploited to such a degree that a clamorous debate arose between Aristotelian anti-Copernicans who were opposed to Galileo, and Copernican anti-Aristotelians who followed Galileo. Gassendi joined the debate, and his writings reflect its course: he began as an enthusiastic Copernican anti-Aristotelian follower of Galileo; he suffered from afar the trauma of the condemnation of Galileo; and he ended his days as a mild Tychonian with most of his anti-Aristotelian fire spent.

In this chapter I propose to describe the shifts and developments in Gassendi's position as he participated in the Copernican debate and tried to cope with the dilemma in which he found himself following the condemnation of Galileo. The period which will be studied opened with the year 1618, when Gassendi began to keep a record of his observations, and concluded in 1655 when he wrote his last pages on astronomical subjects and was forced to call a halt to his observations.

Two years after his appointment to the chair of Aristotelian philosophy at Aix-en-Provence, in the year 1618, Gassendi began to keep records of his astronomical observations. His records opened with a series of observations of the last of three comets which were seen between August and December of that year, and which aroused much controversy.[1] The third comet first appeared late in November of that year, and Gassendi followed its course until the twenty-fourth of December.

Gassendi welcomed this comet at the time when he was embarking on his attack on Aristotelianism in the *Exercitationes* (the only record that remains of his lectures on astronomy at Aix), for it seemed to him at that time to provide a chance to score an easy victory over the Aristotelians. After all, Tycho Brahe, an astronomer of the greatest renown and respectability, had concluded from his observations of the comet of 1577 that the Aristotelian doctrine of comets could not be accepted any more.[2] From accurate observations Tycho had established that the comet of 1577 had less parallax, not only than the Moon, but also than the Sun; hence he concluded that the comet was located above the orbit of the Sun, and was not a sub-lunary phenomenon as Aristotle and the Peripatetics had maintained.[3] Gassendi was glad to have the authority of Tycho Brahe behind him, and in conscious imitation of Tycho he observed the comet of 1618 to have less parallax than the Moon, and also less than the Sun and concluded that it had appeared high above the Sun.[4] Following Tycho, also, Gassendi intended to use this evidence against the Aristotelians; in the preface he stated that he would object against Aristotle's theory of comets in the projected Book 5 of the *Exercitationes* as follows:

> In that book I trace the paths of the comets through the aetherial spaces, and I establish that they are no less permanent bodies than the visible stars.[5]

However, when he came to discuss comets in MS Tours 710 (1643) and later again in the *Syntagma philosophicum* (1649-1655), Gassendi had lost confidence in the polemical value of the observation; instead of weighing in against the Aristotelian theory of comets and the dualist cosmology that underpinned it he merely discussed the arguments in favour of the view that comets were sub-lunar phenomena and of the alternative view that they were located in the celestial regions, and concluded lamely:

> As can be seen, there are difficulties with both positions. Hence it is better that we not pronounce conclusively on the question, but be satisfied to give a report of that comet which appeared not long ago, first as we saw it, and then, by way of conjecture and combining our observations with those of others, to say what can be said with some degree of verisimilitude.[6]

It was the authority of Galileo that had undermined his argument. At the time of publication of the *Exercitationes* (1624) Gassendi did not know of Galileo's theory about comets; he first wrote to Galileo in 1625[7] and stated in the course of the letter that he had not yet been able to read the *Saggiatore* (1623).[8] He evidently had not, as he was under the false impression that Galileo's writings on the subject of comets would furnish him with further arguments that he could use in his demonstration, based on his observations of 1618, that comets were permanent bodies. In an intemperate attack on the Jesuit Orazio Grassi of the Collegio Romano, who published under the pseudonym Lothario Sarsi,[9] Galileo had in fact argued against the Tychonian interpretation of comets as supra-lunar phenomena; he had maintained that they were purely optical phenomena similar to rainbows, mere refractions of light in vapours rising from the Earth. Like rainbows, Galileo maintained, comets appear to be displaced along with the observer as he moves from place to place, and so the argument from the lack of parallax for locating comets in the celestial regions was irrelevant.[10] When Gassendi eventually came to know of Galileo's theory he did not argue against it even though he, Gassendi, had actually observed the comet of 1618 while Galileo had not; nor did he feel inclined to point out that Galileo was arguing in the manner of a conservative Aristotelian.[11] Such was his deference to the great man that he felt obliged to acknowledge that Galileo's arguments gave credibility to the opinion that comets were sub-lunar phenomena.[12]

Gassendi had also intended to use his observations of the comet to disprove the real existence of the celestial spheres, for he intended to trace the paths of comets through the aetherial spaces. He attributed the theory that the heavens were filled with impenetrable crystalline spheres to the whole Aristotelian tradition: Eudoxus, he claimed, was the first to present the hypothesis and Aristotle adopted and expanded the theory of Eudoxus in the *Metaphysics*;[13] in the *Exercitationes* Gassendi rebuked the Aristotelians for continuing to take the theory seriously. He wrote:

> They reflect solemnly on a host of silly subjects which feed their bad dreams, such as the solidity and reality of the celestial spheres, the channels which the stars travel along ...[14]

Gassendi was again following the lead of Tycho Brahe who had attributed the theory of solid spheres to the majority of his predecessors.[15]

It has recently been argued that the belief that the heavenly bodies were carried in their orbits by real, solid, crystalline spheres was not as widespread as Tycho claimed.[16] It is clear that Aristotle's spheres were composed of Aether, the fifth element, which was *not* material: the Aether had neither weight nor lightness; it was a substance unmovable in itself and eternal.[17] While it is as yet unclear who was responsible for turning Aristotle's spiritual orbs into solid material spheres, it is clear that Gassendi exaggerated when he attributed the theory of crystalline spheres to the whole Aristotelian tradition.

Gassendi had also welcomed the comet of 1618 because it provided empirical evidence against the Aristotelian doctrine according to which the super-lunary or celestial regions were immutable and perfect. That a comet should come into view and disappear in the heavens was proof that changes take place in those celestial regions; and since it was further believed that comets came to birth and died in those regions, one could take them as evidence that the heavenly substance was not essentially different from earthly matter.[18]

It must have been particularly gratifying to Gassendi to have been able, as he had at first believed, to contradict the whole Aristotelian tradition using observational evidence that he had obtained himself, and we can appreciate something of his great respect for everything that Galileo wrote when we see him surrender his advantage over the Aristotelians rather than be out of step with one of Galileo's theories. More usually, however, Gassendi found Galileo's influence and leadership very helpful in his anti-Aristotelian polemic. Gassendi concentrated most of his energy in his astronomical writings on the task of supporting the Copernican heliocentric system of the universe at the expense of the Ptolemaic/Aristotelian geocentric system, and he did this after the example of Galileo.

In the preface to the *Exercitationes* Gassendi promised that, in contradiction of the Aristotelian doctrine,

> ... the fixed stars and the Sun will be set at rest, and the Earth as one of the planets will be set in motion ...[19]

From his first letter to Galileo, which has already been cited, we learn that Gassendi was a Copernican in earnest and, what is more, that he was a Copernican as a result of the influence of Galileo. He wrote:

> First of all my dear Galileo, I would like you to be fully assured that I have embraced your Copernican theory in astronomy with the greatest mental delight. I seem to have been liberated by it, for my mind wanders free and untrammelled through the immense spaces, unrestricted by the limits of the system of this world.[20]

Gassendi stated in the same letter of the year 1625 that he had been captivated by Galileo's discoveries and writings immediately, and that he continued to entertain the highest esteem for them. He wrote:

> From the earliest days I have honoured your supreme wisdom and erudition. I cannot express how great was the silent worship I paid to you from the time your interpreter of the heavens revealed those mysteries so unknown by the human race.[21]

Gassendi here referred to the *Siderius nuncius* (1610).[22] He stated that he had read thoroughly both this work and Galileo's three letters to Mark Welser on sunspots (1613).[23] Gassendi's expressions of esteem for Galileo were always highly enthusiastic. In March 1632 he wrote:

> I continually praise the fertility of your genius, and wherever you lead I shall follow ... Proceed, admirable sir,

with your sublime business, which is worthy of the majesty
of nature, worthy of yourself, and worthy of those who long
to imitate you.[24]

In November of the same year he wrote to Galileo to thank him for a copy
of the *Dialogo*[25] which he had received at the author's request from Elia
Diodati, an important associate of Galileo's whom Gassendi claimed as a
friend.[26] Gassendi stated in this letter that, although he had not yet
sufficient opportunity to digest Galileo's latest work, he wished to tell
Galileo without delay:

> ... with what gratitude I received the book, with what
> pleasure I have skimmed it through. Indeed, I am so moved
> with delight as I read it that even now, as often as I recall its
> contents to mind, I am extraordinarily moved.[27]

Even though, as he stated, he had not yet properly read the *Dialogo*,
Gassendi expressed his complete agreement with Galileo's reasoning and
conclusions in the following words:

> I might say more, but if you could but perceive the temper
> of my mind, you would clearly realise that there is nothing
> in your arguments which I am not perfectly disposed to
> accept.[28]

Thus Gassendi clearly acknowledged the influence of Galileo in
attracting him to Copernicanism. Galileo became an ally against the
Aristotelians, for Gassendi, as has been seen, intended to use
Copernicanism against the Aristotelians in the *Exercitationes*, and
presumably he had used it in this way in his lectures from which the
*Exercitationes* was drawn. Once Gassendi stated explicitly to Galileo that he
was using the latter's astronomical reasoning in his anti-Aristotelian
project; he wrote:

> I do not intend to write anything concerning [my own]
> observations of sunspots except insofar as they lead,
> according to your principles, to a refutation of
> Aristotelianism and an exhortation that men adopt a truer
> and better philosophy.[29]

On another occasion, Gassendi's devotion to Galileo led him to fail to
note that other than Galilean/Copernican conclusions might be drawn from
his observations. The observations in question were those of the transit of
Mercury across the Sun in 1631, which have been considered to be
Gassendi's chief claim to fame as an astronomer,[30] and which Gassendi

interpreted as a triumph for Galileo.[31] The phenomenon had been predicted by Kepler,[32] whom Gassendi rightly believed to be a Copernican, but it could equally be accommodated in the Tychonic system according to which both Mercury and Venus describe orbits around the Sun.

From the foregoing samples taken from his correspondence with Galileo, Gassendi can be seen to have been an enthusiastic and somewhat uncritical follower of Galileo who was especially drawn to Galileo's work and to Copernicanism because of their anti-Aristotelian significance. Without doubt Gassendi was interested in Copernicanism for a variety of reasons: because it was modern and revolutionary; because many of the better educated scholars had been converted to it; because the most recent observations confirmed it ..., but he was particularly interested in the Copernican debate in the late 1620s because it suited his anti-Aristotelian concerns so perfectly.

In the years 1628-1629 Gassendi embarked on a nine-month tour of Flanders and Holland - the only journey he made outside France - in the course of which he visited scholars in Liège, Louvain, Anvers, Brussels, Mons, Douai, Arras, Leyden, Amsterdam, Middlebourg, Dordrecht and Gorkum.[33] It was in large part a journey of one Copernican visiting other Copernicans, as Gassendi broadened and deepened his understanding of the theory and its philosophical ramifications. Gassendi recorded very little concerning his discussions along the way but, from the little he did write to Peiresc, we learn that the Copernican theory and questions concerning the motion of bodies figured prominently in the discussions.

At Arras, Gassendi met Fr Malaperti, the Rector of the Jesuit college who, Gassendi noted, was on the point of publishing a book on sunspots, and was withholding publication until Fr Scheiner had published his work.[34] At Amsterdam he met a Sieur Janssenius who informed him that there would soon be a new armillary sphere which would be an improvement on the one which Peiresc had in his possession.[35] When he was passing through Middelbourg Gassendi, much to his regret, did not realise that Philip of Lansberg lived in that town, and so he did not call upon him. Philip of Lansberg was on Gassendi's list of most important Copernicans.[36]

At Dordrecht, Gassendi met the famous Copernican Isaac Beeckman, whom he described as the best philosopher he had met so far.[37] Beeckman led the way in the task of applying the new mechanics to Copernican speculations.[38] According to the record which Beeckman wrote in his *Journal*,[39] the two philosophers discussed the following subjects among a few others: motion and inertia; the surface areas of large and small bodies; sympathetic resonance of strings; the "point of equality in free fall"; the sweetness of musical harmonies [*consonantiarum*]; atmospheric pressure and the *"fuga vacui"* as it is called; Kepler's theories of planetary motion, of light and of magnetism; and sound. Finally, Beeckman gave to Gassendi a copy of the corollaries to the theses which he had defended in 1618 at the

University of Caen: one of the corollaries concerned the superiority of the Copernican system over the Ptolemaic.

At his last stopping place, Gorkum, Gassendi met a Maronite whose opinions concerning the order and arrangement of the universe he found to be admirable. Gassendi did not indicate what these opinions were, but we may presume that they were Copernican. He also recorded that he visited the army barracks and met a certain Monsieur de Fresnes Canaye who introduced him to the mathematician Albert Girard who had been responsible for the reprinting of the mathematical works of Samuel Marolois.[40] Gassendi concluded from his visit that "all these gentlemen were in favour of the opinion of the movement of the earth".[41] It appears that he was able to find quite a strong body of scholarly opinion in favour of the Copernican hypothesis. His position met with peer-group approval and he was not intellectually isolated.

Thus Gassendi's Copernicanism in the late 1620s is well enough documented, and it also seems clear that he saw the relevance of the new mechanics to Copernicanism as a means of demonstrating its intelligibility. It is also clear that Gassendi interpreted the Aristotelian/Ptolemaic and Copernican systems in realist fashion along with, according to the accepted view, Galileo and the generality of astronomers of the early seventeenth century.[42] Gassendi believed that the Copernican system conformed to the nature of things, that the Earth really was a planet that moved around the Sun, and that this view, or "opinion",[43] was confirmed by observations of comets, sunspots, the apparent mountainous character of the Moon, the composition of the Milky Way, the discovery of the satellites of Jupiter, and the tracing of the orbits of Mercury and Venus. After the publication of the *Dialogo* (1632), Gassendi also accepted the movement of the tides as providing probable evidence. As he expressed his thought in the letter to Galileo of November 1632,

> The systems and hypotheses of all the ancients seem mere nonsense and empty dreams when they are compared with your discovery.[44]

In these words Gassendi echoed his statement in his letter to Galileo of 1625 concerning the service of the "interpreter of the heavens" in revealing the unknown mysteries. Galileo had revealed, or discovered, the truth at last. (In the matter of the tides, Galileo was, of course, mistaken. This was the area of Galileo's system that was least satisfactory. But Gassendi was not one to check Galileo's work for errors.)

Gassendi structured his own natural philosophy in a manner which corresponded to the realistic interpretation of astronomical hypotheses by combining physical, or natural, philosophy with astronomy. Indeed, he was working to achieve this combination immediately prior to 1632. He listed in a letter to Peiresc written in 1631[45] the chapter headings of the very first draft of his Epicurean philosophy. According to this list, natural philosophy ("*La physique*") was to be expounded in four books, the first of which concerned nature ("*de natura*"), the second concerned the universe ('*de mundo*"), the third concerned the heavens ("*de sublimibus*", astronomy), and the fourth concerned the Earth ("*de humilibus*"). In the *Syntagma* version, which he prepared between 1649 and 1655, Gassendi connected astronomy and physical philosophy still more definitely by reducing the four divisions to three, of which the first was entitled "on nature in general" ("*de rebus naturae universe*"), the second "on heavenly things" ("*de rebus caelestibus*"), and the third "on earthly things" ("*de rebus terrenis*").[46]

To combine astronomy with natural philosophy in the way that Gassendi did implied that the superlunary and sublunary realms were to be explained by the same principles and according to the same laws of nature. No longer were astronomical hypotheses permitted to be simply devices for saving phenomena: it was required that they be declarations concerning the real nature of things, and therefore had to be stated in a way that was compatible with the laws and theories determined by investigation of terrestrial phenomena. Whence arose the realistic interpretation of hypotheses in the late sixteenth and early seventeenth centuries.[47] Gassendi was fully in accord with the new realism, and he promoted it through the very structure of his systematic exposition of Epicurean philosophy. Furthermore, the realistic interpretation of hypotheses and the corresponding demand that the whole of the universe be understood as subject to the same natural laws would ultimately banish from philosophy the Aristotelian division between Heaven and Earth. Consequently, it was germane to Gassendi's anti-Aristotelian project to combine astronomy and natural philosophy and to adopt a realist interpretation of astronomical hypotheses.

The condemnation of Galileo by the Roman authorities on June 22nd, 1633,[48] came as a profound shock to Gassendi. We learn from a letter that Gassendi wrote to Thomas Campanella in May of that year that he had received information from Galileo himself that conflict with the Roman authorities was looming. Gassendi informed Campanella:

> In recent long letters from Galileo I have learnt that he is soon to be in Rome, whence he has been summoned. I was astonished, for he has not published anything without [Ecclesiastical] approval. But it is not for us to know of such weighty matters.[49]

Even with forewarning from such an entirely credible source as the man himself who had been under scrutiny, some time elapsed before Gassendi could actually believe that Galileo had been condemned. He wrote a letter to Galileo in mid-January of the following year which shows that he was still somewhat incredulous. He wrote:

> I am still waiting to discover what has happened to you,
> great glory of our age. Though a persistent rumour has been
> spread abroad, I cannot trust it until the affair has been
> made fully known.[50]

Gassendi's shock was understandable. Given his enthusiasm for almost everything Galileo did, given the anti-Aristotelian capital he had been making out of Galilean Copernicanism, and given the fact that, as it would seem,[51] he was on the point of concluding a manuscript in which Epicurean philosophy was expounded as the new natural philosophy to support the Copernican system in astronomy, the condemnation of Galileo required that Gassendi completely change the direction in which he had been moving for as long as he had been professing philosophy.

Gassendi was also completely taken by surprise because he had not heeded the warning given to Galileo by Cardinal Bellarmine in Rome in 1616.[52] No doubt, Galileo's own dismissal of the warning in practice during the 1620s encouraged Gassendi to follow a similar course. Gassendi seems to have made but a single reference to the censure of Galileo in 1616, in a very private letter to Peiresc in February 1634, indirectly prompted by the condemnation of 1633. The relevant passage is worth quoting for the insight it gives into the caution that Gassendi considered necessary:

> As for M. Diodati, I am happy that you are doing him the
> favour of sending your copy of Foscarini's book to him. It
> would be just as well, nevertheless, to warn him to take care
> that Bernegger should not mention that it was you who sent
> it. In any case, when I write to M. Diodati I shall give him
> the information which perhaps he does not have, that the
> same Foscarini has been censured, along with Galileo, I do
> not remember in which year, and that I recall having seen
> the censure in the commentary of Mersenne on Genesis. It
> would be well to do this, not to prevent him from doing
> what he wants to do, but so that he will be properly
> forewarned.[53]

Foscarini's work[54] was condemned in a decree of the Sacred Congregation for the Index of Prohibited Books on 5.3.1616. [55] Bernegger and Diodati collaborated to publish Galileo's writings despite ecclesiastical prohibition; whence Gassendi's advice to Peiresc to be cautious. Even in this one reference to the censure of 1616 Gassendi was unclear concerning the precise year in which it had occurred. Evidently, the censure of 1616 had been a dead letter for Gassendi for many years prior to 1633, and his reactions to the events of this latter year, which will be the subject of the pages that follow, provide indications of why he should have disregarded the earlier censure. Especially significant were his reactions to the scriptural objections to Copernicanism and his understanding of the limitations of the authority of the Holy Office: even after 1633 he could barely conceal his disdain for the scriptural objections, and it would seem that it was only because the Roman authorities insisted a second time, in 1633, and with a greater show of strength, that Gassendi felt compelled to take notice.

Gassendi finally realised that it was no longer possible for him to support the Copernican opinion as he had done prior to 1633. But eleven whole years passed before he would even consider the compromise system of Tycho Brahe, and he only adopted this solution in his teaching at the Collège Royal in the academic year 1645-1646.[56] Jean-Baptiste Morin, a close anti-Copernican acquaintance with whom Gassendi had a series of public rows,[57] was also professor at the Collège Royal before Gassendi,[58] and he had accepted the Tychonic compromise in his work *Famosi et antiqui problematis ... solutio* (1631);[59] consequently, Gassendi was apparently presenting what was customary at the Collège Royal when he advocated the Tychonic solution.

During the eleven years between the time that Gassendi ascertained that Galileo had been condemned and the year that he took the chair of mathematics at the Collège Royal, Gassendi continued to work on his Epicurean philosophy, but did not return to the astronomical section until he wrote MS Tours 710 in 1642/1643. In this way he was able to avoid committing himself to adopting an alternative astronomical system during all those years. He was in effect silenced along with Galileo; possibly he hoped for a change in the ecclesiastical and cultural climate; perhaps he even hoped for a reversal of the anti-Copernican judgment.

Only once did Gassendi break his silence on the Copernican question of his own accord during this time, and that was in the two letters entitled *De motu impresso a motore translato* (1642)[60] whereupon he found himself under attack from Jean-Baptiste Morin[61] and from the Jesuit rector of the college of Metz, Pierre de Cazrée.[62] In these letters Gassendi had ventured to discuss, after the manner of Galileo's *Dialogo*, Second Day, the physical arguments used by the Copernicans in defence of their opinions. Gassendi did this by writing an account of his experiments on the motion of projectiles, taking as his basic principle that a body in motion impresses its own motion on anything that it carries along with it, and presenting as his conclusion that the arguments from common sense employed against the Copernican theory had no value. Gassendi emphasised that he was not asserting that the Earth was in fact in motion, but rather that the arguments, based on the motion of projectiles, and offered in support of the theory of the stability of the Earth were not strong enough, and that better arguments must be looked for:

> You will not need me to repeat that I did not do this in
> order to assert that the Earth moves, but, out of love for the
> truth, in order to indicate that the stability of the Earth
> must be established by stronger arguments.[63]

Morin and Cazrée attacked Gassendi mainly on points of his discussion
of the physical arguments, Morin presenting what he claimed to be proofs
for the stability of the Earth, and Cazrée criticising Gassendi's analysis of
the movement of falling bodies.[64] Gassendi responded to Morin in a third
letter *De motu impresso a motore translato* (1643).[65] and to Cazrée in three
letters *De proportione qua gravia decidentia accelerantur* (1646).[66]

At the conclusion of his discussion of the physical arguments against
Copernicanism in the first two letters *De motu impresso a motore translato*,
Gassendi made a brief but succinct statement of the response of the
Copernicans to the objections based on Sacred Scripture. In fact, he
outlined two different responses. The first was of the kind which Galileo
had given in his letter to the Grand Duchess Christina (1615),[67] namely that
the Bible is not a book which is concerned with physical, mathematical and
such-like teaching, but one that instructs men concerning grace and
supernatural salvation; it deals solely with appearances when it speaks of
the motion of the Sun and the stability of the Earth, and it speaks in a
language that is accommodated to the understanding of all men rather than
the language of the natural philosopher. The second response, which
Gassendi claimed was given by a number of Copernicans, was that the
stability attributed to the Earth:

> ... did not refer to the Earth's being stationed in one place,
> but to the constancy of its composition, its incorruptibility
> as a whole; while there are continuous changes of generation
> and corruption especially in its surface parts, the Earth itself
> remains a perduring whole.[68]

In outlining these Copernican responses to the objections that were made
against their theory and which were based on Scriptural passages, Gassendi
was careful to stress that he accepted the ruling of the Roman authorities
according to which the objections were sustained. At the same time, he
could not see that the objections had validity. He wrote:

> Because those texts are explained in a different fashion by
> men who exercise considerable authority in the Church, I
> stand by their judgment, and in this I am not ashamed to
> enslave my intellect.[69]

Cazrée endeavoured to convince Gassendi of the validity of the
objections based on Scripture, but his efforts drew a response which

showed how little value he saw in this type of objection. Gassendi argued that the simple fact that authors quote scriptural passages as objections to the Copernican theory did not render it any more suspect than the opinions that the heavens are round, or that the Earth is surrounded by regions of air, fire and aether, that the heavens are fluid, and so on. Objections based on scripture, Gassendi argued, could and often were made to all these opinions, yet they had never been suspect in the eyes of the Church.[70]

Thus Gassendi considered that the anti-Copernican case could not stand on the physical arguments that had been adduced, and he considered that the objections based on Scripture of themselves were unconvincing to say the least. He made it perfectly obvious that the only reason why he accepted that he must abandon the Copernican theory was the weight of the authority of the Holy Office in Rome. He did not consider the judgment handed down by this authority to be an article of faith, nor did he believe that it had been formally promulgated as something to be accepted by the whole Church. But he did believe that:

> ... the judgment [of the Cardinals of the Holy Office] must be held in special regard, and must be considered to be of the greatest significance by the faithful.[71]

Furthermore, Gassendi rejected Cazrée's claim that Copernicanism had been suspect all along, and he made the counter-claim that from the time of Copernicus onwards learned men had given it their approval, and that these were even men in responsible positions in the Church, interpreters of Sacred Scripture, religious men and Doctors expert in such matters.[72] Clearly, Gassendi's acceptance of the verdict against Copernicanism relied solely upon the authority of the Holy Office in its specific intervention against Galileo in 1633. As a consequence it was a very oppressive verdict for Gassendi. Just how oppressive he felt it to be may perhaps be gauged from the following considerations.

First, Gassendi's distress was particularly acute because for him, as it had been for Galileo,[73] the only option to the Copernican system to be considered was the Ptolemaic system of which the system of Tycho Brahe was considered a version.[74] At this time the options were seen, at least by Gassendi, as being geocentrism and heliocentrism. (It was only in 1645-1646 that, under the stimulus of his new post at the Collège Royal, Gassendi would bring himself to consider and adopt as a compromise the system of Tycho Brahe.) Thus, for example, Gassendi failed to take into account that the transit of Mercury across the Sun in 1631 could have been accommodated in the Tychonic system just as easily as in the Copernican. Again, in MS Tours 709 (1642-1643), Gassendi listed only two major astronomical systems, the Ptolemaic and the Copernican:

It is to be noted that the major opinions concerning the
disposition of the universe are two. One is the common
opinion especially defended by Aristotle which places the
Earth in the centre of the universe. The other is the opinion
which contradicts the evidence of our senses and which was
in former times proposed especially by Plato and
Pythagoras, and recently by Copernicus and his followers.
According to this latter opinion the Sun stands in the centre
of the universe.[75]

However, in the much expanded *Syntagma* version of this passage (post
1649) the major systems were given as three in number, the Tychonic
system being the third and presented as being preferable to the other two
by reason of the judgment of the Holy Office.[76]

Second, it would appear that the most striking evidence of Gassendi's
distress at the condemnation of Galileo is the complete disappearance of the
first version of the *Pars physica* of his Epicurean philosophy. It seems to be
strongly indicated that Gassendi destroyed this version following the
condemnation. In April, 1631, two years preceding the condemnation,
Gassendi wrote to Peiresc giving an account of the progress of his
Epicurean project. He told Peiresc that he was more than half-way through
the *Pars physica*. At the very time of writing he was engaged on the third
book, the *De sublimibus*, or the treatise on astronomy. Thus, during the
years that immediately preceded the trauma, Gassendi was writing the
astronomical section of his Epicurean philosophy. The following were the
first four of the twelve chapter headings of Book 3 as he gave them to
Peiresc: 1. On the substance of the heavens and the stars; 2. On the variety,
position and intervals of the stars; 3. On the size and shape of the stars; 4.
On the movement of the heavenly bodies.[77] Given that Gassendi was an
enthusiastic Copernican following in the footsteps of Galileo at this time,
his text in these chapters could only have contained an exposition of
Copernican astronomy rendered intelligible by the physical philosophy of
Epicurus. And since Gassendi had been working on the project for a
number of years,[78] he would have considered his text as an important
statement.

Following the condemnation of Galileo, however, Gassendi was forced to
reconsider the whole project, and he re-wrote the *Pars physica* in such a
way that his Epicurean philosophy would not contravene the ban on the
teaching of Copernicanism. Nevertheless, his frustration caused by the ban
was scarcely veiled. For when he re-wrote the astronomical section in MS
Tours 710 (1643), and when he prepared the much-enlarged version of the
treatise (between 1649 and 1655) for publication in the *Syntagma*, he stated
that the Pythagorean/Copernican theory was "more probable and
evident",[79] but, because some Church heads had confirmed by decree that
the Earth was stationary in the centre of the universe, those who were

orthodox had to accept their decision with reverence.[80] At the same time, however, the rest of Gassendi's text showed why he considered the Pythagorean/Copernican theory to be superior.[81] Once Gassendi had re-written the astronomical section of his Epicurean philosophy, I suggest, from frustration or for reasons of prudence, or perhaps because of both, he destroyed the first, Copernican, version of the astronomical section of his Epicurean philosophy.[82]

Thus Gassendi was seriously frustrated by the condemnation of Galileo. He was convinced that the physical arguments in favour of Copernicanism far outweighed any physical arguments that could be adduced in support of the Aristotelian/Ptolemaic system. As an orthodox Catholic, however, he felt obliged to accept the ruling of the Holy Office, and he had to cope with that ruling as best he could.

One stratagem that made it more possible to cope with the ban on Copernicanism was to avoid thinking about it. As has already been noted, Gassendi resorted to this stratagem for about eleven years. But such a solution was entirely unsatisfactory for someone like Gassendi who had a professional interest in the matter. As a philosopher, he needed to achieve a *modus vivendi* with this extremely unpalatable but authoritative judgment. And so Gassendi turned to his Epicureanism. He accentuated the theme of Epicurean scepticism which he had been developing in his logical writings, and applied it to subjects of the Copernican debate. In this way Epicurus provided Gassendi with a *rationale* which helped him to accept the condemnation of Galileo and of Copernicanism with a greater degree of *ataraxia*, or peace of mind.

Gassendi had accepted in theory the sceptical interpretation of Galileo's work expressed by Galileo himself at the conclusion of the *Dialogo* when he had Simplicio observe that Salviati's (Galileo's) reasonings were "more plausible ... but not true and conclusive".[83] Apparently not noticing the guile that is sometimes perceived in this passage[84] - though he *did* say that he had not had time to digest the work - Gassendi commended Galileo for the fact that "no matter how plausible your conjectures may be, they never become more than conjectures for you".[85] He simply accepted Galileo's reminder of the need to apply his sceptical principles to Copernicanism, and after 1634 he applied them with stringency as he highlighted the sceptical motif of Epicureanism.[86]

Sextus Empiricus had classified Epicurus as a dogmatist, or one who proceeded upon *a priori* principles accepted as true rather than founded upon experience,[78] and Gassendi discussed this classification in order to modify it. He accepted that it was correct to number Epicurus among the dogmatists, but he asserted that of all dogmatists Epicurus most approached the position of the sceptics. Gassendi claimed of Epicurus that:

Whenever there were many possible causes for the one
effect, it being possible for that effect to be brought about
in many varied ways, then he set these causes and ways in
opposition to each other after the manner of the sceptics.[88]

And Gassendi quoted the following passage from the letter of Epicurus to
Pythocles as evidence of the truth of his claim:

If one were to accept one *modus* and reject another that is
equally in accord with the appearances, one would obviously
stray from the correct way of philosophising about nature
and slip into fables.[89]

Gassendi also pointed to the use that Epicurus made of the term
" προσμένειν " that expressed the need to wait and to examine everything
carefully in order to avoid making rash pronouncements, and of the term
" ἐνδέχεσθαι " which meant "it might be so, and it might be otherwise".
Gassendi claimed that both terms were properly sceptical.[90]

Gassendi's discussion of the sceptical element in the writings of Epicurus
was in his manuscripts before he applied his sceptical principles to
Copernicanism. In MS Carpentras 1832 (1634), Gassendi referred to an
earlier, and untraced, discussion concerning whether Epicurus should be
classified as a dogmatist - one who, according to Gassendi, claims to have
discovered the truth - or as an *"acatalepticus"* (academician) - one who
considers that truth cannot be apprehended.[91] The final version of this
discussion is to be found in the *Proemium de philosophia universe* of the
*Syntagma*,[92] and it was evidently included in much the same form in all the
versions of Gassendi's Epicurean philosophy, including presumably the
version which was destroyed because it was too Copernican.

Now Gassendi was correct in interpreting Epicureanism as a form of
sceptical dogmatism. Ancient Epicureanism had been developed as a
philosophy that could provide an answer to the extreme scepticism of the
Pyrrhonists by establishing that some things at least were certain even in a
world in which nothing seemed to be so.[93] Since the Pyrrhonists maintained
that *nothing* could be regarded as true or certain, the Epicureans countered
by maintaining that sensation and mental perception (understood as an
inner sensation)[94] provided information that was infallibly true. The
corollary of this dogmatic sensationalism was that one had to adopt a
sceptical position concerning all reality that lay beyond the reach of direct
sensation and mental perception.

The insight into Epicureanism just outlined was to prove very helpful to
Gassendi in his struggle to accept the condemnation of Copernicanism, for
he found that Epicurus was particularly sceptical in discussions of
cosmological and astronomical questions. Gassendi was able to rely on the

support and example of Epicurus in adopting a similar sceptical position in the Copernican debate.

Thus Gassendi noted that Epicurus suspended judgment concerning the shape of the world. Far from being worthy of criticism for refusing to accept that the universe is round, Gassendi argued, or for refusing to decide whether the outer spheres (*extremum mundi*) were dense or rarefied, Epicurus was, Gassendi argued, to be commended for his "moderation of spirit" and for showing himself to be a true sceptic by not affirming something for which he did not have indubitable reasons. Then Gassendi went on to write:

> Clearly, having weighed up the various opinions concerning the outer spheres he [Epicurus] saw that considerable probability attached to each of them, but that none of them were recommended for indubitable reasons. So, recognising the plausibility of each one, he preferred to act with moderation and to withhold assent, rather than make confident assertions concerning states of affairs that were so far away and so hidden from mortal eyes.[95]

Gassendi presented these discussions as still being vital at the time of writing (1641), and the sceptical suspension of judgment maintained by Epicurus as still being the correct position to be adopted. He explained that when one claimed that the outer spheres were dense (referring to the theory of the crystalline spheres), there was no means of proving that they were not rarefied, or when one claimed that they were rarefied, there was no means of proving that they were not dense. Then, applying the scepticism of Epicurus directly to the crux of the Copernican discussion, Gassendi claimed that a similar moderation of spirit such as Epicurus displayed is required in discussions concerning the question of the movement of the fixed stars and the Earth, since there was insufficient evidence to prove that either one of the two opinions, the Ptolemaic/Aristotelian or the Copernican, was true:

> In similar manner, how can the one who contends that the outer sphere is immobile demonstrate that it is not moved, especially when we see the bodies that are in it carried from East to West? And how can the one who contends that it is mobile demonstrate that it is not immobile, especially since the appearance that the stars are moved towards the West might be caused by the fact that we are carried to the East, as happens when we seem to see the harbour moved towards the ship, although it is certain that the harbour is at rest and that the ship is moved towards the harbour?[96]

It seems clear that Gassendi applied his sceptical principles to the Copernican question only after the condemnation of Galileo and Copernicanism in 1633. As I have argued, he was spurred on to do this by the need to find a rationally satisfactory means of accepting the condemnation given with official Church authority. At the same time he ensured that his astronomical writings were in harmony with the substance of the decree of sentence of Galileo, for they no longer expressed belief in or commitment to the Copernican doctrine.[97] In this way, Gassendi found some rational justification for accepting the content of the authoritative judgment from his scepticism and that of Epicurus. And at the same time he found a way in which he could draw his philosophy back within the bounds laid down for orthodoxy by that judgment. Consequently, he was able to conclude:

> ... although the opinion that the Earth moves may seem to be proven by some plausible arguments, yet no demonstration can be offered that would prove it to be true. So the opposite view cannot be assailed because it lacks demonstrative proof, nor because it has been disproved by certain arguments.[98]

Gassendi's acceptance of the Tychonic compromise system seems in part to have been stimulated by his appointment to the chair of mathematics at the Collège Royal in 1645. The principal evidence for this is the fact that Gassendi did not accept the system in any of his writings prior to his *Institutio astronomica*, the text of his teaching at the Collège Royal which was published in 1647.[99] But thereafter he presented it at every opportune moment as the most suitable system for an orthodox astronomer. In the *Syntagma* the passages advocating the Tychonic system are invariably additions made by Gassendi after 1649 to his earlier version of MS Tours 710, written in 1643. For instance, to the passage quoted in the previous paragraph Gassendi added the rather awkward sentence:

> Consequently, for those whose religion bars [lit., keeps safe] the Copernican hypothesis, the hypothesis of Tycho Brahe comes to the rescue, and this has the greatest verisimilitude of all the hypotheses.[100]

And in another passage added to the *Syntagma* version Gassendi compared the three systems rather than two, as he had done previously, and he drew the following conclusion:

> Finally, the following is now the customary view: the Ptolemaic hypothesis, especially when presented with solid spheres, and especially because according to the hypothesis

Mercury and Venus remain below the Sun, cannot be satisfactorily defended; th⁻ Copernican hypothesis is generally avoided because it attributes motion to the Earth, which appears to contradict Sacred Scripture; therefore there is no other hypothesis that is capable of saving the phenomena as well as the Tychonic, and this is the one which is best adopted throughout one's astronomy and mostly adhered to.[101]

It is clear from Gassendi's biography of Tycho Brahe[102] that he was genuinely enthusiastic about Tycho and his work. He judged that Tycho was greater than Hipparchus, the astronomer of antiquity to whom, according to Gassendi, Kepler had compared him.[103] Gassendi preferred a grander, mythological allusion, comparing Hipparchus to Atlas and Tycho to Hercules.[104] Gassendi was, I suggest, picking up the thread of Tychonic influence that had been in his life before he came under the spell of Galileo, and in Gassendi's later life Tycho came to assume the position that Galileo had formerly occupied, prior to the condemnation of Copernicanism by the Holy Office in 1633. Tycho's system of the universe had now been confirmed in its position as the more respectable and fashionable hypothesis.

All this clearly indicates that the impetus went out of Gassendi's Galilean/Copernican anti-Aristotelian polemic. The Aristotelians, through the instrumentality of the decree of sentence of Galileo, had won the round. Indeed the position which Gassendi adopted at the end of his career corresponded exactly with that which had been advocated by the Aristotelian Jesuit, Horatio Grassi, in a public lecture delivered in the Collegio Romano in the year 1619. Using his pseudonym Lothario Sarsi, Grassi pronounced:

But consider, let it be granted that my master [Horatio Grassi] adhered to Tycho. How much of a crime is that? Whom instead might we follow? Ptolemy? whose followers' throats are threatened by the outthrust sword of Mars now made closer. Or Copernicus? but he who is dutiful will rather call everyone away from him and will equally reject and spurn his recently condemned hypothesis. Therefore, Tycho remains as the only one whom we may approve as our leader among the unknown courses of the stars.[105]

## CHAPTER 3

## EPICUREAN ANTI-ARISTOTELIANISM

Gassendi was one of the many philosophers of his time who struggled to extricate themselves from Aristotelianism so that they might participate in the new scientific movement which was gathering momentum in the early seventeenth century. We have seen that scepticism was the chief weapon that Gassendi used against the Aristotelians, and he used it with the aim of undermining the reputation for infallibility which the Aristotelians supposedly enjoyed. We have seen that Gassendi used Copernican astronomy as another weapon for his anti-Aristotelian campaign, although it lost much of its effectiveness as a weapon when Copernicanism was condemned in 1633. Now in this third chapter, the anti-Aristotelian character of Gassendi's Epicureanism will be explored, and it will be seen that the adoption of Epicurean philosophy was integral to Gassendi's anti-Aristotelian polemic.

It is not wholly clear why Gassendi should have chosen Epicureanism in the first place, but humanist influences were very significant in his choice. The philosophy was circulating prominently in learned circles in the sixteenth and seventeenth centuries by reason of the popularity of the *De rerum natura* of Lucretius: between 1563 and 1631, twenty-two editions of Lucretius are known to have been published; Montaigne quoted more than a sixth part of the whole poem in one hundred and forty-eight citations;[1] and there was a strong tradition of Lucretian scholarship in France dating from the middle of the sixteenth century and including such names as Lambinus, Turnèbe, Pierre Galland, Henri de Mesme, Dorat, Tourneboeuf and Claude du Puy.[2]

Gassendi originally placed at the head of his writings on Epicurean philosophy an apology for Epicurus entitled *De vita et moribus Epicuri libri octo*, a work which he completed early in 1634,[3] and which was published in 1647,[4] but which was ultimately not incorporated into the *Syntagma philosophicum*. Gassendi wrote a whole new treatise of Epicurean ethics for the *Syntagma*,[5] and the original apology for Epicurus is now to be found among Gassendi's miscellaneous works in the fifth volume of the *Opera omnia*, where its significance is largely lost. It is this small work which makes it most clear that Gassendi took up the cause of Epicureanism in great part out of his humanist admiration for it as an ancient philosophy, and out of his humanist aspiration to restore it to full life and vigour in the seventeenth century.

Gassendi expressed his purpose succinctly in the title which he gave to one of the chapters of his apology: "Epicurus is re-admitted to the company of the philosophers".[6] And in the course of this chapter he showed that he subscribed to the common humanist view according to which there was a period of darkness lasting for many centuries which gave way to the bright period when classical learning was revived. He wrote:

> Throughout almost all those centuries when good literature lay buried, Epicurus was considered to be a disreputable person. But when, about two centuries ago, the dust was shaken from the books of the humanities and they again came to hand, almost all learned men voiced their praises for Epicurus.[7]

Gassendi saw his task as one of rescuing Epicurus from undeserved disrepute and neglect, thereby making a contribution to the revival of learning which he saw as having begun in the fifteenth century. Gassendi quoted passages from the following humanist scholars in praise of Epicurus: Francesco Filelfo[8], Alexander ab Alexandro[9], Ludovicus Caelius Rhodiginus[10], Raphael Maffejus of Volterra[11], Gianfrancesco Pico della Mirandola.[12]He also mentioned Giovanni Battista Guarini, a dramatist, and Marcus Antonius Bonciarius, a Parisian professor, as two others who were reputed to have written in praise of Epicurus some years previous to Gassendi's own time of writing, but whose writings on the subject Gassendi had not been able to trace. He cited also Andreas Arnaudus, a local author, who had written a brief apology for Epicurus,[13] and he concluded with a quotation from the fifteenth-century poet Palingenius in praise of Epicurus[14]. All these features of Gassendi's apology for Epicurus stamp it as a product of the humanist movement.

The humanist character of the apology can also be discerned in the prominence it gave to ethical concerns. Gassendi was chiefly concerned to defend Epicurus from calumnies against his moral teaching, his personal moral integrity and that of the School he founded. The quotations from humanist scholars mentioned in the previous paragraph all supported Gassendi in his attempts to overcome prejudice against Epicureanism that was based on ethical considerations.

The methods of humanist erudition, furthermore, were reflected in Gassendi's researches into Epicurean philosophy. In 1626 he explained in a letter to Peiresc[15] that he was making a study of the ancient commentators on Epicurean philosophy. And in another letter to Peiresc three years later he described in the following words his labours to translate the *Vita Epicuri* of Diogenes Laertius:

> At present I am engaged on a translation of the tenth book
> of Laertius which is devoted to Epicurus but which contains

so many errors that Epicurus is hardly recognisable in all the
most important passages. I have a variety of translations,
notes and manuscripts before me, and by comparing them
all and relying upon the little knowledge that I possess of the
philosophy of this man I am endeavouring to prepare a
translation of my own which I can quote when I use Laertius
as an authority.[16]

Such an approach to Epicurean philosophy as Gassendi described in the
quotation just given, reflected the literary and erudite methods of the
humanists, intent on restoring original texts. In fact, his approach
resembled very closely the methods of Lambinus, the sixteenth-century
editor of the text of the De rerum natura of Lucretius,[17] whose critical
edition was a veritable restoration of the poem and became the
authoritative edition for the next three centuries, and was the edition used
by Montaigne.[18] As Gassendi entered more fully into his task he relied
heavily on the De rerum natura, quoting an estimated 5,347 of the total
7,415 lines of the poem, many lines more than once.[19] As Gassendi did long
after him, Lambinus provided philosophical and historical commentaries on
the text of Lucretius, drawing on the works of Plato, Aristotle, Diogenes
Laertius, Plutarch, Herodotus, Thucydides, Xenophon, Pliny, Strabo,
Arrianus and other classical sources. Whereas Montaigne, for instance, read
the De rerum natura especially for its literary qualities and moral teachings,
Lambinus appreciated the poem also for the natural philosophy it
expressed. Gassendi appreciated the poem of Lucretius above all for its
explanations of the nature of the universe and of the causes of natural
phenomena, and although he did not cite Lambinus, as he did not cite other
editors of classical texts, it is apparent that his commentary on the
philosophy owed more than a little to Lambinus's annotated, critical edition
of the De rerum natura.

At first Gassendi intended that his whole Epicurean project should be an
erudite commentary on the philosophy of Epicurus.[20] But this intention was
not sustained. For a start, as he wrote MS Carpentras 1832 (the second
version of the treatise on logic and the first two chapters of the Pars
physica) and the first two books of MS Tours 709 (the treatises on the
physical universe and on the atoms), his work did retain some semblance of
the commentary form: at least Gassendi could claim that his work was as
much a commentary on the philosophy of Epicurus as the texts of the
Schoolmen were commentaries on the philosophy of Aristotle. However, it
soon became apparent - by Book XIV of MS Tours 709, in fact (and the MS
commenced at Book XII) - that Gassendi was not really writing a
commentary, for his scope was too broad. Writing in 1630 to Golius, a
professor at Leyden, Gassendi described his manner of writing the
"commentary":

You know that I have committed myself to a work on Epicurus. I usually expound his doctrine, but at the same time I explore other doctrines as well. In this way I think over and compare the more well-known doctrines of the ancient philosophers, and since I respect them all I strive to give consideration to each and every opinion ...[21]

Possibly because he had made his task of writing a commentary impossible by attempting to do too much, Gassendi gradually abandoned the idea of writing one and produced instead his own Epicurean philosophy published as "the *Syntagma philosophicum* of Pierre Gassendi".

At the same time, however, Gassendi continued to use his sources for Epicurean philosophy with considerable eclectic freedom. He relied heavily on the *De rerum natura* of Lucretius especially when he strove to be thoroughly mechanistic, as in his treatment of the subjects of motion, alteration and the production of qualities.[22] But when he gave an atomistic account of seminal and vital processes, and when he strove to advocate a theistic Epicurean theory of causality, Gassendi quoted from the Stoic versions of Epicurean teaching, such as those which were given in the writings of Diogenes Laertius, Seneca, and Cicero.[23] The Stoic cosmos was established on an orderly plan, it was designed and purposive and consequently more suited to Gassendi's Christian atomism than the Epicurean universe which was uncreated and governed by chance.[24]

### Epicureanism as substitute for Aristotelianism

Gassendi's humanism, as has already been seen, was of a particularly anti-Aristotelian kind; his restoration of Epicureanism, likewise, was central to the realisation of his anti-Aristotelian designs. Gassendi aimed at bringing about nothing less than the acceptance of Epicureanism by scholars and by the Church authorities - *especially* by the Church authorities - in the place of Aristotelianism, which had been the authorised Christian philosophy since the fourteenth century. In short, Gassendi wanted Epicureanism to be accepted as a substitute for Aristotelianism.

Gassendi announced that the substitution was his main project when he wrote the dedicatory letter to his friend and patron François Luillier,[25] which letter was published at the head of the *De vita et moribus Epicuri*. His design, he told Luillier, was to do for Epicurean philosophy what had been done for Aristotelianism, namely, to render it fit to be approved by the Church authorities. Just as the books of Aristotle had supposedly been expurgated in order to make them fit to be used for public instruction, he said, so he himself aimed to expurgate Epicurean philosophy in order that it might be permitted for use at least in private study.[26] He reiterated that this was his intention in the general philosophical introduction to the *Syntagma*,

seeking to put his project into historical perspective by tracing the rise of
Aristotelian philosophy from a position of low repute comparable to that of
Epicureanism (at the time of writing) to a position in which it won
universal favour and acceptance. He wrote:

> The early Church Fathers were particularly opposed to
> Aristotle and his philosophy, and they displayed extreme
> animosity against the followers of Aristotle. But when some
> philosophers were converted to the faith they began to set
> aside the more serious errors of Aristotle. What remained of
> Aristotelian philosophy was then accommodated to religion
> so successfully that it was no longer suspect and finally
> became the handmaid ministering to religion. Therefore, I
> say, just as it was possible in the case of Aristotelian
> philosophy, which is now taught publicly, so it is possible
> with other philosophies such as the Stoic and the Epicurean.
> All of them have much that is of value and worthy of being
> learned once the errors are eliminated and refuted in the
> same way as the very grave errors of Aristotle were refuted.
> This is the task that I am attempting, as I made perfectly
> clear when I wrote on the life and manners of Epicurus.[27]

Gassendi thus claimed that the task of expurgating and refuting the
"errors" of Epicureanism and making it generally acceptable was no more
daunting than the task of rejecting the "errors" of Aristotle had been
previously when Christian philosophers had attempted the task and had
succeeded well enough to satisfy the Church authorities of the day.

When Gassendi wrote to Galileo in 1625[28] telling him that he was
following his lead in striving to refute Aristotelianism and to advocate a
truer and better philosophy, he already had it in mind that Epicureanism
would be the truer and better philosophy to be substituted for
Aristotelianism, for his predilection for Epicureanism had already
manifested itself in the *Exercitationes* (1624). One can see this predilection
in the summary of the projected seven books of the *Exercitationes* which he
gave in the preface.[29] There Gassendi announced that Book 7 was to be
entirely devoted to presenting Epicurean ethics as an alternative to
Aristotelian ethics. Also, in his description in the same summary of the
other six books he listed many subjects that he intended to deal with. Some
of these were properly Epicurean, such as the doctrine of space which, he
stated, he intended to substitute for the Aristotelian doctrine of place, and
the doctrines of the void, and of multiple universes or, at least, the
immensity of the universe. Others were subjects for which Gassendi later
substituted Epicurean for Aristotelian explanations, such as matter and
form, the nature of celestial bodies, the causes of motion, the nature of
light and celestial phenomena, the nature of the elements and of mixed (*i.e.*

compound) substances. It seems clear that the *Exercitationes*, if it had been completed, would have been an Epicurean work.

Gassendi's above-mentioned remark in his letter to Galileo in 1625 indicated that there was a close link between his Epicureanism and his Copernicanism. Gassendi made a more explicit allusion to the link in the same letter by drawing Galileo's attention to the projected Book 4 of the *Exercitationes* in which, as he had stated in the preface:

> the fixed stars and the Sun will be set at rest, and the Earth
> as one of the planets will be set in motion.[30]

Gassendi told Galileo that from these words Galileo could see that he had been thinking along Copernican/Galilean lines.[31]

The link between Gassendi's Epicureanism and his Copernicanism is also discernible from the information that is available concerning his journey to Flanders and Holland in the years 1628-1629.[32] On this journey Gassendi was much occupied with Copernican questions. However, the Copernican questions were very often Epicurean questions as well. Such was apparently the case in his conversations with the scholars of Leyden,[33] while it was clearly the case in his conversations with Isaac Beeckman whom Gassendi met later on his journey.[34] Beeckman was a Copernican and an atomist who exploited the new science of motion in order to render Copernican astronomy more consistent and intelligible,[35] and when Gassendi returned home he pursued essentially the same aims by combining physical philosophy with astronomy in his Epicurean project.[36] While Beeckman's contribution to Gassendi's philosophical development was apparently not as seminal as it had been for Descartes',[37] since Gassendi was already developing his Copernican/Epicurean philosophy before he met Beeckman, nevertheless the meeting with Beeckman meant a great deal to Gassendi, as both men recorded, each in his own way: Beeckman wrote that Gassendi "approved all [my explanations] and seemed to hear them with joy and wonder",[38] while Gassendi wrote to Peiresc that Beeckman was "the best philosopher that I have yet met".[39]

Despite the condemnation of Copernicanism in 1633,[40] Gassendi continued to work on his plan of providing an Epicurean explanation of motion in general, including celestial motion: thus his Epicurean project continued, regardless. And he still wished to seek the approval of Galileo for what he was doing, for he wrote a letter to Galileo in 1636 expressing a resolve to visit the master before allowing any of his own writings on Epicurus to be published.[41] The visit in fact never took place, but the promise of it shows how fully Gassendi linked his basic Epicurean philosophy with the work of Galileo, despite everything.

The foregoing considerations indicate that Gassendi advocated Epicureanism because he was a humanist and because he was a Copernican, and that he advocated that Aristotelianism, the generally accepted

philosophy, be replaced by Epicureanism for similarly humanist and
Copernican reasons. In urging such a change Gassendi was being quite
revolutionary: it was axiomatic for conservative Aristotelians that
Aristotelianism was a bulwark against all kinds of errors.[42] As a
consequence, Gassendi felt constrained to present Epicureanism as a
philosophy that was not merely as good as, but in fact preferable to
Aristotelianism, in the fight to preserve the faith above all, quite apart
from any other advantages it might be considered to have. If he could not
do this he would have little hope of persuading his readers to abandon
Aristotelianism in order to embrace Epicureanism.

As a consequence, Gassendi's advocacy of Epicureanism acquired a
distinctly apologetic aspect. On the one hand, he aimed to harmonise
Epicureanism with the doctrines of the faith - to pluck from Epicurean
philosophy, as he said, every error, small or great, that could be in the
slightest degree in disagreement with the faith. He wrote:

> Whenever I come upon not only those more serious subjects
> of disagreement between Epicureanism and the Faith, but
> even things that might seem in only a minimal way out of
> harmony with Christian doctrine, it is my intention to
> oppose Epicurus to the utmost of my ability and to uproot
> his doctrine with all the power of reason that I can muster.[43]

On the other hand, he strove to deflect potential criticisms away from
Epicureanism and in the direction of Aristotelianism, thereby elevating the
process of harmonising Epicureanism with the doctrine of the faith to an
exercise in comparative philosophy, comparing Epicureanism and
Aristotelianism according to their "Christian truth" content. From this
latter exercise Epicureanism persistently showed up either as well as or
better than Aristotelianism, the conclusion being drawn - or at least implied
- that Epicureanism was intrinsically more Christian than Aristotelianism.
Let us examine some ways in which Gassendi compared and contrasted
Epicureanism and Aristotelianism, extolling the former at the expense of
the latter in order that he might claim that Epicureanism was more suitable
as a "Christian" philosophy than the old Aristotelianism that had been
generally adopted hitherto.


MATTER AND ITS MODES

According to Gassendi's Epicurean theory the whole of reality is built up
from, and reducible to, atoms and their qualities (shape, size, and weight).[44]
Obviously there are vast differences between such a doctrine and the
Aristotelian doctrines concerning the ultimate principles, matter and form,
the generation of substances, and the nature of qualities.[45] In Epicurean

philosophy a mechanistic theory of the world is presented, according to which the natural ontological unit is a particle of independently actual, substantial matter, completely devoid of any internal processes of change. In Aristotelianism, on the contrary, an organic system inspired by biological models is adopted, according to which a natural unit is a composite of matter and form, two substantial principles, and the natural unit possesses an intrinsic dynamism arising from the formal principle. Yet, despite the fundamentally contrasting character of the two philosophies, Gassendi strove to minimise the differences.

Gassendi gave the following as the title for the concluding chapter of the treatise in the *Syntagma* on the material principle: "It appears that atoms can be accepted as the material principle of things, or as prime matter".[46] This title clearly expressed what his discussion of the variety of theories concerning the nature of the material principle had been leading to. In MS Tours 709, Bk. XV, and in the corresponding treatise in Book 3 of Section I of the *pars physica* of the *Syntagma* Gassendi examined the principal theories that had been proposed concerning the nature of the material principle, especially those of Parmenides, the Milesians, those which presuppose the theory of the four elements, the theories of Anaxagoras, the Chymists, the Aristotelians, the Stoics, the Platonists and the Pythagoreans, and finally the theory of the atomists. Gassendi's conclusion from the whole investigation, as expressed in the chapter mentioned above, was that the Epicurean theory of matter was the most acceptable of all theories presented by either the ancients or the moderns.[47]

At the same time, however, Gassendi gave special attention to the Aristotelian theory, arguing that the Aristotelian and Epicurean theories were similar in important respects, so that the Epicurean theory, he claimed, was fully a match for, and no more worthy of condemnation than, the Aristotelian theory. He pointed out that Epicurus had had the same reason for postulating atoms as Aristotle had had for teaching the existence of prime matter: it was needed for his explanation of change. As Aristotle taught that all things were first generated from and finally dissolved into prime matter, so Epicurus taught that they first arose from and ultimately dissolved into atoms. As did Aristotle, so Epicurus described matter as unbegotten and incorruptible. As is the case with Aristotle's prime matter, so also were the atoms of Epicurus to be understood as immutable, or not subject to processes of coming-to-be and ceasing-to-be.[48] Like Aristotle and all the ancient pagan philosophers of nature, Epicurus accepted the adage *ex nihilo nihil fit* as expressing a doctrine that was fundamental to his description of matter and change.[49]

Gassendi's argument continued along the following lines. While it is a fact that the Epicurean theory can explain in its way everything that the Aristotelian theory attempted to explain, and thus the two philosophies are approximately equivalent in their strengths, so to speak, it is also a fact that they are exactly equivalent in what might be judged as their defects, namely in the fact that they are equally in conflict with Christian doctrine. For, as both theories have been adopted to explain change so both have been adopted to explain the nature and origin of the universe as a whole and in every sense, thereby contradicting the Christian doctrine of Creation. For matter was understood by Aristotle as well as by Epicurus as an absolute principle of the universe, as absolutely unbegotten, incorruptible, eternal, leaving no place for the Christian doctrine that the universe was created out of nothing.[50]

Thus Gassendi argued that Epicureanism was not to be singled out and condemned as atheistic. The corrections that needed to be made to the Epicurean theory were precisely the same as had been necessary in the case of Aristotelianism in former times when the Church authorities had adopted that philosophy. Indeed, Gassendi added, they were the same corrections that would have to be made to Platonism or to any other pagan philosophy which did not allow for the Christian doctrine of Creation. Epicurean atomism was no more un-Christian than the other pagan philosophies, including that of Aristotle, in this respect.[51]

In a passage which he added to the *Syntagma* version[52] Gassendi explained how he considered that Epicureanism could be purged of its errors. First, the doctrine that atoms are eternal, uncreated and infinite in number must be rejected. Second, the doctrine that atoms have an innate mobility which is not derived from a higher motive principle must be rejected. In place of these theories, Gassendi urged, it is possible to subscribe to the view that atoms are the prime matter which was created finite by God in the beginning. God then formed these atoms into the visible world and allowed them to continue in movement on their pre-ordained courses.

Accordingly, Gassendi presented the following as the basis of his Christian/Epicurean explanation of the universe. Atoms have been created by God and all bodies in the natural world are constructed out of atoms. All motion of atoms is likewise created: atoms are mobile and active by reason of the movement with which they were endowed in the moment of Creation. God still co-operates with this movement by his ordinary action of conserving all things in being: "Just as he conserves all things, so he co-operates with all things".[53]

Though Gassendi could claim that such an explanation of the universe was in harmony with Christian doctrines of Creation and Providence, there are some obvious points of possible conflict with other doctrines. Gassendi referred to one such point in a brief passage added to the *Syntagma* version at the conclusion of his treatise on the material principle when he alluded to his treatise on the mind, human reasoning and the sense faculties;[54] any atomistic account of these phenomena would have to avoid conflict with the Christian doctrine of the spirituality of the soul. Gassendi found his solution for this difficulty in the orthodox (Aristotelian/Thomistic) doctrine according to which the human soul is a composite of matter and spirit, the spiritual part having been created separately and infused into the body to become its substantial form.[55] Gassendi thus ensured that his Epicurean philosophy was in harmony with the doctrine of the spirituality of the soul by limiting the domain of his mechanistic explanations in such a way that risk of conflict with the Christian doctrine was obviated *a priori*. Gassendi did not recognise any conflict between Epicurean atomism and the Christian doctrine of the freedom of the will since Epicurus taught that humans had freedom of choice and Gassendi presented the doctrine of Epicurus at length in the *Pars ethica* of the *Syntagma*.[56]

In his third letter *"De proportione qua gravia decidentia accelerantur"* (1642)[57] Gassendi expressed explicitly and succinctly what he tried to demonstrate in his writings on matter in MS Tours 709 and the *Syntagma*: "It is no less tolerable from the religious point of view to affirm atoms than it is to affirm Aristotle's matter".[58] As it was noticeable that, in his attempts to support that claim, Gassendi minimised the differences between Epicurean and Aristotelian doctrines on matter, so also, in his writings on the nature of qualities, Gassendi was concerned to discover concordances between Epicurean and Aristotelian doctrines. His efforts were so plausibly successful that he presented the Epicurean doctrine of modes and the Aristotelian doctrine of qualities and accidents as being, implicitly at least, approximately equivalent.

Gassendi began his discussion of qualities with an assumption that there is a great deal of concordance in the Epicurean and Aristotelian doctrines on the subject, for he compared the various Epicurean and Aristotelian definitions of modes, qualities and accidents and accepted them all as definitions of the same realities. He stated the Epicurean definition first, as follows: a quality is the mode of a substance.[59] He then gave, by way of explanation and restatement of this definition, a second version which one can identify as a Stoic definition: a quality is the condition and state of the commingled principles.[60] Further, Gassendi stated, the (same) notion of quality may be defined as Aristotle defined it: everything by which concrete objects are qualified.[61] Gassendi presented these as perfectly acceptable definitions one and all, thereby implying that the Aristotelian and Epicurean definitions of quality were equivalent.

But an alleged equivalence of definitions was only the first step in Gassendi's concordistic exposition of the nature of qualities. He proceeded to draw a surprising variety of conclusions from the Aristotelian definition already referred to, *viz.* "everything by which things are qualified" or, as it may also be translated: "everything that answers the question, 'What kind of thing is it?'".[62] He claimed that, according to this definition and also according to Aristotle's own view, accidents were one and the same thing as qualities.[63] In order to see the truth of this, Gassendi argued, one must not be misled by the fact that Aristotle separated accidents and qualities into distinct categories, since even for Aristotle the categories were not inflexible.[64] Accidents and qualities were, according to Gassendi's interpretation, equivalent realities: the one same mode of a substance, *qua* mode of substance, is called an accident, and *qua* qualifying, or as a response to the question "What kind of thing is it?" is called a quality.[65] For, Gassendi claimed, all accidents answer the question "What kind of thing is it?" Therefore, all accidents are qualities.

Much the same thing can be said, Gassendi stated, of all the categories except that of substance. They are all categories of things that qualify or answer the question: "What kind of thing is it?" and therefore they are all qualities.[66] In other words, all reality can be said to be composed of substance and qualities, or, in the terms of Epicurus, of substance and modes of substance:

> It follows, therefore, that whatever is observed in physical bodies (the rational soul in man excepted) is either a substance, which is one and the same thing as the body, the conglomerate of material or corporeal principles, or it is a quality, an accident, or a mode of the substance.[67]

Gassendi considered that Aristotle's writings in the *Categories*, from which the Aristotelian definition of quality was taken, and the writings of Aristotelians in their text-books in which the Aristotelian definition was repeated, favoured such a view. And, what is more, he found further evidence to support his conclusion in statements concerning accidents in Aristotle's *Metaphysics*:

> Thus it follows, I say, and Aristotle himself did not deny it, since he considered the substance alone to be properly speaking the being, while he considered the accident to be not so much a being as a being of a being, or a mode of being.[68]

Gassendi had laid the groundwork for his concordistic presentation of the Epicurean and Aristotelian explanations of qualities in the book of the *Syntagma* which immediately preceeded his treatise on qualities. The book in question is entitled "Concerning change and alteration".[69] In the concluding paragraph of this book Gassendi drew attention to the fact that an explanation of the nature of qualities depended on an explanation of change and alteration, saying, "And since all alterations terminate in qualities, the following book must deal with these qualities themselves".[70] Gassendi's explanation of alteration and change was entirely mechanist, and he argued at length that Aristotle's explanation of the same reality was likewise mechanist in orientation. His argument went as follows.

Aristotle and Epicurus were in agreement that all change is local motion for (according to Gassendi) Aristotle held the view that only local motion was change properly so-called, and he demonstrated that other species of change - generation and corruption, accretion, diminution and alteration - did not occur without local motion.[71] The reason why people had not understood this up to the present, Gassendi explained, was that the point in Aristotle's teaching had been obscured by the fact that Aristotle wrote in two different ways on the subject. In his *Metaphysics* and in one place in his *Physics*[72] Aristotle referred to alteration as the genus and change as the species, and according to this teminology Aristotle would seem to be implying that not all alteration is change. In another place in the *Physics*, however, Aristotle referred to change as the genus and to alteration as the species, thereby inferring that all alteration is change. The latter position, Gassendi asserted, represented Aristotle's true opinion. Thus, to re-state Gassendi's argument, since Aristotle taught that all change was local motion and all alteration was change, he also taught that all alteration was local motion. But since all alterations terminated in the production of qualities, Aristotle taught, implicitly at least, that all qualities were produced by local motion. Thus Aristotle gave an explanation of the production of qualities which, because it was based on the notion of local motion, was not really very dissimilar from the mechanist theory.[73]

Gassendi's lists of qualities in the version of MS Tours 709[74] and in the *Syntagma*[75] approximately represented the qualities mentioned by Aristotle in the *Meteorologica*,[76] the *Syntagma* list representing them more completely. Gassendi, however, organised the list in a way different from that of Aristotle himself. Whereas Aristotle's qualities were presented as generated from the elemental qualities of hot, cold, dry and moist, Gassendi's qualities, which included Aristotle's elemental qualities, were presented as derived from the Epicurean elemental qualities of size, shape and weight (*gravitas*).[77] With this list Gassendi completed his argument that the Epicurean theory of qualities was a fitting substitute for the Aristotelian theory. The Epicurean theory, he inferred, could explain everything that had been presumed to have been explained by the Aristotelian theory of qualities; though the Epicurean explanation was somewhat different, it was not really foreign to the genius of Aristotelianism and in fact Aristotle implicitly favoured the Epicurean theory; indeed, the Epicurean theory might be considered to be in some ways a simple improvement on the Aristotelian theory.

By such arguments, then, Gassendi sought to recommend the Epicurean theory of matter and its modes as a substitute for the Aristotelian theories of matter, substance and quality. He argued that the Epicurean theory was acceptable because it was in harmony with Christian doctrine; he claimed that it was at least the philosophical equal of Aristotelianism, and intimated that, in some ways at least, it was superior. In fact, as he developed his argument, Gassendi claimed to discover a large measure of agreement between Epicurean and Aristotelian theory, and in the process of supporting this claim Gassendi's interpretation of Aristotelianism exhibited a mechanist bias.

ETERNITY OF THE WORLD

The question of the eternity of matter is a question distinct from that of the eternity of the world. While the pagan philosophers, according to Gassendi, generally accepted the doctrine of the eternity of matter,[78] there was no such agreement among them on the doctrine of the eternity of the world. And because Epicurus and Aristotle were on opposite sides on this question, with Epicurus opposing and Aristotle propounding the doctrine, Gassendi was able to claim that Aristotle was seriously in error while the views of Epicurus harmonised adequately with the faith. Indeed, Gassendi stated, Aristotle was all the more blameworthy for the fact that he taught in an unwavering and especially emphatic manner that the world is eternal, so that he was recognised as the chief proponent of the doctrine.[79]

To demonstrate how seriously Aristotle "erred" in teaching such a doctrine, Gassendi divided the question of the eternity of the world into two questions, the first being whether the world had a beginning, the second being whether it would have an end. Considering these two matters separately, he felt able to conclude that the doctrine of Epicurus and the Epicureans was more "Christian" than that of Aristotle on both questions.

On the first question Gassendi recorded that Aristotle had been a proponent of the doctrine that the world had not had a beginning, while Epicurus was to be numbered among those who taught that it did.[80] Thus, Gassendi pointed out, Aristotle contradicted, while Epicurus was in harmony with, the true opinion, namely the opinion that was to be held because it was prescribed by holy faith according to the first chapter of the Book of Genesis where it is written: "In the beginning God created heaven and earth".[81]

On the second question, Gassendi recorded that not only did Aristotle hold the view that the world would have no end, but the same Aristotle went so far as to condemn for impiety all those who held the view that the world would come to an end.[82] Thus Gassendi let it be known that Aristotle was to be considered to have seriously erred on this question, and that he was, furthermore, a hostile critic of a view that ultimately became a Christian doctrine.

At the same time, however, Gassendi noted that Epicurus must also be considered to have been in error when he taught that the world would finally disintegrate by its own natural processes and not through an act of God. But, Gassendi immediately pointed out, even so Epicurus was not seriously in error, for at least he did teach that the world would have an end, and to that extent his doctrine was in harmony with orthodox Christian doctrine.[83]

On the other hand, Gassendi urged, the teaching of Epicurus on the ultimate end of the world was marvellously consonant with sacred doctrine.

And the same could be said, he suggested, concerning his teaching on the manner in which the end of the world would come about: it was a teaching that was consonant with the teaching of the "more approved authors" that the world would end, not by total annihilation, but by merely qualitative renewal or change:

> The more approved authors teach that the world will not be annihilated but will simply be renewed by a qualitative, not a substantial change. They teach, in other words, that the same substance of the heavens and the [four] elements will remain, but it will be cleansed of all stain and will be more splendid in all its properties. For instance, the moon will shine like the sun, and the sun will be seven times brighter.[84]

The questions concerning whether the world had had a beginning and whether it was to have an end were comparatively minor subjects in Gassendi's discussion of the relative merits of Epicurean and Aristotelian doctrine. They arose in relation to more significant questions such as the manner in which the world came to be and whether the world was an animate reality or not.[85] But since Gassendi was faced with the task of overcoming entrenched presuppositions in favour of Aristotelianism and opposed to Epicureanism, it served Gassendi's purpose to make even otherwise trivial comparisons if they helped to persuade his readers that there was a greater degree of harmony with the Christian faith in Epicurean philosophy than there was in Aristotelian.

Gassendi further supported his arguments for the superiority of Epicurean philosophy over the Aristotelian by arguments based on observation and natural reasoning. He presented a mixture of new evidence from new discoveries and inventions, and ancient arguments which he adapted from Lucretius: there was the evidence that the universe has been designed, from which it follows that it is not eternal; the various parts of the universe are observed to come to be and to dissolve, and one concludes that the whole is subject to the same processes; there are many signs that the universe is not very old, such as the relative brevity of human history and the fact that we are still making important discoveries.[86] These more empirical arguments lent plausibility to the (Epicurean) teaching that the world had had a beginning and would have an end, and added further credibility to Gassendi's argument that the Epicurean philosophy was superior to the Aristotelian.

INFINITE SPACE

Gassendi stated that the Aristotelian concept of place should be abandoned. Aristotle had defined place as the extreme, or limit, of the containing body.[87] According to the Aristotelian doctrine, Gassendi pointed out, place was an accident of bodies.[88] Instead of Aristotle's concept of place, Gassendi urged that the Epicurean concept of space should be adopted.[89] According to this Epicurean doctrine, Gassendi explained, space is to be understood as a real, existing, non-substantial, three-dimensional reality that transcends and embraces the universe like a container, that permeates bodies when they fill it, and that is interspersed through the universe as minute vacua between particles of matter. In Epicurean doctrine, Gassendi noted, when space is empty of body it may be called "void", and when it is filled with body it may be called "place".[90]

Gassendi's exposition of the 'Epicurean' doctrine of space would seem to have owed more to seventeenth-century mechanical philosophy than to Epicurus. This is to be gathered first of all from the fact that much of the basis for Gassendi's reflections concerning space is to be found in the *Pneumatica* of Hero of Alexandria,[91] which is generally accepted as the seminal work for seventeenth-century studies of the vacuum, and hence of space.[92] Thus, for example, Gassendi adopted Hero's analogy of spaces between grains of sand for the vacua between particles of matter;[93] he also referred to a variety of machines, such as water clocks and perpetual fountains, some of which had actually been described by Hero, while others worked on principles similar to the machines described by him.[94] Gassendi claimed Hero's *Pneumatica* as being a work that belonged to the body of Epicurean literature,[95] even though, as it had been pointed out by Boas,[96] Hero's theory had only a very general similarity with ancient atomism.

However, the clearest indication that Gassendi's reflections on space were more influenced by the seventeenth-century mechanical philosophy than by the writings of Epicurus is the very obvious manner in which his manuscripts reflected the developments in the discussions on the vacuum stimulated by Torricelli's work with the barometer in 1643. The *Syntagma* version of Gassendi's treatise on space, written shortly after 1649, is a very different piece of writing from the MS Tours 709 version written in 1637. The impact of Torricelli's discovery is everywhere apparent in the text. Thus, in the MS Tours 709 version, Gassendi discussed only two types of void, the extra-mundane (*inane separatum*) and the inter-particulate (*inane interspersum*),[97] and in thus restricting the discussion he was explicitly responding to Aristotelian discussions.[98] After Torricelli's experiment, however, Gassendi introduced into the *Syntagma* version a long discussion of a third type of vacuum which he called an "accumulated vacuum" (*inane coacervatum*).[99] He claimed that this vacuum, which could sometimes be produced artificially in nature, was a larger portion of empty space than was natural and was formed by an 'accumulation' of inter-particulate vacua.

But there are other indications of the influence of Torricelli in Gassendi's discussions of space. In the version of MS Tours 709 Gassendi's mechanistic theory had been somewhat primitive: he had accepted the

Aristotelian principle of the repugnance of nature to the void,[100] and had incorporated explanations in terms of sympathies[101] and harmonies.[102] But in the *Syntagma* version he abandoned all these explanations and adopted the new Torricellian principle of atmospheric pressure.[103] Futhermore, whereas in MS Tours 709 Gassendi had merely referred to the various machines that were customarily mentioned in the discussion of the void, asserting that they were so familiar to everyone as not to require explanation,[104] in the *Syntagma* version he gave lengthy descriptions of their operations according to Torricelli's principle.[105] Again in the *Syntagma* version Gassendi incorporated, in a rather untidy manner, a reprint of his commentary on the work of Torricelli which included accounts of his own experiments with barometers.[106] Finally, Gassendi adapted Hero's analogy based on particles of void between grains of sand or, in Gassendi's writings, between grains of wheat,[107] and put it to a new purpose: he used it to explain the mechanics of atmospheric pressure.

Perhaps another indication of the influence of the mechanical philosophy of the seventeenth century on Gassendi's discussions of space is to be discovered in the "parallelism"[108] which he claimed to find between space and time. He presented them as two realities that could not be classified in Aristotle's categories of substance and accident: instead they were to be understood as non-substantial, non-accidental realities which existed independently of bodies and motions. But their "parallelism" or analogous character was not something which he came to appreciate from his reading of Epicurus. As Gassendi himself explained, space and time were extremely dissimilar for Epicurus, the former being an "intactile nature",[109] and the latter being an "accident of accidents".[110] On the other hand, Gassendi could well appreciate their analogous character through his understanding of the new mechanics which represented space and time as mathematical co-ordinates. It is said that, while natural philosophers were accustomed to space co-ordinates, they were not able to conceive of time co-ordinates before Galileo's studies on falling bodies which were published in the *Discorsi* in 1638.[111] In MS Tours 709 Gassendi would seem to have foreshadowed philosophically the mathematico-physical innovation of Galileo when he described the "parallelism" of space and time in his MS Tours 709 treatise (which itself was a second version, and thus perhaps not the first time Gassendi had described it) written in 1637,[112] on the eve of the publication of the *Discorsi*.

One passage, especially, in Gassendi's writings serves to illustrate the manner in which his insight into the "parallelism" of space and time may be considered to have been a philosophical foreshadowing of Galileo's studies on falling bodies in which space and time were linked. After listing a number of ways in which space and time could be considered as similar, Gassendi concluded with the following as being the most striking of all:

Finally, just as place [space] has permanent dimensions into which fit the length, breadth and depth of bodies, so time has successive dimensions that are matched by the motion of bodies.[113]

Then, a few lines further on, Gassendi wrote:

For these reasons it does not seem to be the case that time is something that is based on motion, or that is a consequence of it. It is something that is only indicated by motion, as what is measured is indicated by what is used to measure it.[114]

It would seem to be only a short step from thinking of time in this manner, as an entity measured *by* motion rather than as a measure *of* motion, to Galileo's distinct geometrical representations in the *Dialogo* of times and motions of bodies and of spaces traversed by the same bodies. When time is conceived as a reality measureable in itself and not *in alio*, the challenge is to exploit its independent measureability to obtain new knowledge about the physical world. Galileo responded to that challenge in his experiments with free-falling bodies and his formulations of the laws that governed them in their movements. As soon as he read the *Dialogo*, Gassendi, already conceptualising time as an independently quantifiable entity, was aware of the significance of what Galileo had achieved in representing it as a mathematical co-ordinate. In his first letter *De motu impresso a motore translato*[115] he attempted to explain Galileo's theory of falling bodies; his explanation was somewhat confused, and his mathematics was faulty,[116] but his general aim showed that he understood at least the metaphysical principles and concepts that Galileo had adopted, in particular that change in the form of local motion and time were to be quantified separately from each other.[117] Again, it would seem that Gassendi's so-called Epicurean doctrine of space (and time) owed much more to the seventeenth-century mechanical philosophy than to ancient Epicurean sources.

However, though Gassendi's concept of space may have been only tenuously related to the ancient Epicurean philosophy, he *claimed* it as an "Epicurean" concept, and advocated it as such as a fitting substitute for the Aristotelian concept of place. As part of his apologetical exposition of Epicurean philosophy he sought to demonstrate that his Epicurean concept was at least as acceptable as the Aristotelian concept from the Christian point of view. If he had been satisfied simply to refute Aristotelianism by demonstrating the existence of the void his task would have been simple. Eventually it was done for him by Torricelli. But Gassendi aimed to do much more: he set out to show that Epicurean space as he described it - including as it did an infinite void space outside the world as well as the spaces, both empty and filled, within the world - was preferable on religious grounds to the Aristotelian doctrine.

Aristotle had rejected the possibility of any "place or void or time outside the heaven".[118] For Aristotle, the question of the extra-mundane void was connected with the question of the unicity or plurality of worlds,[119] and it had been the same for Epicurus.[120] The opposition between the Aristotelian and the Epicurean systems was clearly exemplified in their contrasting doctrines concerning the number of worlds. For Aristotle there cannot be more than one world, a conclusion that followed necessarily from his assumptions concerning the natural motion and natural place of the elements: if there were more than one world there would be more than one natural place for an element, requiring the element to move at one and the same time by natural motion towards one of its natural places and by violent motion away from the other, which was an impossible motion in Aristotle's system. The Epicurean system, with its assumptions of infinite space and an infinite number of atoms together with the finitude of our cosmos, entailed the necessity of an infinite number of worlds. The Stoics, on the other hand, had presented the cosmos as a solitary island surrounded by an infinite void.[121] As usual, when the Stoics had presented a version of Epicurean philosophy that was more in harmony with Christian doctrine, Gassendi followed the Stoics rather than Epicurus. He claimed to do the same in this instance.

The question of the plurality of worlds was a sensitive one following the condemnation and execution in 1600 of Giordano Bruno who had championed a pantheistic neo-Pythagorean theory of an infinite number of worlds, but it had not yet become a subject of open debate among freethinkers, and discussion on this question did not begin to pose an appreciable threat to Christian doctrine until after the publication in 1686 of Fontenelle's *Conversations*.[122] Gassendi admitted that there were no demonstrative philosophical arguments to prove that other worlds do not in fact exist, but he considered that a Christian philosopher must accept that there is only one, since Scripture never mentions others, and the Christian doctrines of the Origins of the Universe, of Providence, of Sin and salvation all point to this world's uniqueness. Besides, from an empirical point of view it makes more sense to confine ourselves to this one world which we know rather than to speculate about other worlds which are entirely impenetrable to our senses and minds, there being no good reason to assert the existence of a plurality of worlds.[123]

The Epicurean doctrine of a plurality, even an infinity of worlds may be unacceptable to the Christian faith in Gassendi's estimation, but the Epicurean theory of infinite space was another matter. Gassendi strove to recommend it as preferable, especially on religious grounds, to the Aristotelian concept of place. In MS Tours 709 he argued for the existence of real space by taking one step further the medieval discussions of the possibility of a plurality of worlds[124] in order to conclude that, if it is

possible for God to create further worlds, then space must already exist to
receive them. Furthermore, Gassendi argued, this space had to be infinite
in every direction, for it was understood[125] that God could always create
new worlds, or could always expand this one further into space; therefore
space always had to pre-exist the action of God so that it could receive the
new worlds or the expanded world.

In the *Syntagma* version Gassendi linked the foregoing conclusions with
the theory of "imaginary space", maintaining that this theory was one and
the same as the Epicurean doctrine of infinite void space.[126] Gassendi
explained that it was the theory of imaginary space which was taught by
"most of the Doctors" which he had in mind.[127] The 'Doctors' were rather
obviously Aristotelians, and especially the Jesuits who propagated the
notion of imaginary space in their manuals of scholastic philosophy.[128]
Gassendi's explanation of the theory echoed the one given by the Jesuits,
which indicates that Gassendi was drawing on their works and that he
advocated their orthodox Christian understanding of the theory as being
identical with the Epicurean theory of space. Thus, Gassendi explained that
the imaginary spaces were so named,

> Not because they do not really exist outside the imagination,
> but because we imagine their spatial dimensions as being
> like the bodily dimensions that we are used to observing in
> corporeal things.[129]

This passage clearly drew on the following description of imaginary space
found in the commentary of the Jesuits of Coimbra:

> They are habitually called "imaginary", not because they are
> fictitious, or because they depend only on the idea in the
> mind and do not exist outside the intellect, but because we
> imagine them in space as having proportions corresponding
> to the real and positive dimensions of bodies.[130]

Gassendi even made an identical mistaken interpretation of a passage of the
writings of Augustine as the Jesuits had made, thereby indicating that he
was drawing on their commentary in some measure.[131]

However, Gassendi did not enter into detailed and specific comparisons
between the Epicurean and Jesuit theories. Almost certainly Gassendi was
aware that detailed comparisons would not help his case if he sought
respectability for the Epicurean theory on the grounds that it resembled
that taught by the Jesuits. For one thing, the Jesuits maintained that
imaginary space lacked dimensions, while Gassendi wanted to claim the
opposite.[132] Gassendi had to be content with making a simple allusion to
the theory as propounded by the Doctors and stating, without offering any

proof, that the Epicurean theory of space which he was proposing was identical with it.

Clearly, Gassendi's Epicurean theory of an infinite void space stretching in all directions outside the world was not identical with the theory of imaginary space of the majority of the Doctors. There was some resemblance between Ggssendi's theory, as he enlarged upon it in the *Syntagma* version, and the theory of Thomas Bradwardine (*ca.* 1290-1349) insofar as, like Bradwardine, he linked the infinity of space with the infinity of God.[133] But Bradwardine expressly rejected the idea that the omnipresence of God implied that the infinite imaginary place in which he was present was an infinitely extended space.[134] Nicole Oresme (*ca.* 1320-1382) had likewise claimed that there existed an infinite incorporeal space outside the world, but he identified it with the immensity of God and claimed it to be indivisible or, as it was understood, dimensionless.[135] It is considered possible that Johannes de Ripa (*ca.* 1350) represented the imaginary infinite extramundane void as three-dimensional,[136] but one solitary possible learned precedent, even presuming that Gassendi had known of him, does not add up to the "majority" of the Doctors.

It was the fact that Gassendi attributed three dimensions to imaginary space which distinguished his theory from the traditional doctrines. That the extra-mundane void was three-dimensional was fundamental to the Epicurean cosmological doctrine.[137] But to identify the three-dimensional space of the Epicureans with the imaginary space of the Doctors was to make an important change to the latter doctrine as it had been traditionally understood by the medievals. The medieval philosophers and theologians had invoked imaginary space for the purpose of preserving theological truths, specifically the doctrine of the omnipotence of the Creator;[138] it was not related to questions of natural philosophy.

The properly theological context of the notion of imaginary space can be appreciated from the section dealing with the subject in the text of one of its opponents, Eustache de Saint-Paul, to which reference has already been made.[139] Eustache maintained that there is nothing actually infinite *within* the natural world, all natural things being contained within the finite limit of the sphere of the heavens. He recognised that the contrary view had been proposed on the grounds of the omnipotence and liberty of God, some philosophers teaching that God had the power to create an actual infinite reality. Eustache rejected this opinion, claiming that the impossibility of an actual infinite reality in the universe had nothing to do with God's omnipotence or the lack of it, but that it was a consequence of the condition of a created thing which lacked receptivity to actual infinity. Then, turning to the question of the existence of void space *without* the world (extra-mundane void space), Eustache ruled out the existence of imaginary spaces beyond the heavens for the proper Aristotelian reason that such spaces would not be contained. They would thus be "in no place", it being understood that what was in no place was nowhere in the universe, and consequently did not exist.[140]

Such a metaphysical discussion was somewhat removed from the physical context in which Gassendi chose to use the term "imaginary space". But there had been some precedents for Gassendi's 'physicalisation' of the concept. Giordano Bruno (1548-1600) had supported the real existence of infinite space, arguing from his aprioristic principle of sufficient reason, and linking the medieval discussions of imaginary space with the theory of space of Lucretius.[141] Descartes had asserted in the *Principia* (1644) that the indefinitely extended spaces that we "imagine" were real and that the idea of these spaces included the idea of their extension, which extension was one and the same as the extension of the bodily substance that filled all space. Thus Descartes wrote:

> We know that this world, or the totality of corporeal substance, has no limits to its extension. Wherever we invent such limits we always imagine indefinitely extended spaces beyond them, and we perceive these spaces as truly imaginable or real, and as containing indefinitely extended corporeal substance. For, as has already been shown at some length, the idea of extension which we conceive in any space is evidently the same as the idea of corporeal substance.[142]

It is possible that Gassendi introduced the discussion of imaginary space into the *Syntagma* after he had read the *Principia* of Descartes.[143] It is quite possible, therefore, that Gassendi should have been influenced by Descartes' *Principia* to give prominence to the theory of imaginary space in the *Syntagma* version. Gassendi's view of the imagination, though derived from Epicurus, was not unlike that of Descartes in some important respects, and Gassendi did not quarrel with him on this subject in his critique of the latter's metaphysics.[144] Imagination for both Descartes and Gassendi was a faculty for knowledge of physical reality, and for an idea to be in the imagination was not the same thing as to be fictitious. As a consequence, Gassendi's reading, which was in fact a misreading, of the passage in the commentary of the Jesuits quoted above,[145] gained much plausibility: as the Jesuit Fathers had said, the imaginary spaces were so-called, not because they were fictitious, or because they were purely things of the mind with no existence outside in the physical universe, but because they were *imagined* together with their own dimensions. And for this reason Gassendi claimed with confidence that his 'Epicurean' doctrine of infinite space was one and the same with the theory of imaginary space which was taught by (the Jesuits and) most of the Doctors.

Thus Gassendi argued that the Epicurean doctrine of space should be adopted instead of the Aristotelian doctrine of place. He attempted to forestall expressions of alarm concerning the seeming conflict between the Epicurean doctrine and doctrines of the Christian faith by presenting it as no different from a highly respected doctrine of the medieval philosophers which could be traced back to St. Augustine. Perhaps only a very undiscerning reader would have been convinced, and perhaps the weakness of his argument indicates that Gassendi was preaching to the converted, to those who were already committed to Galilean Copernicanism. Whatever the case, Gassendi's efforts to convince his public that the infinite space of the Epicureans and the imaginary space of the Jesuits and other Christian Doctors were one and the same illustrate the lengths to which he was prepared to go to achieve his aim of establishing Epicureanism as a Christian philosophy that was well suited to take the place of Aristotelianism.

## CAUSALITY

Gassendi's philosophical reflections on the subject of causality were dominated by the principles of the mechanical philosophy, according to which all phenomena were to be explained by accounts of the operations of bodies in motion. In the mechanical philosophy there was room for only one type of cause: efficient cause. Accordingly, Gassendi opened his discussion of causes with the assertion, which he presented as a "presupposition",[146] that, properly speaking, efficient causes were the only causes, and that the other causes to which philosophers were accustomed to refer (material, formal and final) were not causes in the proper sense of the term.[147] With this assertion, which he considered to be obviously true and not needing much support by rational argument,[148] Gassendi replaced Aristotle's system of four causes (and any other system which required more than efficient causality) with the Epicurean theory which, like the mechanical philosophy, had room only for efficient causes.[149]

Again, Gassendi's writings on motion were closely linked to his writings on causality, and from that fact it could be seen how much his reflections were dominated by the mechanical philosophy. Just as Gassendi had recognised only efficient causality in his treatise on causality, so he reduced all motion to local motion in his treatise on motion.[150] As a consequence, Gassendi recognised only one type of cause and one type of motion, a view which was fully in accord with the mechanical theory which attempted to explain all phenomena by accounts of particles in motion and their interactions. In fact, Gassendi was so convinced that efficient causality was the only type of causality and local motion the only type of motion that he had difficulty justifying his action in writing a separate treatise on motion over and above the treatise on (efficient) causality. He clearly felt that there was little more to be said concerning motion, and certainly nothing of an essential nature, apart from what had been said on the subject when he was discussing efficient causality, given that the action of the causes was the same thing as their motion.[151]

Since Gassendi simply asserted his presupposition that only efficient causes were causes properly speaking, he seemed to feel that he was not obliged to offer lengthy or water-tight argumentation to justify the replacement of Aristotelian causal theory by Epicurean at the basic level of physical theory. However, it was a different matter at the metaphysical level where the question of the incompatibility of Epicureanism and Christian doctrine had to be faced. If Gassendi were ever to succeed in his task of sufficiently expurgating Epicureanism of its 'errors' to render it acceptable in the way that Aristotelianism had been expurgated in the Middle Ages for general use by Christians, then he would have to transform it radically, for Epicureanism is the antithesis of Christian doctrine and, indeed, the prototypal materialist philosophy. According to the interpretation of Olivier Bloch,[152] Gassendi found that this task of Christianising Epicureanism was fraught with difficulty. Gassendi, Bloch maintains, struggled hard throughout his work to offset what he perceived to be a real danger that the materialism of his Epicurean natural philosophy might come into conflict with his Christian faith. Bloch sees Gassendi as a philosopher at odds with his philosophy, a materialist *malgré lui*. The struggle, Bloch maintains, became critical after 1641 when Gassendi made substantial alterations to his earlier text that were specifically designed to arrest a bias towards materialism.

I believe that Bloch exaggerates the magnitude of the challenges as they were experienced by Gassendi himself. In fact, my interpretation of Gassendi's state of mind is quite different from that of Bloch: I do not consider that Gassendi was especially concerned at any stage over the materialist tendencies of his own Epicureanism. I am prepared to accept the possibility that he became concerned after 1641 about the way Thomas Hobbes was applying the mechanical philosophy, and I would agree that there may be grounds, as Sarasohn has argued,[153] for detecting that concern in the *Syntagma*, but I believe that such worries would have concerned what he felt were abuses of Epicurean themes, not any particular dangers intrinsic to his own project of Christianising Epicureanism. This is an important discussion for interpreting Gassendi's philosophy, so we need to examine the matter in some detail. First we shall seek to ascertain what were the methods that Gassendi adopted to counteract the materialism of Epicureanism, and then we shall try to establish what kind of changes Gassendi made to the *Syntagma* version that were relevant to this anti-materialist concern.

Gassendi did not seek to make excuses for what he judged to be the all-too-obvious errors of Epicurus on the subject of causality. These errors, as Gassendi saw them, were the atheistic and materialistic doctrines that follow from the premiss that there is no intelligent Designer governing the universe. In particular, Epicurus taught that the world was the product of chance, and that it was not produced for any purpose. Epicurus taught, Gassendi elaborated, that the atoms were the sole causes of all things. Supposedly in motion by reason of their intrinsic weight, the atoms came together haphazardly and produced all that is in the world without any need for an internal or external intelligent Designer.[154]

Gassendi judged that these doctrines were contrary to both religion and reason. He dismissed them in a rather perfunctory manner with arguments from design which he found also in the *De natura deorum* of Cicero[155] and supported these arguments with further examples of his own of what he considered to be evidence of intelligent design and purpose in the natural world.[156] Gassendi clearly considered that the erroneous character of the doctrines was obvious and generally recognised. After all, Gassendi pointed out, they were proposed by only a small number of atheists.[157] Such being the case, Gassendi intimated, these Epicurean doctrines posed no threat to religion. They were so notorious and blatant as to be harmless. In this way Gassendi shrugged off or side-stepped the "errors" which he detected in the theory of causality of Epicureanism and did not attempt to make his usual comparisons of Epicureanism and Aristotelianism according to their degree of compatibility with Christian doctrine. On the other hand he concentrated his discussion at another level altogether, situating it within the context of an exposition of what he considered to be the proper boundaries of the field of natural philosophy. He argued that at this latter level Epicureanism was considerably superior to Aristotelianism. Gassendi developed his theme as follows.

Gassendi praised the Epicurean/Stoic rejection of a distinction between physics and metaphysics. The philosophers of this tradition rejected the division, Gassendi maintained, because they understood that it was the task of a philosopher of nature to search into the causes of things and contemplate the divine and other immortal natures as made known in the creation and government of the universe.[158] He criticised the Aristotelians, on the other hand, because they retained a separation between "theology" (or "first philosophy" - which was called "metaphysics" by later Aristotelians) and physics. Gassendi maintained that as a consequence of their division the Aristotelians forced an unnatural rift between the philosophy of God which they studied in metaphysics (along with other things divine and things separated from body and the most general principles of being) and the philosophy of nature, or natural philosophy.[159]

Thus Gassendi advocated the Epicurean/Stoic tradition of philosophy as one which provided a more suitable model for the construction of a Christian natural philosophy than that provided by Aristotelianism. The Epicurean/Stoic division of philosophy provided the structure for a theological natural philosophy, that is, one which would incorporate the Christian doctrine of causality, as Gassendi understood it, into natural philosophy. Or, to employ a mode of expression that Gassendi himself used, the integration of physics and metaphysics, after the manner of the

Epicureans and Stoics, ensured that the philosopher would follow the "Royal Way" of philosophising, which is the methodological discovery of the First Cause in His works.[160]

Gassendi was himself an enthusiastic follower of this Royal Way: the evidence he discovered of design and purpose in creation provided the dominant metaphysical theme in his physics.[161] This same theme was common in the writings of other seventeenth-century mechanists, but Marin Mersenne's well-known development of it in *La verité des sciences* (1625)[162] could well have served as a model for Gassendi.

True to his conviction therefore, that Epicureanism provided a better structure for the development of a philosophy of nature that followed the Royal Way, Gassendi strove in the various versions of his philosophy to follow the Epicurean model more closely as he sought to achieve a better synthesis of metaphysics and physics in each version. He had the goal still very much on his mind as he prepared the final version, as can be seen from a preface he wrote especially for the first section of the *Pars physica* in the *Syntagma*.[163] In this preface, he drew the reader's attention to the fact that he had departed from the usual practice of writers of philosophical texts in the manner in which he had organised his material. One might expect, he noted, that his *Pars physica* would correspond to the *Physics* of Aristotle; and in fact, he allowed, the reader might find that his work did correspond in some ways to Aristotle's. Even Gassendi's manner of raising the subject in this way shows that he had become more aware of the differences between his *Pars physica* and Aristotle's *Physics*, for in the version of MS Tours 709 he had simply stated that the two corresponded.[164] In the new preface, by contrast, he explained that he preferred to stress the correspondence of his *Pars physica* with the work of Aristotle which was variously referred to under the titles "Metaphysics", "First theology", "Wisdom" and "Theology" (that is, the *Metaphysics*), the work which dealt with "being-as-such", rather than its correspondence with Aristotle's *Physics*, which dealt with specific beings. Gassendi thereupon repeated that the Aristotelian division was a mistaken one, and added that this was demonstrated by the fact that Aristotle himself had failed to observe the division in practice, since he had found it impossible to treat philosophically the immobile substance (God) in isolation from the mobile substance (the natural world), and *vice versa*.[165] Thus this preface, added to his text for the *Syntagma* version and emending the earlier version, is another indication that the integration of the metaphysical and physical branches of philosophy was a highly important goal in Gassendi's writings.

Gassendi's arguments recommending Epicureanism as a substitute for Aristotelianism thus took a rather surprising turn. Despite the supposedly atheistic and materialistic character of Epicureanism, Gassendi argued that it actually provided the structural support for presenting philosophically the relationship between God and nature in a manner which Gassendi and other mechanists considered appropriate. In the course of his argument Gassendi achieved at least two results.[166] First, he implicitly responded to the usual criticisms of Epicureanism: while freely admitting that Epicureanism was an ungodly philosophy in itself, he pointed out that it could be reformed and made to harmonise with Christian doctrine because it allowed the integration of metaphysics and natural philosophy. Though it had no religion it could easily be accommodated to one, and it opened the way for the philosopher to investigate the causes of things until he came to contemplate the divine and other immortal natures as they were made known in created things: that, after all, in Gassendi's view, was the task of the philosopher.[167] Second, he advocated the adoption of Epicureanism instead of Aristotelianism, claiming that the latter did not provide the same kind of structural support for what he claimed to be the appropriate integration of metaphysics and physics. Thus, he argued, Epicureanism was more useful than Aristotelianism for Christian philosophers because it was more amenable to the presentation of a theory of causality that was in harmony with Christian doctrine.

Gassendi gave to one of the earliest chapters of his presentation of Epicurean philosophy in MS Tours 709 the following title: "The goal of Epicurus corrected".[168] The goal of Epicurus, Gassendi explained, had been to find tranquillity, *ataraxia*, through natural philosophy. Gassendi agreed with Epicurus, he stated, insofar as Epicurus claimed that it was the first task of natural philosophy to offset the grave harm done to people and their peace of mind by superstition and spurious religion. However, Gassendi strenuously objected to the claim made by Epicurus[169] that natural philosophy should overthrow all religion, on the grounds that it is nothing more than superstition and fable. Quoting the *Naturales quaestiones* of Seneca, Gassendi asserted that to know the nature of things is to know who is the author and guardian of all things; it is to know who God is.[170]

Accordingly, Gassendi set out to redirect the natural philosophy of Epicurus to a Christian goal. Not surprisingly, the Christian goal as Gassendi described it was that which mechanists generally were pursuing, the contemplation of nature in order to argue from its admirable properties (which Gassendi listed in mechanist terms as magnitude, variety, arrangement, beauty and regularity) to the existence of a most wise, powerful and benevolent God.[171] By such contemplation, Gassendi continued, the ultimate goal of natural philosophy was achieved, that of bringing men to acknowledge that God is to be worshipped for his excellence and beneficence.[172] This is the knowledge, Gassendi claimed, that brings intellectual tranquillity and freedom from perturbation, filling the soul to overflowing with a humane and delightful joy.

However, although Gassendi was redirecting Epicureanism to the specific goal of seventeenth-century mechanical philosophy, the authorities he quoted in support of his action in treating Epicureanism in such a manner were the ancient Stoics, Diogenes Laertius, Plutarch and Cicero. He claimed that these authors reacted to the atheism of Epicurus by asserting that the tranquillity and liberation from fear proposed as the goal of natural philosophy stemmed, not from the overthrow of religion, but from the knowledge of God in nature.[173]

In the light of the foregoing considerations, it appears evident that Gassendi had already settled on what would be his method and strategy for off-setting the materialist orientation of Epicureanism when he wrote MS Tours 709. I do not believe that the *Syntagma* version was marked in any special way, in comparison with the version of MS Tours 709, by a struggle to keep materialism in check. On the contrary, I believe that Gassendi was satisfied that the materialist orientations could be adequately contained by redirecting the goal of Epicurus in the way indicated by the Stoic authors.

Bloch was especially impressed by a particularly obvious difference between the version of the treatise on causality in MS Tours 709 and that of the *Syntagma*: the section of the treatise in the *Syntagma* dealing with the First Cause is considerably expanded by comparison with the corresponding section in the version of MS Tours 709. He considered that this development in Gassendi's presentation of his Epicurean philosophy indicated that Gassendi felt the need to make much greater efforts than he had been making to offset the materialist orientation of his Epicurean philosophy. I have to disagree with this interpretation, though I accept that the substantial expansion of the treatise in the *Syntagma* version requires some explanation.

As Bloch has rightly noted, the treatise on causality in the *Syntagma*, which is entitled "Concerning the efficient principle, or on the causes of things"[174] is an amalgam of Book XVI "On causes, fortune and fate" (minus the section on "fortune and fate")[175] and Book XXI "On God, author and ruler of the world"[176] from MS Tours 709. I agree with Bloch that Gassendi combined these two treatises in order to ensure that the study of secondary causes in the *Syntagma* would be more intimately linked with the study of the First Cause. But I suggest that the new arrangement was part of Gassendi's long-standing plan to combine Epicureanism with Christian theology, and was not, as Bloch saw it, the result of a growing awareness on Gassendi's part that the materialistic orientation of his work might have been becoming too pronounced.

In MS Tours 709, the treatise on causality included a chapter on the First Cause entitled "Besides these causes a first, general, Divine Cause has been acknowledged".[177] As Bloch pointed out, the 'God' section in the new, expanded version of the *Syntagma* contains additional material not found in MS Tours 709 either in Book XVI or Book XXI. However, I do not believe that this signifies any renewed effort on Gassendi's part in striving to offset the materialism of his philosophy. For while half of the new material was taken from the *Pars ethica* of Gassendi's Epicurean philosophy, as Bloch has noted, the other half came from the *Pars physiologica* of Gassendi's *Animadversiones*, a fact not noted by Bloch, and thus it was material which Gassendi had considered as belonging to his natural philosophy.[178] Consequently, I do not believe that the new 'God' material is to be seen as something that Gassendi introduced into the *Syntagma* version because he felt a need to bolster what he feared to be the fading role for the First Cause. Rather, I would see the *Syntagma* version as simply a fuller achievement of Gassendi's original aim of correcting the goal of Epicurus in the manner indicated by the Stoics and desired by seventeenth-century mechanists, thereby giving him grounds for recommending Epicureanism as a substitute for Aristotelianism as a Christian philosophy.

Thus, I consider, Gassendi was generally fairly satisfied with the way he had offset the materialism of Epicureanism in the MS Tours 709 version of his philosophy. He did make a number of alterations to his text and sometimes to his philosophical positions for the *Syntagma* version,[179] but these can be explained, I believe, without postulating a significant change of direction or emphasis in his effort to neutralise the materialism of Epicureanism.

It was Gassendi's theology that permitted him to be so sanguine: since he was a Catholic priest in good standing, educated in the scholastic tradition (however deficient may have been the version which he received of the theology of that tradition), the Christian doctrines of Creation and Providence were primal in his world-view and not matters of question or debate, much less could they be seriously threatened by any pagan philosophy. But more importantly, Gassendi was a voluntarist, and this is the feature of his theology which exempted him from the efforts to harmonise Christian doctrine and Epicurean atomism that a philosopher who followed a more intellectualist tradition of theology, an Aquinas, a Descartes or a Leibniz for instance, would have felt compelled to make.[180]Gassendi stressed Divine Omnipotence and the primacy of God's will and providential activity in his creation, presenting God's relationship to the natural order as one in which the mediation of secondary causes, forms and laws is subject to God's absolutely free choice; purposes and designs in nature are all imprinted by God in a manner extrinsic to the inner constituents of things and by an absolutely unconditioned act of the Divine Will. Thus, for Gassendi, God's control over his creation was paramount and fundamental; the fact that the natural philosophy of Epicurus was tailored to fit an atheistic metaphysics was easily corrected: one simply added God, Creation and Divine Providence to the system and it was 'converted' to Christianity. The atoms which Epicurus claimed to be eternal and uncreated, Gassendi pronounced to be the product of a creative act of God and thus to have had a beginning in time. And, whereas Epicurus explained the evolution of the universe and everything it contains as the result of the chance activity of innately active and mobile atoms, Gassendi insisted that the mobility of the atoms was created together with the atoms themselves, and that nothing comes about in the universe except by design and Divine Providence. Even though, according to Gassendi, God normally acted through secondary causes, the operations of these causes, he affirmed, were entirely subject to God's will.[181]Whenever Epicurus asserted some unacceptably materialist doctrine Gassendi simply ruled it out of order with reference to the relevant christian doctrine, and proceeded to offer an 'Epicurean' theory more in harmony with Christian teaching.

Thus, according to my interpretation of the evidence, Gassendi was not concerned about the possibility that the atheism and materialism of Epicurean natural philosophy would prove intractible or even escape his control as he strove to Christianise it. With the Almighty in his heaven, the atomistic system of Epicurus was no longer auto-sufficient, and Gassendi could introduce God's power, wisdom and providential guidance to neutralise at every turn the anti-religious features of Epicureanism. Gassendi's solution to the challenge to harmonise Epicurean atomism and Christian doctrine may seem arbitrary, lacking in systematic cohesion, a distortion of Epicureanism and little more than a facile reliance on a *deus ex machina*, but our quarrel, if there be one, is with the tradition of theological voluntarism as much as with Gassendi himself. Gassendi's overriding concern was to present an alternative to Aristotelianism, and theological voluntarism enabled him to do this, so he at least was satisfied. Our discussion that follows of Gassendi's explanation of celestial motion provides us with a further opportunity to appreciate how useful Gassendi found his theological voluntarism to be.

## CELESTIAL MOTION

By discounting the 'Aristotelian' theory of solid spheres[182] Gassendi rejected the physical supports provided by that theory for the celestial bodies and their rotations; he declared that the celestial spaces are not crammed with crystalline spheres but that they are empty, totally free of all bodies apart from the visible heavenly objects themselves and corpuscles of light which travel at great speed in all directions.[183] In addition Gassendi made specific objections to the Aristotelian explanation of celestial motion on the grounds that it accounted for the phenomena without reference to an impetus and relied on the operations of motive forces that were external to the heavenly bodies. For Gassendi, any explanation of movement that relied upon external causes alone was inadequate.

After first noting that Aristotle's statements in the *Physics* and *Metaphysics* are not easily reconciled, Gassendi interpreted Aristotle's account of the cause of celestial motion to be the following: the heavenly spheres are animated by a rational soul which enables them to perceive beautiful, good and desirable objects; the heavenly spheres do in fact apprehend certain beautiful, good and desirable separate intelligible substances, or Movers, which are present to each sphere and which, without being moved themselves, move the spheres by their influence upon them as desirable goals to be attained; the heavenly spheres, in striving to reach the intelligible substances, move as their circular form determines, in continuous and eternal revolutions. Gassendi objected to the fact that the separate substances, the Movers of the heavenly spheres which the Aristotelians variously identified as Intelligences and Angels, operate as final causes: final causes are not physical motive forces and thus cannot perform the role of efficient causes, the only kind of cause that Gassendi recognised as real.[184] Consequently, Gassendi asserted, Aristotle had not succeeded in explaining celestial motion. Moreover, Gassendi added with a certain note of triumph, in explaining the motions of the celestial bodies by the operations of purely external causes, the Aristotelians reckoned the heavenly bodies to be exceptional in nature:

> [According to this theory] the celestial bodies would be in a poorer condition than all other natural things such as fire, stone and, indeed, animals, all of which move themselves and do not depend on external agencies in order to move.[185]

Thus, Gassendi implied, far from exalting heavenly matter, the Aristotelians in fact degraded it, according to their theory.

It was more reasonable, Gassendi claimed, to declare that the celestial bodies were moved by their own internal principle, by their own 'forms', by their own motive power.[186] For this reason, he stated, his Epicurean theory was superior to the theories of the Aristotelians, for, according to his theory, the heavenly bodies had as their internal cause of movement the "innate form, contexture and constitution"[187] of atoms. The atoms, coming together, gave to the bodies into which they were formed their determinate and permanent motions,[188] a permanent impetus. From the atoms, therefore,

> there comes not only circular motion, but also its perpetual character. Since the compaction [of atoms into large-scale bodies] is permanent, so also is the global character of the bodies and the action of the causes which push the bodies in a circular motion.[189]

Gassendi's Epicurean explanation of celestial motion was simply his explanation of atomic movements writ large. For all the inconsistencies that might be found in his writings on matter and motion,[190] one fundamental point upon which he was entirely consistent was that the motion of the atoms constitutes the internal cause of motion at all levels:[191] when atoms come together to form composite bodies, their motions are combined and absorbed into the motion of the new body so that macro-motions, insofar as they are produced by forces internal to the bodies, are the resultants of the myriad micro-motions of the atoms that compose them.[192] Gassendi acknowledged that in addition there are a variety of external causes of motion, the two most important being impressed force and the force of attraction,[193] but Gassendi believed the heavenly bodies to be free of external forces, so that their movements are entirely dependent upon the atoms that constitute them.

Gassendi enunciated a version of the principle of the conservation of motive force applicable to all levels of matter by universalising his considerations of the movements of the atoms. There is, he stated, no loss of motion or creation of motion in the universe, the sum of motion being now what it always has been since the beginning (*i.e.* since the Creation).

> This [motive] force which is inherent in the atoms does not perish but is only held back when concrete things begin to slow down; nor does it increase when things begin to move, but it is simply liberated. So, in the light of these suppositions, we can say that the impetus continues constant in things in the same quantity as it was in the beginning. Hence it is, that one atom colliding with another pushes it just so much as it is repulsed by it, and the impetus neither increases nor decreases; it always remains the same because of the compensation that is made, and the movement continues the same as long as the atom passes through empty space and does not meet resistance.[194]

Then, making one of his leaps from the micro-level to the macro-level, Gassendi went on to state:

> So we can understand that when composite things collide with and repel each other they so affect each other that if they come together with equal forces there is that compensation by which just that amount of motion continues as has been received by both together.[195]

This principle was also expressed more succinctly in the statement: "All impressed motion is of its nature indelible".[196]

Gassendi likewise enunciated the theory of inertia by extrapolating from his Epicurean atomic theory. He claimed that atoms move because of their "weight" (*pondus, gravitas*), which he described in MS Tours 709 as:

> A power or impulse of nature [in atoms, carrying them] from one part of the universe to another without terminus.[197]

While in the *Syntagma* version he described the theory of atomic "weight" (*pondus, gravitas*) which he claimed to find in the writings of Epicurus as:

> An innate vigour or internal energy ... which causes [the
> atoms] to move through space in such a way that, space
> being infinite and having no centre, the atoms will never
> cease from their natural motions, but will continue in them
> through all ages unless other atoms or composite bodies
> obstruct them and cause them to change their paths.[198]

Gassendi explained that this "inclination" (*propensio*) of the atoms, their
"weight", understood as an active force, was not towards the centre of the
Earth,[199] and that, in effect, there were no privileged directions in the
universe.[200] It is to be noted that Gassendi's "theory of inertial motion" was
an impetus theory.

Gassendi made the leap from micro-theory to macro-theory without
hesitation. In the one same section of the *Pars physica* in the *Syntagma*,
under the title "On natural things in general",[201] he combined a study of
nature both at the micro-level and at the macro-level, and when writing on
motion specifically, Gassendi made the extrapolation from atomic motion to
the motion of large-scale objects by using explicit phrases such as, "As
with the motion of atoms ... so with the composite objects ...",[202] and, "In
what pertains to motion in a straight line ... whether of atoms or of
composite objects ...".[203] For Gassendi, the movement of bodies throughout
the whole of nature was explained by the same physical principles.

Gassendi simply applied his general theory of the internal physical cause
of motion to the movements in the heavens and thereby arrived at his
explanation of celestial motion. The causes of the movements of the
heavenly bodies, he stated, and also of the circularity of their movements,
are identical with the material composition, the "innate form, contexture
and constitution",[204] of the heavenly bodies themselves, the atoms with
their indelible motions. The atoms, coming together, give to the bodies into
which they are formed their determinate and permanent motions,[205] a
permanent impetus. From the atoms, therefore,

> there comes not only circular motion, but also its perpetual
> character. Since the compaction [of atoms into large-scale
> bodies] is permanent, so also is the global character of the
> bodies and the action of the causes which push the bodies in
> a circular motion.[206]

This was a more reasonable theory than the Aristotelian, Gassendi
claimed, because according to this explanation the celestial bodies were
moved by their own internal principle, by their own 'forms', by their own
motive power.[207] Nevertheless, Gassendi did not propose his theory in
dogmatic fashion: though he considered that the Aristotelian theory ran into
difficulties in attempting to explain how incorporeal substances could

impart impetus to corporeal substances, he was willing to allow the possibility that God could in fact have chosen to keep the heavenly bodies in motion by some such agents as the Aristotelians postulated. However, he found no reason to accept their theory.[208]

Overlooking the possibility of extending his last objection (the difficulty of conceiving interaction between incorporeal and corporeal substances) to his own creationist doctrine, Gassendi linked his theory of celestial motion with his theological voluntarism, claiming that the inner contexture of atoms had been imprinted and their natural and permanent impetus imparted by God, so that the resultant motions of the celestial bodies composed of these atoms had all been engineered by the Creator. He wrote:

> It must be added that the internal contexture of atoms ... had Almighty God as its Author, as also did the very principles [atoms] to which the permanent impetus was imparted. As a consequence, the reason why the stars presently move in one manner rather than in another is because it was so arranged from the beginning by the Author of nature, who willed motion to begin and to continue.[209]

By completing his Epicurean theory of celestial motion with these assertions from his voluntarist theology, Gassendi recommended his theory as a substitute for the Aristotelian theory. Just as he had argued concerning his Epicurean philosophy generally, Gassendi implied that his theory offered at least as much support to Christian faith as the Aristotelian theory could afford.

Before arriving at his final explanation of celestial motion Gassendi had run into problems on account of the condemnation of Galileo in 1633. As has already been noted,[210] Gassendi's early Epicureanism was intimately linked with Copernicanism. The discussions he had with Isaac Beeckman in 1629 were largely concerned with the application of the mechanical philosophy to Copernican astronomy. Gassendi's own first exposition of Epicurean philosophy (1631) was expressly structured with a view to combining Epicureanism with Copernican astronomy. Even the second version, that of MS Tours 710 (1643), showed that Gassendi was more sympathetic towards the Copernican system than any of its rivals, giving only grudging acknowledgment of the fact that Copernicanism had been condemned.[211] However, the change in mid-stream from the Copernican to the Tychonic system had no noticeable effect on Gassendi's theory of motion, and it would seem that the reason for this is simple. Gassendi had originally intended to use Copernicanism, which he considered to be the true system, in his polemic against the Aristotelians. To support the Copernican system, he developed his Epicurean theory of motion which, while appropriate for the Copernican system, was also in itself anti-Aristotelian. Consequently, there had been two distinct but related lines of anti-Aristotelian polemic in Gassendi's early astronomical writings, one Copernican and another Epicurean, the first based on speculations about astronomical phenomena, the second based on a new explanation of celestial motions as such. Gassendi lost the support of the first line of argument because of the intervention of the Church authorities in condemning Copernicanism.[212] However, the second line retained its strength, for the celestial motions needed explanation, regardless of what system might be invoked to describe them. Gassendi was able to pursue his aim of providing a better account of motion, including celestial motion, than that given by the Aristotelians even when it became unwise to persist with his original plan of using his theory to support the Copernican theory.

However, Gassendi did not leave the matter there: he had a fresh thought which he incorporated into what became in the *Syntagma* the third part of his *Pars physica*: "Concerning terrestrial things".[213] It was a new and surprising thought, probably dating from 1645,[214] according to which Epicurean cosmology was geocentric and geostatic. Gassendi considered that the evidence for this conclusion was to be found in a passage of Lucretius.[215] Nevertheless, the very fact that Gassendi should have expressed the thought at all indicated that he was still pursuing the same end: given that Copernicanism had been ruled out by the Roman authorities, he looked about for ways in which he might commend Epicureanism as a suitable philosophy for orthodox Christian philosophers. He had, he believed, more than ample philosophical reasons already to support his argument that Epicureanism should be accepted in the place of Aristotelianism. Nevertheless, without going so far as to claim that Epicureanism was more suitable than Aristotelianism, being more in harmony with the approved astronomical system, Gassendi did seriously suggest that Epicureanism, in allegedly supporting the geocentric and geostatic system, was thereby at least as suitable as Aristotelianism.

Thus it is clear that although Gassendi was very much under the influence of Galilean Copernicanism when he wrote the early versions of his Epicurean philosophy he by no means ceased to function as a philosopher on account of the condemnation of Copernicanism. On the contrary, for the most part at least he continued to develop and elaborate his Epicurean themes without any apparent adjustments. The only modifications that one can perceive as having been determined by the new situation for astronomers following the condemnation were those obvious changes to his text whereby he tempered his support for the Copernican system and obediently promoted the system of Tycho Brahe as the one most acceptable.

CONCLUSION

Gassendi's Epicureanism was integral to his humanism and to his humanist anti-Aristotelianism. We have seen that Gassendi made it his special project to restore Epicureanism in such a way that he might explicitly recommend it as a substitute philosophy for Aristotelianism. Gassendi expressly claimed that he could make Epicureanism acceptable as a Christian philosophy just as Aristotelianism had been made acceptable in the fourteenth century. Gassendi's efforts to accomplish this have been displayed in this chapter by examining his writings on a series of specific philosophical topics.

The ambitious project of rendering Epicureanism acceptable and advocating that it be substituted for Aristotelianism took up most of Gassendi's time and energy as a philosopher. It became his main interest and concern throughout his working life, and thus represents an important key for understanding his philosophy.

# CHAPTER 4

## EMPIRICAL ANTI-ARISTOTELIANISM

Let us again recall Gassendi's philosophical origins. He began his academic life as an Aristotelian scholastic, first as a pupil and then as a teacher. His personal rebellion against Aristotelianism began from within the Aristotelian tradition, largely stimulated by the humanist movement towards the rejection of Aristotelianism. He had two specific complaints against Aristotelianism: first, that it did not teach one how to live; and second, that it did not teach one how to explore nature and make progress in knowledge.[1] Gassendi was in that frame of mind, then, when he turned from Aristotelianism to Epicureanism, a philosophy which he claimed to be the most sceptical of all the so-called dogmatic philosophies.[2] He was reacting against what he judged to be a highly dogmatic Aristotelianism and was reaching out for a more humane, less pretentious and less dogmatic classical philosophy which might take the place of Aristotelianism, with its claim to certain knowledge.

The Epicureanism which Gassendi presented was a mutant of the ancient system, an eclectic synthesis of Stoic and Epicurean presuppositions and doctrines emasculated by theological voluntarism. Gassendi had no firm commitment to the principles of Epicureanism; he was ready to modify and adapt the system in quite fundamental ways in order to shape it to serve his purposes as a Christian philosopher. Yet, for all the philosophical liberties he took, he has been hailed as a pioneer of modern empiricism,[3] and even commentators who would consider such an accolade be be an overstatement consider that Gassendi's role was not an insignificant one. It is considered, for instance, that Gassendi's writings on cognition, especially his sensualism, had some appreciable influence, at least indirectly, on the development of Locke's theory of the way of ideas and that Locke's distinction between "nominal essence" and "real essence" is identical with Gassendi's distinction between "appearances" and "true natures". Such similarities of doctrine are considered to be too striking to be merely the product of a common source of inspiration, and possible channels of Gassendi's influence on Locke have been explored.[4] Whether Gassendi's influence was substantial or not, his Epicurean theory of knowledge and of the processes of cognition did provide a foundation for the form of empiricism that was coming to prominence in the seventeenth century.

That Gassendi should have reflected modern philosophical movements at such a high theoretical level is cause for some astonishment: what we have

seen so far of his philosophical approach hardly provides grounds to expect
more than superficial reflections of liberal trends adorning an essentially
Renaissance *corpus* of doctrines. Yet Gassendi's understanding of the role
of logic, and his description of the physical, physiological and psychological
processes of cognition reveal that his eclectic Epicurean and sceptical anti-
Aristotelianism enabled him to mark out a ground plan for the new
understanding of science. My purpose in this chapter will be to explore the
steps which Gassendi took to arrive at such a result. It will be observed that
the same themes that dominated Gassendi's work elsewhere, anti-
Aristotelian scepticism and anti-Aristotelian Epicureanism, played a
fundamental part in determining the development of his theories. Our
exploration begins with the various versions of Gassendi's logic.

### Logical writings: from Aristotelian dialectic to Epicurean canonic

The final version of Gassendi's logic as found in the *Syntagma*[5] is difficult
to follow. The text is a poorly co-ordinated assembly of writings which deal
in various ways with subjects that traditionally belong in a treatise on logic
and which date from differing periods of Gassendi's career. To begin to
understand Gassendi's purposes or themes in these writings one needs to
compare the earlier versions and the final treatise in the *Syntagma*.

Gassendi wrote four versions of his logic. Of the first we have no more
than the chapter headings which he sent to Peiresc as part of a list of all the
books and chapters of the version of his Epicurean philosophy that he was
working on during the year 1631.[6] The second version is that of MS
Carpentras 1832, which Gassendi composed in the year 1634.[7] In a long
series of letters to Louis of Valois, his protector after the death of Peiresc,
Gassendi included a lengthy description of a third version that was in
manuscript in 1642.[8] This version has not survived. The fourth version,
which dates from 1649, is that of the *Syntagma*.[9]

We learn from the chapter headings which he listed in his letter to
Peiresc that Gassendi gave a straight-forward exposition of the 'Canonic' of
Epicurus in the first version.[10] 'Canonic' was a term used by the Epicureans
to refer to their theory of knowledge, and by 'canon' they meant a measure
or yardstick - a criterion - for determining the true and the false. Thus,
according to their theory the *senses* were the first canon or criterion for
determining truth; the "anticipations" or universal ideas[11] were the second
criterion; while the affections or passions were the third, used specifically
for determining moral truth.[12]

The reason why Gassendi gave the above-mentioned exposition of
Epicurean canonic became clear in the second version, that of MS
Carpentras 1832. The title of the first of the three books in which the
canonic of Epicurus was explained in this manuscript made it plain, for it
reads: "Concerning canonic which is substituted for dialectic".[13] Just as

Epicurus, Gassendi noted,[14] had proposed his canonic as a substitute for the dialectic of the Stoics, so he (Gassendi) was proposing the same canonic in a similar way as a substitute for dialectic in the seventeenth century, and especially for the dialectic of the seventeenth-century Aristotelians which he had already bitterly attacked in the *Exercitationes*.[15]

Gassendi pointed out that Epicurus had not rejected dialectic because its teachings were false, but for two different reasons: first, its extreme complexity and second, its uselessness.[16] These criticisms found in the teaching of Epicurus corresponded exactly with Gassendi's criticisms of Aristotelian dialectic in the *Exercitationes*. Gassendi claimed in that work that dialectic was an extraordinarily complicated and artificial branch of philosophy[17] which the Aristotelians had further complicated by bringing into it the most difficult and abstruse questions and disputations of the whole of philosophy. Gassendi further claimed that dialectic was a most unsuitable study for students beginning philosophy,[18] and he especially complained that it did not prepare students for the study of the sciences.[19] In fact, he complained, dialectic was quite useless.[20] The following passage from the *Exercitationes* conveys Gassendi's opinion concerning the uselessness of dialectic:

> Is it not a fact that [Aristotelian dialectic] does not open up nature, but only acts like the man who promised the discovery of a treasure saying, "Search where it is hidden and you will find it"?[21]

Thus, in the first two versions, Gassendi's anti-Aristotelian purpose was clear. Just as Epicurus, according to Gassendi, had substituted dialectic by "a few canons to help the intellect in its investigation of truth",[22] so Gassendi aimed to substitute Aristotelian dialectic with those self-same canons of Epicurus. In the later versions, however, and especially in the much expanded and extensively re-organised *Syntagma* version, Gassendi's anti-Aristotelian purpose was obscured. The *Syntagma* version was no longer a simple anti-Aristotelian exposition of the canonic of Epicurus, but had become a fairly comprehensive logical treatise in which the reaction against Aristotelian dialectic which had inspired the two early versions found no clear expression.

Thus, while the *Syntagma* version retained the early theme that logic is meant to assist the intellect to discover truth, it was now no longer expressed in the context of opposition to Aristotelain dialectic, and consequently the theme lost much of its anti-Aristotelian point. Furthermore, many of the principles which Gassendi enunciated, often for the first time in the *Syntagma* version, were not obviously dissimilar to classical Aristotelian logical principles. On the contrary, they were often identical. For instance, in the *Syntagma* Gassendi proposed a definition of logic that he had not previously employed, *viz.*, "the art of thinking well".[23] He enlarged upon his definition by explaining that logic was the art concerned with providing the rules to direct the intellect in its contemplation of nature:

> Here we speak of the art of the intellect. This art is not itself involved with the objects wherein truth is being investigated - that is the task of physics or natural sciences - but it has the role of providing the rules by which the intellect can be directed as it contemplates nature.[24]

Later in the *Syntagma* version, he described logic as the art that directs *all* the sciences, as follows:

> Physics and the other sciences are involved professedly with their own particular subject matters and with the examination of the truth to be found in them. Logic presides over the several sciences and holds up a torch for them by providing general precepts and rules common to them all. If they make use of these precepts and rules they will not wander from the way of inquiry into truth, or else when they have wandered they will be warned of their error and will set themselves on a more correct course.[25]

In both these quotations Gassendi gave a reasonably apt description of the art which Aristotle described throughout the *Analytica posteriora* - the art which governed the construction of demonstrative sciences as such.[26]

But similarity or lack of similarity between Gassendi's logical writings and classical Aristotelian logic are not the point of the present discussion. What is at issue is whether or no Gassendi was reacting against latter-day Aristotelians when he wrote his text. The answer to that question is affirmative: in the *Syntagma* version his anti-Aristotelian themes continued to dominate, in particular the theme that logic should be a discipline which like Epicurean 'Canonic', established the rules for the observation of nature correctly, and not as it was in the Schools (according to Gassendi), a useless dialectical exercise. Gassendi's advocacy of an empirical way to knowledge of nature, especially as outlined in Epicurean canonic, for all its similarity to the empiricism of Aristotle, was expressed as a reaction to the dialectic of the Aristotelians which he had attacked in the *Exercitationes* for being too complex and for being useless for the investigation of nature.

### Cognition: the physical and physiological processes

Gassendi commented in a passage concerned with the sense of vision that he was following the way of speaking adopted by authors generally when he spoke of sight taking place on the retina of the eye. Strictly speaking, he said, it would be better to say that vision takes place in the brain. However, he excused himself by saying that he always bore in mind the fact that he was referring only to the external sense organ, which organ moved the faculty in the brain to perform the act of sight.[27] That Gassendi should feel the need to make this comment seems to show that he was aware of a relatively new trend in the seventeenth-century discussions of cognition: what had hitherto been discussed as one philosophical subject, the act of cognition, was increasingly being discussed as a series of separate subjects concerned with distinct processes which were, by turns, optical, physiological and psychological.[28] This trend corresponded to the decline of Aristotelianism, a philosophy according to which the process of cognition was one process of species transmission from object to cognitive faculty.[29] The trend corresponded likewise with the rise of mechanistic philosophy in which the process of cognition was studied and explained as a series of subordinate processes.

For Gassendi, who was intimately involved in the decline of Aristotelianism and the rise of the mechanistic hypothesis, finding satisfactory explanations of the subordinate processes was an important task. The Aristotelian explanations having been found unacceptable, he sought to provide Epicurean explanations of what it was that was transmitted from object to cognitive faculty, and how it was transmitted. My argument in the pages that follow is that Gassendi's writings relating to the processes of cognition were dominated by that task: he sought simply to provide a suitably modernised Epicurean theory of cognition which would take the place of the Aristotelian theory. Furthermore, I argue, he showed little concern with the question of the validity of the knowledge gained according to the processes as he explained them.

Gassendi made his purpose clear in a letter to Fortunato Liceti which, along with three other letters on the same subject, was published under the title, "On the apparent magnitude of the sun when it is low and when it is high".[30] Liceti was an Aristotelian who corresponded with Galileo on diverse topics including the question of the nature of light.[31] Gassendi became involved in a discussion with Liceti when the latter was sent a copy, according to Gassendi's own wishes, of a letter which Gassendi had written to his friend Gabriel Naudé on the subject of the apparent variation in the size of the sun according to its position in the sky.[32] Liceti responded by publishing his objections to Gassendi's views expressed in the letter to Naudé.[33] Gassendi thereupon responded directly to Liceti in a second letter.[34]

The problem that had prompted Gassendi's original letter to Naudé was one which had been posed in a letter attributed to Epicurus in Diogenes Laertius, *De clarorum philosophorum vitis*, Bk. X:

The sun and the other stars are for us the size that they
appear to be ... in themselves, though, they may be [a little]
greater in size than they appear, or a little smaller, or
equal.[35]

This doctrine is strange in every context except that of Epicurean
philosophy. It was a general law of Epicurean physics that objects at a
distance appear smaller than objects close up, the explanation being that the
images emanating from objects became 'worn at the edges' in transit.[36]
However, Epicurus taught that luminous bodies - that is, highly visible
bodies such as the sun, the moon, the stars and earthly fires - transmit their
light and colour in such a forceful way that their images retain their form
and size practically undiminished and unaltered. Subsequently, luminous
bodies are exceptions to the general law. However, the viewer does not
always see absolutely exact images of luminous bodies because the contours
of these images become blurred by the effects of radiation, so that
variations in their apparent magnitudes occur. But this effect, it must be
stressed, is a phenomenon in the images of the luminous bodies themselves,
somewhat similar to a halo around the moon, and it does not signify any
defect in the faculties of perception.[37]

The foregoing laws of Epicuren physics were intentionally anti-sceptical
and formed part of the reply of Epicurus to the extreme scepticism of the
Pyrrhonists. Epicurus had based his theory of knowledge on the value of
experience as the source of knowledge, claiming that the senses and the
mind, which was viewed as a more refined sense, were infallible.[38]
Epicurus thus contradicted the Pyrrhonists: where the latter maintained that
nothing can be regarded as true especially since information gained from
the senses cannot be considered to be true, Epicurus countered by
maintaining that all sensations and mental perceptions are true.

Gassendi completely ignored the anti-sceptical intention of the doctrine
of Epicurus on the differing apparent sizes of the sun. His earliest reaction
insofar as it can be gauged from his correspondence, indicated that he did
not realise that the doctrine was an integral part of the response of Epicurus
to the sceptics for, influenced by the scorn of authors such as Cicero, he
was sceptical as to whether Epicurus had ever taught it.[39] In his letters "On
the apparent magnitude of the sun" the anti-scepticism of the doctrine of
Epicurus was totally left out of the discussion as Gassendi proposed to give
an explanation of the variation of the size not, as Epicurus had stated it, of
the sun itself, but of the appearance of the sun. Gassendi had thus either
not understood or had chosen to ignore the point of the discussion in
Epicurean philosophy, and had likewise not understood or had chosen to
ignore the distinction which Epicurus had made between ordinary objects
of vision and luminous objects. Once the question had become a simple one
of a variation of appearances which needed an explanation Gassendi treated

it as a purely optical problem whose solution was to be found in the Epicurean corpuscular theory of light and Keplerian optics.

In presenting his solution, Gassendi limited the discussion to the well-known phenomenon of variation between the apparent size of a celestial body at the horizon and its apparent size at the zenith. His preferred explanation of the phenomena was that the vapours near the horizon disperse the corpuscular rays issuing from the bodies and make their images larger and less strong. Consequently, the pupil of the eye dilates in the weaker light so that the larger images penetrate the eye and project themselves over a larger area of the retina. Thus it is that a larger image is seen when it issues from the sun or the moon when near the horizon than when they are at the zenith.[40]

Gassendi's solution to the problem found in Epicurean sources resembles so closely Kepler's solution to a problem posed by Tycho Brahe that one must conclude that Gassendi found his solution in the optical writings of Kepler. Tycho had drawn attention to the fact that the diameter of the moon as measured by the use of a pinhole camera appeared smaller during a solar eclipse than at other times although it was no further away.[41] Kepler explained the phenomenon in terms of his optical theory of radiation through small apertures, illustrating his solution by the use of a model in which a book represented the luminous source and a thread represented light rays propagated rectilinearly onto a surface on which the "image" was formed. The crucial point demonstrated by the use of the model was that the size of the image projected depended upon the size of the aperture, and changes of the latter brought about changes of the former.[42] Gassendi did not mention the pinhole camera in his solution to the problem of Epicurus, but based his conclusions on measurements taken by means of a shadow-making apparatus which he was accustomed to use for measuring the diameter of the sun and the moon.[43] However, his solution relied upon Kepler's findings concerning the variability of the pupil of the eye and the control it exercises over the amount of light that is projected onto the retina.[44] The only non-Keplerian feature of Gassendi's solution was his corpuscularian account of the nature of light.

Gassendi's linking of the corpuscularian theory of light with Keplerian optical theory was always more or less explicitly anti-Aristotelian. In 1634, a little over two years before he wrote his first letter on the apparent sizes of the sun, Gassendi had collaborated with Peiresc in a series of dissections of eyes of various animals, birds and fish.[45] The purpose of these experiments had been to investigate the truth of Kepler's theory of the retinal image, and it was with considerable excitement that they ascertained the existence of such an image.[46] Gassendi accepted the discovery as evidence supporting the view that the retina was the place of vision against the Aristotelian view that the crystalline humour performed that function. Subsequently, in his second letter on the sizes of the sun which he wrote to the Aristotelian Liceti in 1640, Gassendi supported his anti-Aristotelian

Keplerian position. He pointed out to Liceti that the reasons offered by the Aristotelians to support the view that the crystalline humour was the place of vision were at least as favourable for the retina. He quoted Liceti back at himself:

> The function of seeing must take place especially in that part [of the eye] in which the species of all visible things and the images of all colours can be received and held.[47]

Gassendi argued that the retina fitted this requirement better than the crystalline humour since the former is positioned at the back of the eye, and thus the *species* would be received and held by it after they had passed through the diaphanous medium of the crystalline humour. Liceti had claimed that the place of vision must itself be diaphanous and colourless, which the retina was not. Although Kepler had described the retina as "reddish-white",[48] Gassendi claimed in his letter to Liceti that it was colourless. He stated that, though he had examined the retina a hundred times he had never found it to be as Liceti described it, an opaque reddish-white body crammed with a multitude of arteries and veins filled with bright red blood. On the contrary, he maintained, the retina is simply the optic nerve spread out to form a very thin, very smooth and very transparent membrane which is passed directly over the choroid to form a mirror surface.[49] (Gassendi seems to have been exaggerating in opposition to the exaggerated description of Liceti. He also seems to have been following the description of Felix Plater who declared that the principal organ of vision was the optic nerve which dilated to form the grey, hemispherical retina inside the eye.)[50] And thus it is, Gassendi concluded, that the corporeal visual spirits pass along the optic nerve, animate the retina and foster the faculty of sight in that part where the image is located. Thus vision takes place on the retina lying against the choroid at the back of the eye.[51]

It would seem that Gassendi's description of the colour of the retina should be taken as an indiction that he was not thoroughly conversant with Kepler's writings, rather than that he consciously chose to differ from Kepler. For, on another subject Gassendi clearly corrected himself upon becomping better acquainted with Kepler's work. This occurred in his discussions on the inversion of the visible image. Gassendi observed for himself that the image on the retina was inverted and reversed from right to left. It seemed necessary that the images should be the right way up and the right way round for us to see objects as we do. Kepler had argued that geometrical laws required that the image on the retina be inverted and reversed, and accepted that it was a problem, but proclaimed it to be not an optical problem.[52] Gassendi, on the other hand, when writing to Liceti in 1640,[53] supposed that when the corpuscular species penetrated the eye after passing through the pupil, the crystalline humour acted as a refracting medium which prevented the images from reaching the apex so that they appeared on the retina according to the required alignment. This solution was that found in the medieval treatises on optics.[54] But when Gassendi came to write on the subject of the sense of sight in MS Tours 708 (1644-1645) which was published in the *Syntagma*,[55] he followed Kepler without any comment or attempt to improve upon his theory, thereby indicating, it would seem, that he had read Kepler's text more carefully and brought his own treatment of the subject up to date with the latest optical theory.

While the visual apparatus was not the only channel by which Gassendi understood that information passed from objects to the mind, nevertheless he considered it to be the primary channel,[56] and his writings on the sense of sight may be taken as representative of his theory concerning the physical and physiological processes involved in the act of cognition. Gassendi's theory of these processes was an Epicurean theory which was designedly anti-Aristotelian. The very fact that his first writings in which his theory was expressed led to a confrontation, brought about by Gassendi himself, with Liceti, shows that Gassendi presented his theory with explicit anti-Aristotelian animus. Liceti, it is worth noting, was accused by Galileo of being an extreme Aristotelian.[57] Gassendi also considered that his theory was anti-Aristotelian because it was supported by experimental evidence while, he accused, the Aristotelians had not performed any experiments in support of their theories. Indeed, he told Liceti he had adopted his theory which was "abhorrent to a Peripatetic" because the Aristotelian theory was not able to explain the (experimental) phenomena.[58] And above all, Gassendi's theory was anti-Aristotelian because it was part of his grand design to substitute Epicurean for Aristotelian philosophy. In this context he advocated corpuscular, material images, the Epicurean films which were composed of atoms supposedly thrown off from the surfaces of objects, in place of Aristotelian immaterial forms. Thus he proposed a mechanistic explanation of the transmission of information from objects to the organ of vision as a replacement for what he considered to be the inadequate Aristotelain explanations.

Thus, in his writings on the physical and physiological processes of the act of cognition, Gassendi's principal concern was to promote a theory of these processes alternative to that of the Aristotelians.

### Cognition: the 'psychological' processes

An examination of Gassendi's writings on the cognitive processes which occur after species have impinged upon the external sense organs leads to a conclusion similar to the one which was drawn at the end of the examination of his writings on perception by the external senses: Gassendi was intent upon completing his project of providing an Epicurean explanation of the processes involved in the act of cognition which might be accepted as a substitute for the Aristotelian explanations. However, there are many indications that Gassendi was unable to achieve the same results in his explanation of the psychological processes as he had achieved in his explanation of the physical and physiological processes. No doubt the comparatively inchoate state of the disciplines which dealt with what we today have come to term neurophysiology and psychology made it difficult for Gassendi to present an equally clear alternative to Aristotelian theory as he had been able to present in his explanation of the physical and physiological processes associated with vision.

I propose to examine Gassendi's explanation of the nature and functions of the imagination and intellect. It will become apparent that he was less clear about the ways in which these faculties operated than about the types of knowledge that they supposedly yielded. His theory was a somewhat makeshift, perhaps unfinished, explanation. It was devised to provide a foundation for a number of suppositions concerning human knowledge of the natural universe that Gassendi was anxious to promote, especially the empirical basis for all such knowledge and its probabilistic character. However, the validity of the knowledge of the natural universe thus gained was not one of the suppositions Gassendi sought to defend through his explanation; rather, he simply took it for granted.

When Gassendi linked the Epicurean theory of the emission from objects of images composed of ordered patterns of atoms with the geometrical optical theory of Kepler and other theorists, he departed from classical Epicurean philosophy. Kepler's optical theory, and all optics after Kepler, was concerned solely with the phenomena that occur in the field between the object and the retina. In the ancient Epicurean explanation of vision there had been no such cut-off point: Epicurus gave one single explanation of vision that embraced the whole process from object to mental perception. He maintained that the larger atoms of the film-like *species* which were emitted from objects struck the external sense organs and were perceived in the act of sensation. Finer atoms penetrated right through to the mind and thus caused a mental perception. And so it was that, for Epicurus, objects were perceived by the mind by contact in essentially the same way as they were perceived by the senses.[59] Gassendi could have no use for this explanation. He was committed to providing a philosophical framework for contemporary optics as an alternative to Aristotelian explanations of vision, and the ancient Epicurean theory, being so *simpliste*, was not even a rival for the Aristotelian theories.

In Gassendi's philosophy, therefore, we have an example of what had occurred in theories of vision universally after Kepler: the interior processes of vision that occur beyond the retina had become a newly-demarcated field of study.[60] Gassendi's theory of these processes is of interest as an example of a very early theory which was propounded to plug the theoretical gap that Kepler had left behind him. It is also of some interest because, in Gassendi's manuscript from which the *Syntagma* was printed (MS Tours 708) we find a change of text and change of explanation which seems to have been brought about by Gassendi's reading of Descartes' *Le traité de l'homme*.[61] And, I maintain, it is just such aspects of Gassendi's writings on the processes of cognition that are their principal points of interest. Gassendi strove for completeness in presenting his Epicurean philosophy for, as the title *"Syntagma philosophicum,"* was meant to indicate,[62] he aimed to present "an orderly account of the main things in philosophy".

MS Tours 708, from which the pertinent *Syntagma* text was taken, shows that Gassendi's explanation of the processes within the eye, the nerves and the brain, derives from two different periods. In the first period, 1644-1645,[63] Gassendi wrote the body of the text, while at some time later, probably in the period 1649-1654 when he was preparing his manuscripts for publication, making corrections to some and re-writing others, he made some corrections and additions to MS Tours 708. His explanation of the processes which occurred between the external sense organ and the brain differed in the later, corrected version from that of the first version.

In the first version of MS Tours 708, at f.1216v, Gassendi explained that the nerves were comprised of a double layer of skin filled with soft matter. The double skin, he stated, was continuous with the double membrane enclosing the brain, and the soft matter was the same as the soft matter of the brain. Gassendi referred to Galen's description with approval, according to which the nerve was nothing more than a small and slightly harder brain, and the brain was nothing more than a very ample and very soft nerve.[64] The animal spirits, Gassendi continued, were generated in that part of the brain from which the nerves originated and they filled all the soft matter of the nerve until the nerve was fully distended. Then, when the nerve was pressed, the spirits within were pushed along so that they pushed those next to them, and a chain reaction was set off along the length of the nerve, reaching right up to the spirits at the root of the nerve in the brain. The sense faculty located in the brain was thereby moved, and it perceived (or apprehended, knew, felt) the 'touch' that had taken place.

The second version consisted of this first version, together with some additions in the margin and at the foot of the text and some simple changes to the text itself. First of all, Gassendi added a reference to the anatomists, especially to one by the name of Laurentius, who can only be the Provençal André du Laurens of Montpellier whose text-book,[65] published in 1599 and frequently re-printed, was the most popular of the time. Then Gassendi made changes to his text that caused it to read quite differently from the first version; yet he worked in these textual additions in such a way as to leave the original text intact. In the revised version Gassendi stated that the Galenists were only guessing when they described the nature of the substance inside the nerve, and that no such soft matter could be detected. On the contrary, Gassendi asserted, the substance appeared to consist of a cluster of many extremely fine threads arranged in a series along the length of the nerve. These threads, he claimed, were hollow and filled with animal spirits. The extremely fine threads, he claimed, were like hairs which, he further claimed, and wrongly, were to be seen under the microscope to be hollow, even though they did not appear to be so to the naked eye. And so, instead of the motion being passed along the spirits that were crammed into the relatively uncluttered nerve cavity as described in Gassendi's first version, it was passed along the spirits filling the hollow centres of the threads or "little nerves" which in turn filled the nerve cavity.

The new version did not represent a major change to Gassendi's original explanation. The basic mechanism in the second version was still a quasi-hydraulic one, and Gassendi had really done no more to his own theory than accommodate within it a piece of new information from experimental anatomy. Gassendi may have read about the "threads" in the "nerve cavity" in the text-book of du Laurens without any prompting from other persons.[66] However, it seems distinctly possible that it was through reading Descartes' description of the threads in the nerves in *Le traité de l'homme* that Gassendi was spurred on to bring his anatomy up to date. According to what Descartes wrote to Mersenne,[67] the former's treatise was practically complete in July, 1633. Thus Gassendi had had ample time to read a copy of Descartes' much more detailed explanation of the same processes before he revised his manuscript after 1649. And so it would seem plausible that Gassendi corrected his explanation of the mechanism by which information is passed along the nerves, upon learning of new developments in anatomical theory.

Such, then, was Gassendi's explanation of how sensible objects make contact with the brain. It was a purely mechanical process in which all that was transmitted was a corporeal impulse. Gassendi described the process in the *Syntagma* as follows:

> A motion occurs when external senses perceive objects. It occurs when the external sense organ itself is encountered by a species or quality of the sensible thing; it occurs also as the nerves pass on the effect [of the encounter] to the interior of the brain where the nerves terminate or, rather where they take their rise. Thus nerves filled with spirits can be thought of as bundles of spiritous rays; and a spiritous ray of this kind, stretching from the brain to the external sensorium, cannot be pressed or pushed even in a light manner without the brain to which the external sense organ is linked being affected as a result.[68]

Beyond this point in his explanation of the processes, Gassendi's account owed at least as much to the declining Aristotelianism as it did to his own philosophical acumen. In a way it was to be anticipated, for as Gassendi came in his explanation to the limits of what had traditionally been considered the bodily processes and approached the rational processes, he was moving into theological territory, no lines of demarcation having been drawn between the psychology of the mind and the theology of the human soul. In Thomistic Aristotelianism, for instance, the intellect was treated as a faculty of the self-same soul which, according to Christian doctrine and tradition was a spirit created by God and immortal.[69] As a consequence, explanations of the mind were dominated by the Christian doctrines of the spirituality and immortality of the soul, its separate creation and infusion into the body by the Creator, and the reuniting of souls with their bodies on the Last Day. No clearer indication of this dominance could be found than the fact that the mind and its functions were treated at length by Aquinas in his *Summa theologiae*.[70]

Gassendi's explanations of the mind and its functions were dominated by Christian doctrine, and in fact they often reflected the Thomistic/ Aristotelian tradition. Thus Gassendi maintained that: "the soul is quite rightly reckoned to be a substance and a substantial form".[71] He used the following statement as a chapter heading in the *Syntagma*: "The rational soul is an incorporeal substance created by God and infused into the body as a form that informs the body [as opposed to merely assisting it]"[72] and he quoted Aquinas in defending this Thomistic doctrine against other Catholic theologians such as Cajetan.[73]

So Gassendi's explanation of the composition of the mind as a whole reflected the theological/Thomistic Aristotelian tradition, although he did not follow the doctrine of Aquinas strictly. He claimed that the human soul is not a simple substance, but a composite of two substantially distinct parts, a corporeal part in which the vegetative and sentient faculties, including the imagination (a point on which scholastic tradition and Epicurean philosophy agreed), reside, and an incorporeal part in which the intellectual and rational faculties reside. The mind is not joined to crass body immediately, but first it is joined to the vegetative and sentient parts of the soul (the corporeal part) and through them the mind informs the whole body, since these parts are spread throughout the whole body. The mind, or rational part of the soul, on the other hand, is located in the brain where the operations of imagination and intellection take place.[74]

As the soul is composed of two substantially distinct parts, a corporeal part and an incorporeal part, so, Gassendi claimed, there are two sets of cognitive operations, one set in each of the faculties of (corporeal) imagination and (incorporeal) intellect. Furthermore, he argued, these two sets of operations paralleled each other. For, he wrote, we observe animals, which are endowed with the faculty of imagination but not of intellection, to perform the operations of apprehension, judgment and at least rudimentary and simple processes of argument that may be analogically called reasoning. Hence we may conclude that these operations are proper to the faculty of imagination as well as to the intellect, although they are performed by the intellect in man in a superior fashion. In man, Gassendi concluded, the imagination and the intellect operate 'in tandem' (*pari passu*),[75] each performing distinct but linked operations of apprehension, judgment and argument.[76]

Taking Gassendi's explanation thus outlined of the composition of the soul and the operations proper to its various faculties and parts as being the theoretical context, it is possible to follow more easily his account of the processes involved in the act of cognition which occur once the motion that originated with sensible objects has been received by the brain. When the motion, or the impressed *species*, reached the brain, Gassendi explained, the faculty of the imagination which was located in the brain turned to and apprehended the sensible object from which the species originated. The species was not a picture representing the sensible object but was the means by which the object was known:

> The species is not a picture, and is not itself looked at. It is simply the ground for knowing the object by which the species is imressed. In the same way the species impressed on the eye is not what is seen but is simply the ground for seeing the thing which emitted it.[77]

Thereupon, since the imagination and the intellect were intimately present to each other, when the imagination turned to and apprehended the object by way of the species, the intellect also turned and apprehended the object in its own way. Gassendi wrote:

> When the imagination is struck the intellect acts along with it. Of course, the intellect cannot be struck by a corporeal species or by the movement of the spirits ... since it is incorporeal. But in the instant in which the imagination is struck ... and beholds the object ... the intellect which is intimately present to and linked with the imagination also looks at the same object.[78]

One finds clear echoes of Thomistic doctrine in the foregoing theory, even though Gassendi's description of the functions of the imagination and of the similarity of the operations of that faculty to the operations of the intellect differs substantially from the doctrine of Aquinas. Gassendi's assertion that the imagination "turns towards" the thing to be known upon reception of the species reflects the explanation of the operation of the intellect given by Aquinas.[79] Also Gassendi's description of the species as being a pure ground for knowing an object and not as being a thing which is known in itself exactly reflects the doctrine of Aquinas.[80]

Aquinas, however, had offered arguments to support his doctrine. Gassendi, for the most part, simply made assertions. Evidently he relied upon the traditional explanations that had been current since medieval times, and did not seem to see the need of a theoretical basis for his explanations such as Aquinas had provided for his theory.

Gassendi's account of the powers of the intellect showed still more clearly that he was content to repeat commonly-held doctrines without attempting to justify them by rational argument. Gassendi asserted that the intellect could perform feats of which the imagination was incapable. It could apprehend things that did not affect the senses: incorporeal things, such as God and space; abstract natures, essences or universals, such as humanity, whiteness and sweetness; differences, relations, and many other things. The intellect could also have reflexive knowledge of its own operations: it could know itself as knowing and think that it was thinking. The imagination, on the other hand, could not imagine itself to imagine, any more than vision could see itself seeing.[81] In all these cases Gassendi simply asserted that the intellect had the powers of apprehending, but he offered no explanations of how it could have these powers.

Gassendi also offered an explanation of how general ideas, or universals, were formed, and again his reliance on the traditions of commonly-held doctrine seems to have resulted in his making little effort to provide rational support for his assertions. Gassendi stated that both the imagination and the intellect produced universal ideas in two ways: by combining many similar particular ideas into one common idea which is then a collective idea containing all the common elements of the particular ideas and representative of them; or by abstracting what is common in many particular ideas from their particular differences and thereby forming a common or universal idea.[82] While Gassendi did claim that these were two distinct operations, one might be pardoned for finding it difficult to discover any difference between them.

To conclude the description of Gassendi's doctrine on the powers of the intellect, it may be noted that he asserted that the intellect not only apprehended universals, something which the imagination could do in its own way (although the latter was a corporeal faculty), but it could also perceive the very condition of universality of universals, so that it could recognise that a universal was more complete (*perfectior*) as it was more remote from the individual differences of singular things. And therefore the intellect could form a Porphyrian tree of universals, arranging general ideas in ascending order of universality beginning with, for example, Socrates, and concluding with 'being'.[83]

It would seem that Gassendi, like the Stoics before him,[84] had felt it necessary to introduce modifications to the original Epicurean explanation of the formation of general ideas. Whereas Epicurus had maintained that general ideas were produced from repeated sense experiences of objects, and for that reason the ideas were infallibly true,[85] Gassendi introduced theories of operations other than experience into the process of the formation of general ideas. One particular un-Epicurean modification which Gassendi introduced was the mental process of comparing ideas and thereby making judgments;[86] Epicurus had rejected such operations because he considered that they left the door open to the intrusion of opinion and false supposition.[87]

But one might judge that Gassendi's unconcern for providing rational justification of the doctrines of the 'interior' processes of cognition which he was presenting is most clearly illustrated in the few remarks which he made concerning what has come to be referred to as 'the mind-body problem'. He treated the problem as one that was already existing, not as one that he had created, and not, therefore, as one that was of pressing concern for him to solve. His seeming lack of interest in the question is shown in the opening remarks of his brief treatment of the question in the *Syntagma*:

> We need not delay inordinately over the fact that the intellect, which is an incorporeal faculty, immediately uses sense images, which are corporeal species. There is no more of a problem here than in the common doctrine that the incorporeal soul is joined immediately to the body and that it uses corporeal limbs in order to move.[88]

Hence it would appear that, in general, Gassendi's writings on the processes which occur after species have impinged upon the external sense organs resembled what he wrote concerning the processes involved in the act of cognition which occur before that instant. Gassendi was trying to present an alternative to Aristotelian theories. Although the alternative was not Epicurean, nevertheless the influence of mechanical models can be discerned, especially in Gassendi's explanations of the nerves and their functions. Gassendi supplied current anatomical theories for what he considered to be lacking in Epicurean theory. The major difference between Gassendi's writings on this subject and his other writings is that, in describing the soul and its intellectual functions, he relied heavily upon Aristotelian theory. There can be little doubt that the major reason for doing so was that this field of psychology was dominated by Christian doctrine and theology. For once, Gassendi either was not inclined or saw no reason to propose an alternative to Aristotelianism.

### Empirical anti-Aristotelianism

Gassendi's description of the physical, physiological and psychological processes of cognition provided him with a theoretical basis for the kind of science that in his project was to replace Aristotelian science. His explanation of these processes supported his claim that we do not know the inner nature or essences of things - a claim that he had made in the final *exercitatio* of the second book of his *Exercitationes paradoxicae adversus*

*Aristoteleos* (1624).This *exercitatio*, the last pages that Gassendi wrote before permanently interrupting the *Exercitationes* project, was entitled: "That there is no *scientia*, especially *scientia* as the Aristotelians describe it".[89] As Gassendi explained, 'science' as the Aristotelians understood it was based on a knowledge of the essences of things. For, they claimed, when one knew the essence or nature of a thing, one knew the "fount, root, principle and cause of all its properties",[90] and one knew how events proceed as effects from their causes in the inner natures of things. This kind of 'science', which was also referred to as knowledge *per causas*, was impossible for human beings while they lived in the bodily state;[91] with the faculties of knowing that were granted to man it was impossible to attain to the intimate natures of things, and thus to have a knowledge of essences.

The consequence of such a limitation was that all that men could know were the appearances of objects, their sensible accidents or, to use an Epicurean metaphor, the "outer bark" of objects.[92] The sensible images that men perceived did not come from the inner nature of objects; they were nothing but surface emissions, "*adiuncta sensibilia*'. All that men could do was to "deduce ... or, in a manner of speaking, gain some inkling"[93] that there were essences or natures beyond the appearances, which natures were the principles and causes of those sensible properties; but it could not be seen how the effects proceeded from their intimate causes.[94]

In adopting the foregoing view, Gassendi rejected the most fundamental presupposition of Aristotelian science, for the possibility of that science was based upon the presumption that one can know with a certain and evident knowledge, and make infallible statements concerning, what a thing is by its nature and by reason of its inner necessary causes.[95] Gassendi rejected such a presumption as altogether false. One can have knowledge of appearances, he maintained, such as the sweet taste of honey, and so a science of appearances was possible. But one could not know that honey was by its nature and in itself sweet because one could not attain to the necessary cause that determined it to be so, and one consequently could not provide a necessary demonstration that proved why it could not but be so; indeed, Gassendi claimed, there were many reasons that could be offered in support of an argument that it was not so.[96]

Thus, at the end of his long explanation of the processes by which knowledge is acquired Gassendi had worked his way back to the point he had just been making when he interrupted the *Exercitationes*. Gassendi's dominant concern in expounding his theory of cognition was anti-Aristotelian. Gassendi's polemic against the Aristotelians on this subject, as on most subjects, had more forcefulness in the *Syntagma* than it had had in the *Exercitationes* because his rejection of Aristotelian, in favour of Epicurean, theories was substantiated by much more theory and detailed description. Gassendi might almost have considered that he had demonstrated the truth of his theory of a science of appearances in the

*Syntagma*, whereas he had little more than asserted it as a fact in the *Exercitationes*.

Gassendi considered his position to be a *via media* between Aristotelian dogmatism as he described it and scepticism.[97] One needs only to recall his selective dependence on the work of Gianfrancesco Pico della Mirandola. Pico's *Examen vanitatis* was one of the sources that provided Gassendi with his array of criticisms of Aristotelianism, and it seems that, specifically, his rejection of Aristotelian demonstrative science based on a knowledge of essences was a clear reflection of Pico's views on this matter.[98] However, whereas Pico used the arguments from ancient scepticism to support his claim that the senses were fallible and knowledge was impossible and thus promoted an extreme form of scepticism, Gassendi accentuated the positive capabilities of the senses and gave an account of knowledge based on observation by way of the senses whose fallibility he admitted. Gassendi noted that the sceptics had no quarrel with a knowledge of appearances.[99] He took their point that such knowledge was not knowledge of the truth of things, 'in themselves' (to use a Kantian turn of phrase), but he insisted that to know the appearances was to know something. In fact, Gassendi concluded, all science of the natural world is more or less true knowledge of appearances: we do not know truth, but we do attain to varying degrees of truth-seemingness or "verisimilitude".[100]

Thus Gassendi did not adopt the conclusions of the sceptics and did not agree with the negative, anti-rational scepticism of men like Pico. Gassendi emphasised the role of observation and advocated what Popkin has termed a "constructive scepticism", a scepticism which was creative because it assisted the development of the natural sciences. In just such a spirit, Gassendi urged that the philosopher has no call to feel frustrated at not being able to attain the truth of things, but he should strive unceasingly to reach even higher degrees of verisimilitude; he should take great comfort from the fact that the image of the truth does not lead him astray. In a lyrical passage that calls to mind Plato's allegory of the cave,[101] Gassendi wrote:

> It is the greatest of pleasures to dispel the darkness and thick mists from the soul in such a way that, even though it is not permitted to us to see the light of truth shining like the sun, yet we come into the dawn of verisimilitude. Though we do not perceive causes that are certain and indubitable, yet we attain those which have some aspects of probability.[102]

Furthermore, Gassendi urged, the principal task of the philosopher of nature was to search and seek to discover the internal causes or natures of things, even though they remained well beyond his reach.[103] In fact, he gave evidence of a degree of ambivalence in his writings concerning what might be hoped for from such a search. On the one hand he stressed that knowledge of the intimate natures did not belong to mortal men, endowed as they were with such weak powers of perception. Such knowledge, he claimed, belonged to God alone, for it is the maker alone who knows the secret construction of the artefact,[104] and the philosopher will be very pleased if he can attain to some degree of verisimilitude, considering it to be well worth his while to grasp even the shadow or fleeting image of the truth.[105]

Such were Gassendi's views when countering the Aristotelian pretensions to know the inner natures of things. On the other hand, when he was expounding his atomist theory he wrote with an optimism founded especially on the usefulness of the 'engyscope' or microscope. He dreamed of the possibility that one day men *would* see into the corpuscular essences of things. All that would be required, he stated, were much sharper eyes or an extremely good microscope.[106] Gassendi did not pursue the thought any further, but his remarks at least show that he seriously harboured the hope of observational verification of the truth of atomism as an explanation of the natures or essences of things in the natural world.

In his explanation of the act of observation as the way to progress in knowledge, Gassendi referred to signs and criteria. He described signs by using the analogies of smoke in the air which indicated the existence of fire and drops of sweat on the skin which indicated the existence of pores in the skin. Epicurus had made little mention of signs[107] but, reflecting his reading of Sextus Empiricus who had referred to the doctrine of the "Dogmatists" (Stoics) (though he might also have referred to the doctrine of the Aristotelians)[108] Gassendi attributed an important role to signs in his Epicurean theory. On the other hand, Epicurus had placed emphasis on the role of criteria, or standards of apprehension, and had listed three in number: sensation, preconception and passion.[109] The Stoic/Epicureans added voluntary mental acts to the theory of cognition presented by Epicurus,[110] thereby presenting the mind or intellect as one of the criteria. Gassendi again followed suit and claimed that there were two criteria: the senses, by which the signs are perceived (the signs being the appearances), and the mind or intellect by which we reason to the knowledge of the things which are indicated by the signs. Thus, according to Gassendi, smoke or drops of sweat (signs) - are perceived by the senses, and the mind by reasoning comes to know the fire or the pores in the skin. Gassendi accepted that the senses can sometimes be misleading, thus rendering the sign dubious, but the mind can make up for the deficiencies of the senses by using its powers to reason and make judgments.[111]

Furthermore, Gassendi continued, in the process of reasoning from the signs presented to the senses and making conclusions concerning the things indicated by the signs, the mind relied on principles that are not doubted and which have been arrived at by induction from sense experiences. For instance, he explained, the principles that no body passes from place to place without passing through the medium between the two places, and that two bodies cannot occupy the same place at the same time are assumed when the mind reasons to the existence of pores in the skin, or to the fact that light is composed of corpuscles, and to the fact that there are pores in the glass through which the light corpuscles pass.[112]

The validity of the two-fold criterion, the co-operation between mind and senses in providing knowledge of things, has often been demonstrated, Gassendi argued. He pointed out that we often find that the conclusions drawn by the mind are verified upon closer inspection. Furthermore, he observed, the recently discovered 'engyscope' and telescope are especially valuable instruments in this process of verification. Thus, for instance, whereas previously people had reasoned to the conclusion that fleas possess legs, now we can actually see the legs by the use of the 'engyscope'; and as Democritus had reasoned to the fact that the Milky Way was composed of myriad stars, so now the truth of his reasoning has been verified by the use of the telescope.[113]

Thus Gassendi presented an account of knowledge which he claimed to be attainable by observation, and so his account sought to offer a *via media* between dogmatism and scepticism. The role of the "evidence"[114] acquired by observation was central in his account. He described evidence in the following way:

> Evidence is that which presents itself to the senses in such a way that it cannot be disputed, since it fully recommends itself and nothing can be more probable.[115]

In the 1642 version of his logic which he described in his letters to Louis of Valois, Gassendi linked evidence with true opinion rather than knowledge. Thus, he stated, opinion can be true if the evidence of the senses supports it or does not oppose it[116] - that is, in our twentieth-century terms, if the opinion is either verified or not falsified by experience. In expressing himself in this way, Gassendi was following the terminology of Epicurus[117] who linked evidence, understood as the testimony of the senses, with true opinion. But Gassendi adopted this Epicurean manner of expression only in that one version of his logic. In the *Exercitationes* he had used the term "knowledge" rather than "true opinion". Thus he had stated that he had no objection to the non-Aristotelian use of the term "knowledge" in such expressions as "I *know* that honey appears sweet to me because I taste its sweetness", and so, he had claimed, one should allow the use of the term "knowledge" when it signified an experiential acquaintance with things that appear.[118] In the *Syntagma* Gassendi's position on this question of terminology was expressed with more definiteness and at greater length.[119] He dropped the use of the term "true opinion" altogether and used instead the term "knowledge", linking evidence not only with knowledge but also with certitude. In so doing he explicitly rejected the doctrine of the Aristotelians who considered knowledge to be solely of a discursive or demonstrative kind described as "certain, evident and causal".[120] Gassendi simply dropped the third adjective and required as a consequence only two conditions for knowledge: evidence and certitude.[121] These conditions, he stated, were often present, not just in the case of universals as the Aristotelians maintained, but also and more especially in the case of knowledge of singular objects such as the sun and the moon. Thus, Gassendi continued, we can have knowledge of the size, colour, strength and character of *this* man, of the specific kinds of trunks, leaves, fruit and scent of *this* tree, of the specific kind of energy, property, *etc.* of *this* mineral.[122]

For all its inconsistencies, Gassendi's explanation of cognition reflected the new scientific outlook which became widespread in the seventeenth century. His description of the physical, physiological and psychological processes of cognition provided him with a basis for the kind of science which, in his view, was to replace Aristotelian science, and that new science was a form of the empiricism which was coming to prominence. His Epicurean science was based on sense perception: all definitions, all principles - metaphysical, physical, moral, mathematical[123] - would be arrived at through experience. The Aristotelian universal idea, in which it was claimed that the true natures of things were expressed, would be replaced by an idea composed entirely from sensible impressions produced by emissions from the "outer bark" of objects. The new science which Gassendi presented was a science of the appearances of things, a science in which the mind worked on phantasms only, and never penetrated to the essences of things. The accounts of natural phenomena in this science were all probabilistic, provisional, open to refutation and reform. Gassendi claimed to derive all this empirical theory from Epicurean sources.

Thus, upon completion of our investigation of Gassendi's writings on logic and cognition we arrive at the conclusion that Gassendi's principal concern in these writings was to present an Epicurean account that would be acceptable in place of the Aristotelian theories. Gassendi's theory of knowledge and account of science were anti-Aristotelian in the attempts he made to provide an Epicurean account of the channels by which cognition is acquired, and in the sense that doctrines and theories about the natural world were claimed to be a science of appearances only, and not a science based on a knowledge of essences. The whole of natural philosophy, in effect, insofar as it relied on human reasoning unaided by supernatuiral revelation was for Gassendi a more or less systematic body of probabilistic explanations of the causes of phenomena.

## The 'sceptical crisis'

Before concluding these considerations of Gassendi's empiricism, we need
to pay some attention to an interpretation of Gassendi's scepticism that has
been influential in the last two decades, and which would link Gassendi
with what is claimed to have been a deep and general crisis in the
seventeenth century. The view that some kind of crisis of considerable
moment occurred in the seventeenth century is firmly established in general
histories of the period, but there is no consensus among historians
concerning its causes or its nature.[124] Gassendi has been cited as a key
figure in the crisis, along with Mersenne and Descartes, by R.H. Popkin in
his *History of scepticism*.[125]

Popkin's interpretation of Gassendi's scepticism differs considerably
from the one that I have been presenting. I have been claiming that
Gassendi's scepticism was integral to his anti-Aristotelianism, that it was, at
least as a rule, a weapon used by Gassendi in his anti-Aristotelian polemic.
According to the thesis argued by Popkin, however, Gassendi's scepticism
had a wider significance for he elaborated his scepticism and his sceptical
philosophy as a whole in response to a "sceptical crisis" which occurred in
Europe in the early decades of the seventeenth century. Gassendi is thus to
be seen as a close collaborator with Mersenne in advocating a constructive,
or mitigated, scepticism in response to the crisis, and to have thereby
become a pioneer of the modern scientific outlook.[126]

Popkin has presented a very impressive thesis which links theology and
natural philosophy in a manner that is highly plausible. According to
Popkin's account, philosophers of the seventeenth century were influenced
by the *'Nouveau pyrrhonisme'* of a number of Catholic theologians who used
scepticism in religious controversies as a means of defending the faith
against attacks made upon it. The stratagem of these theologians was to
counter the rational arguments of their opponents by sceptical objections
against the rational processes that underpinned their arguments. But what
began as a stratagem devised by theologians for strictly theological or, more
exactly, apologetical purposes, was soon adopted beyond the confines of the
field of theology with the result that sceptical assaults were made against
the bases of all knowledge, ultimately provoking a general crisis of
knowledge and certainty in every field.[127] Thus it came about that the
seventeenth century was marked by a sceptical crisis. The quest for absolute
assurance concerning religious truth, or the religious rationalism of the
Reformation, led to a general epistemological crisis.[128] As men searched for
a criterion of truth in theology, so they were compelled to look for a rule of
truth in natural philosophy, and thereupon, "the *crise pyrrhonienne* ...
overwhelmed man's quest for certainty in both religious and scientific
knowledge."[129]

Gassendi, according to this account, responded to the sceptical crisis: he strove to discover some rule of truth that could withstand sceptical attacks, and believed that he had found it in his mitigated scepticism which he described as the *via media* between Pyrrhonism and dogmatism.[130] A mitigated sceptic did not claim to attain to necessary truths but did claim to arrive at probable knowledge, especially knowledge of appearances, which might be claimed to be knowledge in a lesser sense of the term. It is this *via media* which is often considered to characterise the scientific outlook. Thus, Popkin wrote, Gassendi was able

> to formulate quite fully a scientific outlook devoid of any metaphysical basis, a constructive scepticism that could account for the scientific knowledge that we do, or can possess, without overstepping the limits of human understanding revealed by the Pyrrhonists.[131]

And a little further on Popkin wrote:

> Mitigated or constructive scepticism represents a new way [i.e. novel for its time], possibly the closest to contemporary empirical and pragmatic methods, of dealing with the abyss of doubt that the crisis of the Reformation and the scientific revolution had opened up.[132]

My interpretation of Gassendi's intentions as I have presented it in this and previous chapters corresponds with some points of Popkin's theory. Gassendi did advocate an empirical and probabilistic methodology for natural philosophy; one can, therefore, find similarities between what Gassendi promoted and what many, especially those who adopt positivistic positions, consider to be the "modern scientific outlook". However, I maintain that there is no satisfactory evidence to support the view that Gassendi proposed his views about knowledge in response to a sceptical crisis which is alleged to have been seriously disturbing Europe in the early decades of the seventeenth century. To be sure, it seems evident that Mersenne was concerned to respond to what he perceived as a sceptical threat.[133] And Descartes in his turn, to some extent under the influence of Mersenne, was concerned to answer the sceptics.[134] However, there are grounds for questioning whether Descartes was stimulated to answer the sceptics out of concern about a sceptical crisis, or whether he was not almost entirely moved by his more positive rationalist aspirations to erect a sure and certain system of knowledge.[135] As for Gassendi, while he did consider the views of sceptics, he considered them along with every other shade of opinion and theory of knowledge and its validity, and there is much less evidence in his case to substantiate the view that he was concerned about a sceptical crisis. Rather, I have argued, Gassendi was reacting with considerable vigour and single-mindedness against what he considered to be the obstructive dogmatism of Aristotelianism. If at the same time and in the process of foreaking Aristotelianism and adopting Epicureanism he was anxious to avoid scepticism as an opposite extreme to Aristotelianism - if, in other words, he was involved in an attempt to plug an epistemological gap left by the collapse of Aristotelianism - then it should be possible to find evidence of the fact. But I have not found such evidence. All the evidence, on the contrary, points to a signal unconcern on Gassendi's part about the dangers of scepticism.

If Gassendi was also responding to a sceptical crisis when he wrote the versions of his logic in 1631, 1634, 1642 and 1649, then there are no signs of such a response. When presenting Epicureanism as a dogmatic philosophy which he considered to be the most sceptical of all the dogmatic philosophies, [136] he did so in reaction to Aristotelian dogmatism, not in reaction to scepticism. Insofar as he did treat of the sceptics and their principles in his logical writings, his reference was exclusively to classical sceptics and classical sceptical writings. For instance, he surveyed all the opinions concerning criteria for knowledge - the opinions of those who argued against them and those who posited them - without mentioning a single non-classical source.[137] Thus, Gassendi's sceptical opponents, insofar as he identified them in his logical writings, were to be found in his library of classical authors.

Again, in his writings on the physical, physiological and psychological processes of the act of cognition, and in his empirical account of knowledge, Gassendi's principal concern was to promote a theory that would serve as an alternative to that of the Aristotelians. He manifested a signal lack of concern about epistemological questions: he made no obvious attempt to establish the trustworthiness of the processes by which knowledge is acquired, even though the objective of the ancient Epicurean doctrine, which Gassendi claimed to present, had been to proclaim the credibility of sense experience. Gassendi referred throughout his explanations to Epicurus, Sextus Empiricus and the Aristotelians, and never to a non-classical sceptic. He gave no inkling of concern that the human quest for certainty had been overwhelmed by a *crise pyrrhonnienne*.[138] He proposed observation and evidence as the way to overcome the suspension of judgment of classical scepticism, as the *via media* between the positions of the dogmatist and the sceptics as described by Sextus Empiricus. Gassendi's account of knowledge was a humanist statement, to be interpreted as a contribution to a perennial classical discussion, not as a response worked out to a specific sceptical crisis.

Thus, Gassendi's restoration of Epicureanism resulted in the redeployment of a specifically anti-sceptical theory to serve an anti-dogmatist purpose. Gassendi would appear to have been so unconcerned about the alleged sceptical crisis that he was not moved to emulate the anti-scepticism of his chosen philosophical model. Consequently, I conclude that there are no indications in Gassendi's writings that he should be numbered as one who shared Mersenne's concern about the threat that scepticism was considered to pose to the foundations of philosophy - there are no signs that I can discover to indicate that Gassendi was reacting to a sceptical crisis.

# CHAPTER 5

## "A TRUER PHILOSOPHY"

In the first letter which he wrote to Galileo (20.7.1625), Gassendi made early mention of his project of persuading his contemporaries to adopt "a truer and better philosophy" than Aristotelianism,[1] and when Gassendi was well on the way to completion of his project Thomas Hobbes is reported to have read his manuscripts and to have approved of what he read in them because he considered that Gassendi's Epicurean philosophy was "much truer" than Aristotle's.[2] Gassendi deliberately chose the comparative "truer" (*verisimilior*) in preference to the absolute term "true" in order to distinguish his goals from those of the dogmatic philosophers, those who claimed to have knowledge of the essences of things and those who, like Robert Fludd, claimed to have found the "philosophical key" to the universe.[3] Yet there were times when Gassendi, too, was tempted to expound his corpuscular theory in more dogmatic style, for he evidently believed that the obstacles to verification of the corpuscular explanation of natural processes were technological, and that it is only our divinely-willed human frailty that prevents us from appreciating the full truth of the Epicurean doctrines.[4] However, he did not succumb to the temptation, for the whole thrust of his reaction to Aristotelianism depended on his not crossing the divide between scepticism and dogmatism. He was content to maintain that his Epicurean philosophy was "truer" than all the others, and our task in this chapter will be to give an account of his grounds for believing it to be the case.

Gassendi gave an outline of what he considered to be those features of his Epicureanism which made it superior to the entrenched Aristotelianism in the *Liber proemialis* which he placed at the head of the *Syntagma*.[5] Although the *Liber proemialis* was written at some time later than MS Tours 709 and other early manuscripts, it expressed concerns that had been constant for Gassendi throughout his philosophical career, and he considered that he had thematically addressed them in the length and breadth of the *Syntagma*. His central concerns as they are expressed in the *Liber proemialis* are in the main predictable in the light of what we have already seen of his philosophy. He emphasised that the pursuit of truth should relate to practical ethics, insofar as the goal of all philosophy is to promote peace of mind, tranquillity of soul and true religion;[6] the classical division of philosophical schools into Dogmatic and Sceptic, and Gassendi's categorisation of Epicurus as a sceptical dogmatist feature prominently, proclaiming it to be his project to overthrow the dogmatism of the Aristotelians and replace it with an empirical and probabilistic science;[7] the division of philosophy by which Gassendi combined *metaphysica* with *physica* is also outlined, for this inclusive style of natural philosophy was crucial for his recommendation of Christianised Epicurean cosmology as a replacement for the Aristotelian.[8] It was Gassendi's conviction that all these features of his version of Epicureanism made it a suitable replacement for, and in a manner of speaking a truer philosophy than, Aristotelianism.

However, Gassendi was at pains in the *Liber proemialis* to draw another distinction between the philosophical schools which, by dint of a little delving in the manuscript material and in the *Syntagma*, can be detected as thematic in his restored Epicureanism. It was a distinction which, Gassendi believed, placed his Epicurean philosophy in a special class along with very few others in the whole of philosophical tradition, and which made it "truer" than many other styles of philosophy besides, and including, the Aristotelian. The distinction was between philosophies that were "clear" (*perspicua*) and philosophies which were "obscure" (*obscura, occulta*).[9] Gassendi divided the ancient Greek philosophies according to whether they belonged to the obscure tradition or to the tradition in which philosophy was expressed in a clear manner. In the obscure tradition he placed Homer, Hesiod and Orpheus, Empedocles, Xenophanes, Parmenides, Aesop, Pythagoras, Plato, Heraclitus and Aristotle, while in the clear tradition he placed Aristippus, Zeno, Pyrrho and "especially" Epicurus.[10] The obscure tradition, Gassendi concluded, was continued even in his own age; and he aimed to ensure that the clear tradition would be continued pre-eminently in his Epicurean philosophy. The significance of this distinction is less immediately apparent in the *Syntagma* than the themes mentioned in the previous paragraph, but upon closer reading the force of it can be seen everywhere: it influenced the expression of Gassendi's corpuscular philosophy and further explained why he should have considered his philosophy to be truer than that of all other schools, including that of the Aristotelians.

Gassendi's chief criterion for obscurity in a philosophy was the use of fables and symbols in an endeavour to express mystical or occult concepts.[11] Gassendi quoted the following as being a dictum of Epicurus:

The wise man does not make up fables about what lies beyond the scope of his wisdom; rather he clings to what is true. In this way he places no obstruction to wisdom.[12]

But Gassendi's criticism extended to any deliberately mystifying forms of discourse. After accusing those who teach in fables of providing occasions for the talking of nonsense, Gassendi continued:

> In fact the same may be said of those who conceal what they
> teach in symbols, intricate questions and riddles. For they
> likewise make serious things ludicrous, and from the very
> mouth from which they wish to appear to pronounce the
> truth they pour out darkness that obscures it. The same is to
> be said of those who affect any obscure manner of speaking.
> Even if they were not to be disapproved of for anything
> else, one could not condone the time wasted in all that
> conjecturing, puzzling, mental juggling and interpreting,
> time which would be better spent in striving to make
> progress in more fruitful ways.[13]

In Gassendi's opinion, such obscure philosophies make nonsense of
philosophy, dissipate energy, waste time and do not lead to progress of any
kind.

Gassendi generally wrote in a respectful manner concerning many of the
philosophies which he categorised as obscure; it was the modern versions,
especially neo-Platonism and neo-Pythagoreanism along with Renaissance
Aristotelianism, which he classed as obscure. He had been involved in first-
hand research into one such philosophy, that of Robert Fludd who belonged
to the extreme conservative wing of the "obscure" philosophies, displaying
in caricature the principal features that Gassendi found objectionable in all
the others. In the year 1628, Marin Mersenne requested[14] Gassendi to
support him in his public controversy with Robert Fludd, the Hermeticist
and Rosicrucian. Gassendi responded to Mersenne's appeal by writing a
treatise entitled *A consideration of the philosophy of Robert Fludd* (1630).[15]
This was a forthright condemnation of Fludd and the Rosicrucian
Fraternity, an elusive society of *illuminati* for which Fludd acted as
mouthpiece.

In complying with Mersenne's request for support Gassendi was as
zealous in his condemnation of Fludd as Mersenne had been,[16] and his
objections, like those of Mersenne, were on grounds both of religion and of
natural philosophy. Although he did not agree with Mersenne when the
latter labelled Fludd as an evil magician and an atheist, he did share
Mersenne's view that he was a heretic, and he believed that as such Fludd
was a serious menace to the Christian Faith. Gassendi wrote:

> I do not consider him [Fludd] to be an evil magician or an
> outright atheist. However, I do suspect that he dissents from
> our religion and that we should consequently consider him
> to be a heretic. Indeed, he holds opinions concerning God
> which, if true, might seem worse than atheism. It is clear
> that he is not an atheist from the fact that he ceaselessly
> proclaims some sort of Divine nature, also from the fact that
> he cites the testimony of Sacred Scripture throughout his

writings. He accepts that there is a God, and agrees that this God is the One who brings into being, fosters, causes to act and governs everything that is ... But truly, because he understands the Divine nature in his own particular way, making it the Author of a composite reality composed of itself and of that [vulgar] Spirit, claiming this composite to be Christ the Messiah, and because he wishes to maintain that angels and souls are particles of that composite, together with other views that follow as a consequence, then one must judge that these are ideas that are clearly irreconcileable with Holy Religion. Indeed, who could not consider these opinions to be more dangerous than atheism itself? It was Plutarch who clearly implied that it was far preferable to deny the existence of God altogether than to hold opinions that are superstitious or even just wide of the truth.[17]

Thus, in Gassendi's opinion, the reason why Fludd should be condemned was because he was a heretic, though he found Fludd's doctrine as a whole absurd and impious.[18] Later in his treatise Gassendi condemned the alchemical practices of the Fraternity, criticising the members for blasphemously mixing things sacred and profane:

In no way can this profane abuse be excused. These people mix pure things with impure. They trample all over the Sacred Scriptures, the mysteries of the Faith and the rites of religion. There is nothing sacred which they do not violate and turn into alchemy.[19]

Gassendi judged Fludd's version of the doctrine of the Soul of the World to be pantheistic,[20] which is to say that he believed that Fludd identified God and creation, claiming that God is all things and all things are God, and that Nature is divine and self-creative, God being the immanent creative force. Fludd's pantheism, Gassendi accused, offends Divine simplicity and immutability, leads inevitably to the divinisation of creatures including demons, to idolatry, to the conclusion that animal souls are immortal, and to the conclusion that everything that is done on this earth, both good and bad, is done by God.[21]

Gassendi's philosophical objections were likewise numerous. He complained that Fludd cultivated secrecy and relied on symbols as explanations;[22] that Fludd's philosophy was dogmatic rather than sceptical and probabilistic;[23] that it was arbitrary, especially in its theory of the Monochord, in contrast to the attempts of Kepler and Mersenne to ground their Monochord theories in observations and measurements;[24] his explanations are non-explanations for, even if one were to suppose that

Fludd has attained to the first principles of all natural things, he cannot explain why specific effects follow from these principles;[25] his philosophy was sterile, non-progressive. Gassendi's general reaction is summed up in the following words from the covering letter to Mersenne that he sent when he despatched the completed critique:

> You see practically no-one who philosophises from nature itself, but only from their own or other people's dreams. While no-one studies things in themselves the commentaries that tell us about them are immense. What else can these be but empty commentaries since, unless the human mind is governed by experience and observation, it is utterly sterile, fruitless and extremely fertile in nonsense? You have perceived this very clearly, and consequently you want either to experience everything for yourself or else to trust only to the experience of men worthy of trust ... the book of nature is what we must read if we are to learn anything for certain.[26]

This treatise on the philosophy of Robert Fludd shows that by at least the year 1630 Gassendi was fully in agreement with the views of Kepler and Mersenne concerning the methods to be employed in natural philosophy. His critique thus provides us with important insights into Gassendi's way of thinking as he foresook the *Exercitationes* project and embarked upon his life's work of restoring Epicureanism. He had already assessed the usefulness of his Epicureanism, which at that time was little more than an outline of a project, for achieving his goal of displacing the "obscure" philosophies with an eminently "clear" alternative. Epicureanism did not use fables, nor did it use symbols or riddles; in Epicurean philosophy natural phenomena were explained by means of totally corporeal atoms, corpuscles and the motions of corpuscles. Epicureanism, as Gassendi intended to develop it, would be plain and in principle intelligible to everyone, in conscious contrast to the occult philosophies of Fludd and other philosophers of the Renaissance who, in Gassendi's judgment, expounded pseudo-mystical syntheses of doctrines from neo-Platonist and neo-Pythagorean sources. It would not be a closed, dogmatic philosophy, but open, empirical and probabilistic, closely related to nature itself. It would be a philosophy of progress.[27]

Evidence of the determination with which Gassendi set about the task of ensuring that his Epicureanism would meet such standards of clarity is to be found in the emendations he made to his presentation of the doctrine of atoms and the void and to his presentation of the doctrine of physical causality. We shall now turn our attention to the way Gassendi dealt with these subjects.

### Atoms and the void

The text of Gassendi's treatise "Concerning the material principle or the prime matter of things"[28] is modelled on a section of the *De natura rerum* of Lucretius.[29] Gassendi argued that all philosophical opinions concerning the nature of the material principle are defective, except that of Epicurus. Thus Gassendi first rejected the opinion which supposed the four elements to be the principles of all things; and during the course of his discussions of various poetic/religious versions of this theory he mentioned a version found in the writings of Hermes Trismegistus.[30] Next, he rejected the opinion according to which prime matter has both primary and elemental qualities (heat, cold, wetness, dryness) and secondary qualities (colour, odour, taste, light, rarity, density, *etc.*),[31] remarking that this opinion had recently enjoyed a resurgence and was flourishing among the alchemists. He then proceeded to attack the alchemists for their claim to know the ancient and secret arts.[32] Next, he set out to disprove the theory of five elements adopted by the Chymists, and in the *Syntagma* version[33] added critiques of Telesio, Patrizi, Campanella and Digby. And finally, by way of prelude to a consideration of the theory of Epicurus, Gassendi criticised the opinion according to which matter was entirely without qualities - "without quality, without form, without appearance, without shape".[34] After giving a very brief account of the Stoic, and a longer account of the Aristotelian version of the theory, Gassendi described at length the Platonic and Pythagorean versions, emphasising the connection between this theory of matter in these philosophies with the theory of the World Soul and the theory of universal harmonies.[35] After rejecting all these theories, Gassendi proposed in their stead the Epicurean doctrine of atoms endowed with the three qualities of size, shape and weight.[36]

Gassendi's understanding of the nature of the Epicurean atom was absolutely materialistic. He was perfectly clear that the Epicurean atom was a corporeal 'nature' without any admixture of incorporeal 'nature', a solid particle that was inert except for the motion indelibly imparted to it by the Creator. Gassendi's earliest discussion of the atom in MS Tours 709 reflected a passage from the letter of Epicurus to Herodotus[37] concerning the physical indivisibility of the atom. Gassendi wrote:

> [An atom is] a solid nature that is full and without any admixture of void, so that there is no possibility of a fissure developing through which it might be broken in pieces.[38]

Further, Gassendi prefaced his treatise on atoms in MS Tours 709 by stating that it was necessary to correct a common misunderstanding, according to which Epicurus taught that atoms were mathematical minima.[39] In the *Syntagma* he wrote:

> I am glad to note that [Epicurus] did not call it an atom for
> the reason that it is commonly supposed (and as some
> scholars interpret), namely that it is without parts, and
> entirely without size, so that it would be nothing more than
> a mathematical point.[40]

One of the most important features of the theory of Epicurus concerning
the atom in Gassendi's estimation of it, was that the materialism of the
theory clearly distinguished it from neo-Pythagorean theories of atoms.

Gassendi's description of matter was in total contrast to the conceptions
of matter entertained almost universally in the Renaissance. In the sixteenth
century, and into the seventeenth as well, neo-Platonism and neo-
Pythagoreanism, taking inspiration from the *Timaeus* of Plato,[41] largely
determined the fundamental assumptions of philosophers concerning the
nature of the universe, and in particular, the Platonist assumption of the
fusion of the spiritual and material in the universe was fundamental to
Hermetic theory and the practice of alchemy. According to the *Timaeus*,
the marvel of creation consisted in the transformation of transcendent Ideas
into corporeal realities. The assumption that such a transformation had
produced the universe as they knew it is to be found in the writings of,
among others, Paracelsus, van Helmont, Nicholas LeFèvre, Agrippa,
Giovanni Pico della Mirandola, Johann Reuchlin and Robert Fludd, all of
whom were neo-Platonists.[42] Hence, when one contrasts Gassendi's
emphatically materialistic description of the atom with the vague concepts
of the atom that were widespread, and which were essential to the
alchemical theory of philosophers such as Robert Fludd,[43] one is led to
conclude that Gassendi promoted the Epicurean concept of the atom at least
partly in order to counteract the theories of matter of the "obscure"
tradition of philosophy.

Gassendi's formulation of the doctrine of Epicurus on atoms remained
basically the same in both MS Tours 709 and the *Syntagma*. Gassendi was
satisfied that his presentation of the Epicurean doctrine on that subject was
suitably "clear". On the other hand, however, Gassendi's formulation of the
Epicurean doctrine on the void evolved noticeably, and I believe that there
are indications that the evolution was largely determined by Gassendi's
concern to propose an Epicurean doctrine of space that was in
unmistakeable contrast to obscure doctrines. At least this much is certain:
the developments in Gassendi's presentation of the Epicurean doctrine
resulted in a more unambiguously "clear" account of space in the *Syntagma*
than that which is to be found in MS Tours 709.

Gassendi found himself confronted by the awkward fact that some of the
Epicurean terminology appeared ambiguous, seeming to admit
interpretations that would mesh with certain well-known Renaissance
opinions about the nature of space that Gassendi would describe as obscure.

There were two specific sources of possible ambiguity: one was the Epicurean use of the term "nature" in reference to the void, and the other was the fact that Epicurus, according to Gassendi, probably classified the void as an incorporeal substance. Gassendi took steps to eliminate possible ambiguities arising from both these aspects of Epicurean doctrine: he ensured that it was clearly understood that space was in fact as Epicurus described it, a void, and consequently not a *plenum*, and furthermore that it was inactive, non-substantial and non-spiritual.

Since the term "nature" as used by Epicurus in reference to the void[44] was a potential source of ambiguity, Gassendi let it slip almost totally out of use in his Epicurean writings. He began in the first book of MS Tours 709 with an exposition of the Epicurean doctrine concerning the composition of the universe under the heading, "According to Epicurus the universe is composed of two natures, one corporeal and the other incorporeal".[45] But then Gassendi quickly began to abandon the term in reference to both the atoms (corporeal nature) and space (incorporeal nature). He was quite deliberate about it, and he came to a decision on the matter in the course of writing the very next book of MS Tours 709. He crossed out the second part of the title of that book (Book XIII) so that whereas it originally read "Concerning atoms, that is, simple corporeal nature", it came to read simply "Concerning atoms".[46] Then, when he came to write the next book again (Bk. XIV), which dealt with the corresponding subject of the incorporeal nature, Gassendi did not use the terminology he had begun with when he commenced his examination of the composition of the universe according to Epicurus, but simply began the book with the title, "Concerning the void, or place ...".[47]

In themselves, the foregoing are slight details, but they take on significance in the light of the way in which Gassendi developed his exposition of the two correlative concepts of atoms and the void. While he was to use on infrequent occasions (but in the case of the void, only in quotations from his Epicurean sources)[48] the term "nature" in reference to both atoms and the void, he generally chose other terms by preference. However, there was a significant difference in the type of alternative terminology he chose for atoms by comparison with that which he chose for the void. When referring to atoms, Gassendi used terms that were synonymous in his vocabulary with the term "nature", such as "elements" and "principles".[49] Thus, for instance, the heading of Book XV of MS Tours 709 reads "Concerning principles or elements", the word "elements" having been substituted for "the matter of things", which was Gassendi's original choice for the latter part of the heading and which he crossed out.[50] Again, he referred to "material principles or elements" in the title of the first chapter of the same book.[51] In that way he substituted words that had some parity of meaning to the term "nature" when he chose terms like "principles" or "elements" to refer to atoms in its stead. But he did no such thing when he abandoned the term "nature" in reference to the void.

Instead, he chose to describe space as a totally neutral and designedly lifeless, non-substantial and non-accidental reality.[52]

In Bk. XV of MS Tours 709, which dealt with the Epicurean doctrine on the principles or elements, the final chapter "Concerning matter according to the opinions of Epicurus, Democritus and others who uphold the existence of atoms"[53] contains a passage which seems to explain why Gassendi ceased to use the term "nature" (synonyms: principles, elements) when referring to the void. The possibility of confusion concerning the correct meaning of the doctrine of Epicurus, Gassendi stated, arose because some interpreters of Epicurus made the erroneous judgment that the Epicureans had postulated two principles or elements of all things: atoms and the void. The truth was, Gassendi asserted, that in Epicurean doctrine atoms alone were regarded as elements or principles. Consequently, he inferred, there was nothing of the character of an element, principle or nature about the Epicurean void. Therefore, finally, he inferred, there was no similarity at all between the Epicurean and doctrines of space that attributed life, divinity, or spiritual sources of activity to space. Space, Gassendi insisted, was passive and in no way spiritual or divine.[54]

The second source of possible ambiguity was an issue only in MS Tours 709 for, when Gassendi came to write the *Syntagma* version, he had clarified his doctrine and was able to present it in a manner which avoided all possibility of confusion, including confusion with "obscure" doctrines. According to Gassendi, Epicurus implicitly considered the void to belong in the category of substance. Gassendi's patently anachronistic argument proceeded as follows. Epicurus ostensibly divided the universe into corporeal nature and incorporeal nature, and he permitted no third division. In fact, however, Gassendi added, Epicurus did allow a third category, that of accidents. Thus Epicurus actually taught the same doctrine as Aristotle, that "Being" is divided into substance and accidents.[55] Thus Epicurus divided reality into things that exist of their own nature, substances (corporeal nature and incorporeal nature), and things that do not exist of their own nature, accidents. Consequently, Gassendi claimed, the void, or space, belonged to the category of substance in the philosophy of Epicurus.[56] In MS Tours 709 Gassendi rested with that conclusion, evidently satisfied that it represented the doctrine of Epicurus: and he prepared to present it as his own Epicurean doctrine as well. Space, or the void, as far as he was concerned, was a substance. The doctrine was a little difficult to accept, he agreed, but the difficulty he commented upon was not the fact that space was categorised as a substance, but the fact that another kind of incorporeal substance was being postulated apart from the generally recognised incorporeal realities of ancient and modern philosophy. He wrote:

> It can seem difficult to accept [*durus*] that, since the void
> pertains to substance, Epicurus should call it not only

"being" but even "being existing of itself". However, from what will be said later concerning [the similar natures of] space and time, it will be seen that such is quite possibly the case. But it is not the fact that Epicurus divided substance into corporeal and incorporeal that is so much a cause for concern, but rather the fact that by "incorporeal" he did not mean the Divine nature, nor the nature of the Demons and Intelligences, nor the nature of the soul.[57]

In this passage Gassendi was reacting especially against the Aristotelian rejection of three-dimensional void space.[58] Since according to Gassendi's interpretation of both Epicureanism and Aristotelianism, place/space was necessarily either a substance or an accident, he sought the authority of Epicurus to claim that it was a substance, indeed, a three-dimensional substance. Again, Gassendi thereby claimed, Epicurean doctrine was more satisfactory than Aristotelian doctrine.

But it would seem that Gassendi was reacting against other doctrines as well, and it is possible that Gassendi's acquaintance with Thomas Campanella was important to him at this point in the development of his ideas. Campanella, as Gassendi recorded in the *Syntagma*,[59] was very anti-Aristotelian. It therefore seems likely that the similarities that are to be found between Gassendi's description of space and that of Campanella were not coincidental. Campanella had maintained in his *De sensu rerum et magia* (1620)[60] that space was a substance, just as Gassendi did in 1637. He had also insisted that space was a finite, created reality, and Gassendi found himself faced with a difficult task of attempting to defend the opposite view, namely that space is an infinite and uncreated reality.[61] But Campanella had also taught that space was a three-dimensional incorporeal reality, which was the doctrine Gassendi claimed to find in Epicureanism.[62] All this was anti-Aristotelian doctrine, and of interest to Gassendi for that reason alone. But Campanella's theory of space was also formulated in explicit opposition to doctrines according to which space was treated as something mystical and divine - Campanella went to considerable lengths to stress that space was not God. It seems more than likely, therefore, that Gassendi promoted Campanella's doctrine of space as a three-dimensional, incorporeal substance - the doctrine which he partly discovered anew in the philosophy of Epicurus - not only because it was an anti-Aristotelian doctrine, but also because it was explicitly de-divinising doctrine.

Against this conclusion it could be objected that in the *Syntagma* Gassendi adopted the doctrine of space that was made popular by a philosopher whom Gassendi considered one of the most obscure of them all, Francesco Patrizi (1529-1597). For Patrizi as for Gassendi, the categories of substance and accident were inapplicable to the reality of space, space being neither a substance nor an accident but a third type of reality. Patrizi published his doctrine in the work to which he gave the Lucretian title *De rerum natura*[63] and which he re-published in 1591 as part of his *Nova de universis philosophia*.[64] Gassendi acknowledged the similarity between their doctrines in the following words:

> He [Patrizi] taught exactly the same doctrine concerning space or place, that it has the three dimensions of length, breadth and depth, as I have argued earlier.[65]

But Gassendi wrote those words as part of a long addition to the final *Syntagma* version which he prepared between 1649 and 1655. Over half a century had elapsed since Patrizi had published his theory and, at least insofar as Gassendi took notice of it, Patrizi's concept of space had become detached from the metaphysics of its author.

   One is able to gauge Gassendi's distaste for Patrizi's metaphysics from the account of it which he added to the *Syntagma* version. Gassendi stressed the obscure character of Patrizi's philosophy in his account. Gassendi wrote, in part:

> Last century ... Francesco Patrizi wrote a "new, true, and complete" (these are his words) philosophy of the universe, and said that he had confirmed his teachings with the help of divine oracles (by which he meant not only oracles of Moses, but also of Zoroaster, Trismegistus, Orpheus, *etc.*), and by necessary geometrical reasonings, philosophical arguments and most evident experimental demonstrations.[66]

Gassendi inserted the account of Patrizi's philosophy towards the conclusion of a lengthy critical review of the obscure tradition of philosophy.[67]

### The substance of physical causes

Having rejected the notion that space was counted as one of the principles of Epicurean philosophy, proclaiming it to be an erroneous interpretation of Epicureanism that atoms and the void were the two principles of all things, Gassendi went on to state that there were, indeed, two principles in nature, *viz.* matter and efficient cause. He presented this as the constant doctrine of the mainstream philosophical tradition. For, he maintained, the chief philosophers and poets established the fact that there were only two principles of all things, the material and the efficient principles. He offered the following quotation from Seneca as a passage that was supposedly representative of the whole tradition:

Our Stoic philosophers ... say that there are two things in the universe from which everything comes, namely, cause and matter. Matter is inert, ready for everything, but unmoved if no one sets it in motion. But the cause, or reason, forms matter and turns it in any way it chooses. Through the cause all the variety of things are produced. There must then be something from which things come to be and something by which things come to be. The latter is the cause, the former is the matter. All art is an imitation of nature, so now apply to art what I was saying about the universe. A statue has matter which is moulded and a sculptor who gives a shape to the matter. Thus in a statue the matter is the bronze, the cause is the sculptor. The same applies for all things: they consist of what is in being and of what brings into being.[68]

This quotation is something of a red herring. In its position in the *Syntagma*, at the very beginning of Bk. III, "On the material principle, or the prime matter of things",[69] which treatise was followed by Bk. IV, "On the efficient principle, or on the causes of things",[70] the quotation gives the impression that Gassendi had adopted the Stoic distinction between matter and the efficient principle. In giving that impression, however, the quotation is misleading. It is worth noting that in MS Tours 709 it was located at the beginning of Bk. XVI, "On causes, fortune and fate",[71] which was preceded by Bk. XIII "On atoms"[72] and Bk. XV, "On the principles or elements".[73] Although the quotation in this latter position could likewise give the impression that Gassendi's doctrine on the principle of motion was Stoic rather than Epicurean, it was less misleading in MS Tours 709 at the head of the treatise on the efficient principle than it was in the *Syntagma* at the head of the treatises on both principles. Evidently Gassendi could not resist including this quotation, although it had less relevance to the contents of his discussion than he seemed to indicate.

Gassendi expounded what he claimed to be the Epicurean rather than the Stoic doctrine on the cause of motion, or the efficient principle.[74] For Epicurus, Gassendi explained, and as we have already noted in our examination of Gassendi's theory of celestial motion[75] atoms were in motion because they were endowed with the property of "weight" (*pondus seu gravitas*), an internal principle of motion, a native force or impulsion, which moved the atoms continually. Gassendi described this principle many times, the following being a few selections:

We must now examine heaviness, or weight, from which the motion of atoms is derived. By weight in this case, we must not understand an inclination of atoms toward the centre of the universe ... but a 'force' or natural impulse [moving atoms] from one part of the universe to another without end.[76]

Then, after quoting a few lines from the *De rerum natura* of Lucretius, Gassendi continued:

> Thus Epicurus considered all atoms to be endowed with a certain internal energy, or innate 'force', by which they move and drive themselves through the void in such a way that they will continue on endlessly unless something gets in their way.[77]

He added the following two passages to the *Syntagma* version:

> [Weight is] a natural, internal faculty or 'force' by which an atom can move of its own self; or, rather, it is an in-born, innate, native and indelible inclination to motion, a propulsion and impetus from within.[78]

> It can be supposed that each individual atom, no matter how small, received from God the Creator its bodily character, its size and shape, and in inexpressible variety; likewise it can be supposed that each received its appropriate power to move, travel and detach itself, consequently its power to extricate itself, to emerge, to spring out, to collide, to check and return.[79]

There is a passage in MS Tours 709 concerning the Aristotelian doctrine of the material cause in which Gassendi made a statement which would seem to indicate that he wished to reduce efficient causes to matter-in-motion. It was a statement concerning Aristotle's doctrine of the material cause. Having first remarked:

> To speak the truth, it seems that matter cannot be called a cause except improperly: one cannot properly ask "out of what cause" is a statue made.[80]

Gassendi went on to allude to the relationship of matter and efficient cause in the doctrine of Epicurus, saying:

> Although Epicurus could call matter a cause because of the perpetual motion of the atoms, Aristotle could not do so, for he considered matter to be inert.[81]

But the reductionism of this statement seems to have been an accident: Gassendi omitted the latter sentence from the *Syntagma* version. Gassendi, like Aristotle, believed that a further principle, more specific than matter, even matter in motion, was required to explain motion.

It is important to note Gassendi's reaction to Aristotle's criticism of Leucippus and Democritus for, as Aristotle claimed, leaving the principle of motion unexplained.[82] Gassendi's reaction did not take the form of arguing that Leucippus and Democritus had perhaps provided an explanation of the principle of motion that satisfied their own (mechanist) requirements if not the requirements of Aristotle.[83] Rather, Gassendi argued that they did explain the principle of motion, and in the process of defending them from the criticism of Aristotle he presented Leucippus and Democritus as offering an explanation that was at once ostensibly mechanist and yet satisfied the requirements of Aristotle. It was an ostensibly mechanist explanation insofar as matter and efficient cause were held to be substantially one and the same: they taught that there was no efficient cause apart from matter. At the same time it was an explanation which satisfied the requirements of Aristotle that there be a specific and positive causal principle for motion, for Leucippus and Democritus, Gassendi claimed, held the same doctrine as Epicurus, *viz.* that weight was the principle of motion. Epicurus, according to Gassendi, had simply expressed more clearly than his predecessors the doctrine which was common to them all when he made weight the principle of motion.[84]

Gassendi offered very little by way of evidence both for his interpretation of the doctrine of Epicurus and for his claim that Epicurus spoke for Leucippus and Democritus. He referred to the *De rerum natura* of Lucretius and quoted passages in which reference was made to the fact that the atoms were carried on their courses by their own weight.[85] He also quoted a passage from the *De fato* of Cicero in which an interlocutor is presented as arguing against the need for an atomic swerve, since the atomists already had the impulse which Democritus called a "blow" and which Epicurus called "weight":

> The atomists have another motive force given them by Democritus, the impulse which he called a blow, and which, you, Epicurus, called heaviness and weight.[86]

Gassendi deliberately aimed to make his explanation of the relationship between matter and efficient cause Epicurean rather than Stoic, despite what we might be led to believe from his prominent use of the quotation from Seneca. The Stoic doctrine, as Gassendi observed, made a distinction between passive body (matter) and active body (efficient cause). As Gassendi expressed it, the Stoics distinguished efficient cause and matter "not only in number, but also in substance".[87] The doctrine of Leucippus, Democritus and Epicurus was more satisfactory, Gassendi claimed, since in their philosophy the efficient cause was not substantially distinct from atoms or prime matter. For them, atoms were all active and all participated in the action of the efficient cause.[88]

At the same time, however, Gassendi's interpretation of the doctrine of Epicurus, and thence of the doctrines of Leucippus and Democritus, was certainly influenced by Stoic interpretations of the same philosophies. The influence of the passage from Cicero quoted above is an evident example of such influence. It would seem that Gassendi attributed to all matter the role of a principle of movement which the Stoics had reserved for active matter alone. To arrive at this interpretation of the doctrine of Epicurus, Gassendi first accepted the Stoic interpretation of the original atomist doctrine of Epicurus and then, second, he implied that Epicurus taught that all matter was of the kind to which the Stoics attributed innate activity.

Thus Gassendi categorised "cause" as a substance; indeed, the third chapter of Book XVI of MS Tours 709 was entitled "The substance of physical causes"[89] Although Gassendi did not use the term "substance" in reference to cause in the *Syntagma*, he was nonetheless anxious to develop his Epicurean doctrine of cause in such a way as to distinguish it from the doctrines of causality of the "obscure" philosophies, which relied upon a variety of substantial spiritual causes. In accordance with his Epicurean doctrine, Gassendi pronounced that physical or efficient causes were entirely corporeal. He listed as proponents of the contrary view (*viz.* that efficient causes were incorporeal) Pythagoras and the Aristotelians, adding Plato to the list in the *Syntagma* version. He wrote:

> Now it follows that we should investigate what the philosophers thought about the substance of these causes. Some considered them to be incorporeal, as did Pythagoras ... [added in *Syntagma*: "and Plato"], and as did all who wanted to attribute a soul or form to the world, the particular forms of all things being particles of this soul [added in the *Syntagma*: "and from these forms there springs all efficiency in things"]. This appears to be the Peripatetic doctrine also, insofar as they want the forms to be simple actualities of things, and describe these forms as incorporeal.[90]

Other ancient philosophers, he claimed, taught that efficient causes were corporeal, and he mentioned in particular the Stoics, and Leucippus, Democritus and Epicurus.

We have seen that Gassendi classified Pythagoras, Plato and Aristotle as belonging to an "obscure" tradition of philosophy, while he classified the Stoics and Epicurus as belonging to a "clear" tradition. This division between "obscure" and "clear" philosophy was presupposed in all of Gassendi's discussion of the theories of corporeal and incorporeal efficient causes; in particular, it influenced his critique of the Aristotelian doctrine of forms and of the panpsychist doctrines popular with Hermetic philosophies. There are indications, also, that Gassendi came to be persuaded that there was an affinity between the Aristotelian theory of forms and "obscure" doctrines of efficient causality.

We have an indication of the manner in which Gassendi exploited the Epicurean theory of causality to counteract the obscurity he detected in the Aristotelian doctrine in his critique of Aristotelian forms. The criticisms of this doctrine that Gassendi presented in the *Syntagma*[91] are of two clearly defined types, one of which made its appearance early in MS Tours 709 (before the end of Book XVI) as well as in the *Syntagma*, while the other appeared only after Book XVI of MS Tours 709.[92] The earlier criticisms, those which first appeared in the early books of MS Tours 709, were based on the alleged incompatibility of the doctrine of forms with other Aristotelian doctrines, while the later criticisms were largely inspired by Gassendi's clearer perception of the "obscurity" of the Aristotelian theory, and his arguments were consequently less scholastic. I shall now examine both the earlier and the later arguments that Gassendi adduced in order to see the way his philosophy was developing to be the pre-eminently "clear" philosophy he intended it to be.

In his description of the Aristotelian doctrine that he gave in both the early books of MS Tours 709 and the *Syntagma*, Gassendi wrote:

> There is in any thing an intrinsic and substantial form which perfects matter and fills its substantial deficiency. This form establishes a substantial composite with matter, a being *per se*. When the form perfects the matter it is called the *entelecheia* [or] *perfectihabia* [= full reality], and *energeia* [or] *actus* [= activity]. It actuates or informs the matter. It determines the matter to be actually a certain *genus* of being. It confers on the composite the power to act. It is the source of the principal properties and accidents of the being.[93]

Gassendi's first criticism of this description of forms was that it was largely a fabrication of the Aristotelians. He claimed that Aristotle actually wrote practically nothing about forms. This sort of accusation, that the Aristotelians invented much of what passes for Aristotelian doctrine was fundamental in Gassendi's anti-Aristotelian polemic.[94] But at least in this instance it seems to be largely an unwarranted accusation. The doctrine of forms figured prominently enough in Aristotle's works.[95] Furthermore, the above description of the doctrine, far from being a pure fabrication of the Aristotelians, as Gassendi would have us accept, is a reasonably adequate presentation of important aspects of Aristotle's own exposition of the doctrine in the *Physics*.[96] At the same time, it must be admitted that the doctrine of forms had been extensively elaborated by the Aristotelians. And so it would seem that Gassendi was over-reacting in his criticism of the doctrine to the involved treatises on the subject that were produced by the Aristotelians.

However, Gassendi's most important criticism of the doctrine in this first period was based on its alleged inconsistency with other Aristotelian doctrines. Gassendi gave three instances of this inconsistency. First, according to Aristotle, a principle is something permanent. But forms, which are known as substantial principles, are not permanent since they come to be and cease to be. Second, for Aristotle a principle is something which does not proceed from anything else. But if, as some say, the form is educed from matter, then the form proceeds from something else, namely matter.[97] Third, to say that the form comes from privation is patently absurd, for such a statement contradicts the axiom that 'being' cannot come from 'non-being'.[98] Thus, in the first period Gassendi's objections against the doctrine of forms tended to carry on the scholastic disputes. The objections he put were of the type that might be put in any disputation on the subject within the Schools.

On the other hand, Gassendi's later criticisms of the doctrine, those which are found only after Book XVI of MS Tours 709 and in the *Syntagma*, were all related to the question 'Where do the forms come from?'. He first formulated this question in a letter to the Aristotelian, Fortunato Liceti, dated 1640 and entitled "On the apparent magnitude of the sun when it is low and when it is high".[99] It was a new question about forms in Gassendi's writings, and it changed the terms of his earlier critique of the Aristotelian doctrine as described above. Further, I suggest that the question was prompted by Gassendi's reflections on efficient causality: his explanation of efficient causes in MS Tours 709, and especially his comparison of theories that presented them as incorporeal or corporeal (distinct from matter or identical with matter) provided the philosophical matrix for this new question about forms which was to dominate Gassendi's discussion of the Aristotelian doctrine thereafter. The Aristotelian forms, Gassendi asserted, were proposed as incorporeal causes,[100] and his rejection of incorporeal causes thereafter provided the basis for his later rejection of Aristotelian forms.

Thus, when writing on the subject of generation,[101] Gassendi asked where the form was considered to be before it appeared and what it was supposed to be. In reply to both questions, he noted, the Aristotelians stated that the form was 'in' the matter, but not as an actuality - only as a potentiality.[102] To this, Gassendi responded with the further questions: If the form is in the matter how can the matter await it as though it were absent? And, if it is not an actuality, how does it become actual? The Aristotelian reply, he noted, was that the form was educed from matter by the power of the efficient cause. But, Gassendi objected, the power of the efficient cause was not the point at issue. The difficulty arose from the fact that a form was presented by some as being a 'substance', a true entity in itself, a thing distinct from matter. Yet at the same time it was said to be educed from matter. How, Gassendi asked, could a form be educed from matter if it had nothing of that matter in itself? An alternative solution chosen to avoid this difficulty was to claim that the form was not educed from matter but was created out of nothing by God. Gassendi dismissed this solution. Frequent recourse to miracles was unacceptable as a reply, if for no other reason than that it denied to the powers of nature the capacity to produce forms - an ability which Gassendi considered to be entirely natural.[103]

Gassendi's principal objections against the doctrine of forms in the later period may be summed up in his own words as follows:

> Neither Aristotle nor his interpreters state where the form or actuality comes from and whence it has its active power ... They are accustomed to say that the form is educed from matter. It is beyond comprehension that they should say this when they wish to present the form as an entity distinct from matter. For they do not permit even the least particle of matter to carry over into the form. So they claim that the form is entirely divested of matter, even though it is educed from matter. To be precise, they say that the form is educed from the potentiality of matter; but these are mere words. If, however, they were to claim that the form is educed from matter in the way that it is only a mode of matter as the shape of a statue is a mode of bronze or wood, then they would say something one could accept. But in such a case the form is merely passive just as the matter of which it is a mode is passive. The form would in no sense be an active principle.[104]

So, I may sum up the account which I have been presenting as follows. Gassendi associated the Aristotelian doctrine of forms with the doctrines of causality which he attributed to Pythagoras and Plato, classifying all three as doctrines which advocated theories of incorporeal efficient causes. Further, he classified all these philosophies as belonging to what he called the "obscure" tradition of philosophy, which tradition, he claimed, continued even in his own times, especially in the many different styles of neo-Platonist and neo-Pythagorean philosophies. But it should be pointed out that Gassendi changed his criticism of the forms, and the change occurred with his new emphasis on their incorporeal or spiritual nature. His early criticisms were legitimate enough within the rules of scholastic disputation; his later criticisms were no longer of the same type, for in his later writing Gassendi treated the forms as substances, *i.e.* as individual subsisting entities, whereas the original Aristotelian doctrine had considered them as substantial principles which only together with matter form a substance.

Gassendi's reactions to the doctrine of the World Soul likewise showed his determination to provide a "clear" explanation of physical causality. This was a doctrine that was commonly presented as an all-embracing theory of incorporeal causality, according to which life, activity and movement were the operations of one life-giving principle which animated the whole universe.

Gassendi recognised that there were a number of different types of theories supporting varying degrees of unity in the universe. He then went on to state that it was held by many but not all that the world was composed of parts that:

> commingle and coalesce and are bound together by a force that permeates them, after the manner of a plant or an animal.[105]

Moreover:

> Many, but not all, say that there is a kind of force diffused through the whole world which binds its parts together. It is the kind of power that constitutes the soul in an animal. It is that kind of internal energy that is in us and in our members, the force by which we live, feel, imagine and move. If it departs we die and we perform no more of these kinds of functions.[106]

This energy, Gassendi explained, is called the Soul of the World.

Gassendi noted that the doctrine originated from Pythagoras and Plato.[107] At the same time he claimed that these philosophers presented no more than conjectures, and very vague conjectures at that, since they merely presented an hypothesis.[108] The people chiefly responsible for raising the doctrine from the status of mere conjecture, he claimed, and for propounding it as a fundamental doctrine, were the Cabbalists and the Chymists. In order to give their teaching greater credibility, Gassendi asserted, they claimed support from the philosophers and poets who celebrated the omnipresence of the Divine Nature, maintaining that this Divine omnipresence was a Universal Soul, and that the individual souls of men and animals were particles of the one Universal Soul. Gassendi, in other words, charged that the doctrine of the World Soul as propagated in his time by Cabbalists and Chymists was Pantheistic, and therefore heretical, as well as lacking the support in the philosophical writings of the ancients that was claimed for it.[109]

However, although Gassendi expressed such critical views on the doctrine of the World Soul, he was at times relatively tolerant in his attitude towards the doctrine. Although he condemned the doctrine in 1630 as it was propounded by Robert Fludd, he was willing to grant that some versions of it should not be judged contrary to the Christian faith. In the course of his attack on Fludd he wrote:

> One may consider that the Faith suffers no detriment if there were understood to exist some kind of form, which would be called a special type of soul distinct from the regular vegetal, sensitive and rational souls, and which would be judged different from human souls because incapable of spiritual grace and happiness.[110]

Indeed, in one passage in MS Tours 709 he displayed an attitude of tolerance that bordered on a spirit of co-operation. The topic under consideration was the question of the existence of a First or Supreme Cause in the universe who might be identified with God. To lend weight to his argument, Gassendi mentioned the doctrine of the World Soul. He claimed that it mattered little that some called the Supreme Cause of the world "the Soul of the World, or Mind, or God, or whatever".[111] It was sufficient that they taught the existence of "practically the same reality"[112] as he did, namely that:

> The Divine Nature is everywhere, inwardly permeating all things by its essence, presence and power, conserving all things, co-operating with all things, and the Author of all things.[113]

Gassendi later added in the margin of the manuscript the words "Nature, Necessity and Fate' with an indication that they should be inserted into the text after "Soul of the World, or Mind, or God". The addition was no doubt made in conjunction with Gassendi's considerations on the subjects of Necessity and Fate later in Book XVI of MS Tours 709. Hence, in the emended text of the manuscript the fact that people had postulated the existence of realities called "Nature, Necessity and Fate" was presented as further support of Gassendi's argument concerning the existence of a First Cause in the universe which might be identified with God.

But by the time he came to write the *Syntagma* version of the passage (after 1649), it is clear that Gassendi had had second thoughts about mentioning the World Soul as being practically the same thing as God, the Supreme Cause. In the *Syntagma* he gave the text of MS Tours 709, together with the marginalia, but with one item conspicuously absent, namely the Soul of the World. Thus the sentence in the *Syntagma* reads:

> It does not matter whether they [all ancient philosophers except a few atheists such as Epicurus] called this Cause

God, or Mind, or Nature, or Necessity, or Fate or whatever.
It is enough that they held practically the same doctrine as
we acknowledge.[114]

I suggest that the excision of the Soul of the World from the list was a
significant act, deliberately calculated to put Gassendi's doctrine of the
First Cause at a distance from the doctrine of the World Soul in all its
versions. It was a doctrine which Cabbalists and Chymists such as Robert
Fludd had taken over and developed in ways that were unacceptable to
Gassendi. This last consideration, it would seem, came to determine
Gassendi's definitive attitude to the doctrine. It was patently incorrect for
him to have said that his voluntarist doctrine of the Divine First Cause
complemented by his Epicurean doctrine of secondary causality was similar
to the doctrine of the World Soul, and he took greater care in the *Syntagma*
to distinguish his doctrine from neo-Pythagorean and neo-Platonist theory.
It was perhaps for this purpose that he added a quotation from Seneca to
the *Syntagma* version. The passage was from Seneca's *Quaestiones
naturales*, and reads as follows:

> Do you wish to call Him [God] Fate? You will not err in so
> doing; it is on Him that all depends, the Cause of Causes. Do
> you wish to call Him Providence? You will be speaking
> correctly; it is by his deliberation that this world is provided
> for, so that it might flourish undisturbed. Do you wish to
> call Him Nature? You will not do wrong; for it is in Him
> that all things take their origin and in His spirit that we live,
> *etc.*[115]

By quoting this passage in the *Syntagma*, Gassendi made it clear that his
view of the omnipresence of the Divine First Cause was akin to the
doctrine of the Stoics rather than that of the Cabbalists and Chymists.

Another step which Gassendi took in the *Syntagma* version, by which he
aimed to make it clear that his Epicurean doctrine was not to be confused
with "obscure" doctrines of the World Soul, was to add a passage in which
he again discussed legitimate and illegitimate ways in which one might
suppose that the world had a soul. He maintained that if the Soul of the
World were understood as another term for God, insofar as He was an
'assisting' but not an 'informing' soul - God being presented as a moderator
and ruler of the world according to the analogy of a pilot in a ship - then
the term would be acceptable. But in such a case God would not be
presented as being part of the world. Or if by the term 'Soul of the World'
nothing else were meant than the heat which 'everyone' believed to be
diffused through the world, then there would be no reason to object to the
doctrine.[116] In both these uses of the term the world is only improperly and
by analogy considered to be animate or to have a soul. But Gassendi

considered that it was difficult to see how one could claim, without misusing the term 'soul', that the world had a soul such as one understood vegetative, sentient and rational souls to be souls.[117]

Thus Gassendi went to considerable lengths to emphasise the difference between his Epicurean doctrine of causality and the doctrine of the World Soul, an "obscure" neo-Pythagorean, neo-Platonist theory of incorporeal causality with which he was particularly acquainted through his earlier work on the philosophy of Robert Fludd. Gassendi was really doing no more than develop his Epicurean philosophy in the direction that Mersenne had encouraged him to follow when he enlisted his support against Fludd.

Gassendi's concern to develop a "clear" philosophy to stand in contrast to the "obscure" philosophies that were abroad in the seventeenth century found expression throughout his Epicurean explanations of natural processes. All his writings on generation and growth show that he had made a determined effort to provide explanations of these phenomena that eschewed sterile 'mystical' notions of causality.

His Epicurean theory on the generation of plant seeds and the growth of plants, for example, was developed in explicit contradiction to the theories of concordances and stellar influences.[118] According to Gassendi, one might choose between two theories. The first theory suggested that God directly created the seeds and all seminal virtue when He created atoms, and that He dispersed these seeds according to the design of His own Divine Wisdom through the earth. Gassendi wrote:

> You may ask, when were these seeds in the earth created? ...
> We can say that they have been there since the creation of
> all things, that they were made by God and spresd over the
> earth in the manner most suitable to each, and that God
> commanded them to germinate and produce all the species
> of plants and trees.[119]

The second theory was obviously less concordant with the literal interpretation of the first chapter of the book of *Genesis*.[120] Nevertheless, Gassendi maintained, there was no reason why one may not hold it. According to this theory, at the time of creation God fashioned atoms of various shapes and weights and endowed them with a variety of motions. These atoms thereupon procreated all kinds of molecules, including the seeds of plants. God 'pre-programmed' the atoms, as it were, so that they would come together in certain configurations, and thereby form themselves into living seeds, and ultimately living plants.

In both these theories Gassendi provided a specific cause for the specific effect, *viz.* the generation of seeds and plants. According to the first theory God was more involved directly with the process of generation than He was according to the second theory, since, in this latter theory Gassendi's Epicurean principle of motion (weight) was given a greater role. Gassendi explicitly opposed both theories to what he described as a "common" theory[121] which he explicitly identified as a Cabbalist theory, and to which he presented his own two possible theories as alternatives. According to the common theory, Gassendi explained, it was the Sun which provided the seminal virtue, or else it was the stars which provided it.[122] This theory, Gassendi observed, was linked with the theory that there are correspondences between metals and the planets, and between plants and the stars, and he quoted the following Cabbalist saying as an expression of the theory:

> Every herb and plant here below has its star in the firmament which taps it and says to it, "Grow!".[123]

However, the truth of the matter is, Gassendi claimed, that the power that emanates from the Sun and the stars is not a specific, internal cause such as natural philosophers seek, but only a general influence. He wrote:

> The Sun's heat breaks up the compressed earth and loosens the substance of the seeds. This heat is only an external cause which does no more than remove the barriers that restrain and hold dormant and inert the seminal or formative virtue.[124]

Gassendi even expressly rejected the theory that there exist various dispositions in the Earth which are worked upon by the celestial influences so that they become the various species of plants.[125]

Thus Gassendi explicitly opposed his Epicurean theory on the generation of seeds and plants to the 'Cabbalist' theories of concordances and stellar influences, which theories relied on neo-Pythagorean and neo-Platonist docrines.[126] He explained the generation of stones and metals by the same Epicurean principles as he had called upon to explain the generation of plant seeds and the growth of plants. He taught that stones and metals also grow from seeds in a manner which is analogous to the growth of plants. The seeds, he stated, possess a lapidific or metallic internal power. This power may also be termed a "seminal" power, but must not be identified with heat and cold, which are also termed "seminal" powers, but which are no more than external influences. Gassendi wrote:

> It is essential that there be an interior power which works to shape the stones, and which can be considered a seminal power. This power must be acting in the process of formation of stones over and above the power of heat or any other extrinsic agent.[127]

Gassendi also termed this internal power an "elaborative spirit" and a "soul", emphasising at the same time that it was a soul *sui generis*.[128]

Despite the animistic sound of Gassendi's statements, he intended them all to be understood in the context of his basic Epicurean theory. He intended his writings on the generation of stones and metals to be read as descriptions of particular cases that were explained by his theory, and his terms "seeds", "growth", "seminal powers", "elaborative spirit", and "soul" have only the meaning that can be attributed to them by that theory. Gassendi had deliberately set out to explain the lapidific spirits, and the supposed growth of stones and metals, by his Epicurean theory, and all these phenomena were thus to be explained ultimately by atoms possessing shape, size and weight, together with the resultant movements and interactions of these atoms.

Furthermore, Gassendi explicitly identified the theories he was specifically writing against in this section. First, there was the theory of the fixed creationists who claimed that stones and metals were not generated; second, there was the theory of the medieval Aristotelians who claimed that stones and metals were formed by the sole efficient causality of the stars; and third, there was the theory of the later Aristotelians and some Chymists who proposed that they were formed either by heat and cold, or by mud and sap.[129]

Gassendi criticised all three of the rival theories. He stated that the theory of fixed creationism contradicted experience, insofar as it is evident, he claimed, that many stones are still in the process of formation. He did not respond in this treatise to the theory of the medieval Aristotelians, but he had already ruled out the influence of the stars, claiming that such an influence constituted at most no more than a general or unspecific causal influence.[130] Finally, he ruled out the theory of the later Aristotelians and Chymists as being inadequate. He paid most attention to this last theory, arguing that a further active principle, over and above the simple elementary substances, was needed to produce the multiplicity that is to be found among stones and metals.[131]

But these were particular theories related specifically to the process of lapidification. Beyond them, especially the theory of stellar influences and the elemental theories of the Chymists, there were more general neo-Pythagorean and neo-Platonist theories that explained the same processes and phenomena by incorporeal causes. Gassendi's Epicurean theory of the development of seeds, and generation from them, responded ultimately to those more general theories.

There is another passage in which Gassendi used his theory of seeds in which it is clearer that he proposed his theory as an alternative to the more general neo-Pythagorean and neo-Platonic theories. The passage deals with the subject of the six-cornered snowflake, and was inspired by Kepler's discussion of the same phenomenon.[132] The phenomenon that gave rise to the discussion was the regularity of the construction of snowflakes. Whereas

Kepler had tried in his discussion to fuse the Pythagorean mathematical world-view with mechanical philosophy, attempting to interpret material processes by means of the harmonies and regularities of the celestial spheres, Gassendi offered his theory of seeds and internal causality. He wrote:

> Because all natural things have specific seeds they all have their specific shapes. Just as animals, plants and stones have their own peculiar profiles, are not all things likewise shaped the way they are because they are so determined by their seeds? ... In the same way snowflakes, too, can be shaped as they grow by reason of their own proper determinants (*ratio*).[133]

Gassendi offered his solution in this case in express opposition to two other explanations, the one that there is a World Soul instructed in geometry, the other that Divine Wisdom itself operates directly on matter.[134]

Thus, when we consider Gassendi's theory on the generation of plant seeds and the growth of plants, together with his theory of the generation of stones and metals, as well as his theory of the process that gives rise to the snowflake, we obtain a more adequate insight into the reasons why Gassendi proposed his Epicurean theory of generation that stressed the need for explanations in terms of internal causes. Gassendi considered his theory to be more satisfactory than not only the particular theories of the fixed creationists and Chymists and the theory of stellar influences, and consequently than the astrological cosmology upon which it was based, but also he considered his Epicurean theory to be more satisfactory than the neo-Platonic general theory of the World Soul and the quasi-pantheistic theories that mingled Divine Wisdom too intimately, in Gassendi's opinion, with the processes of the material world. Gassendi required a "clearer" account of natural causes than was given in any of theories he sought to replace.

Gassendi's discussion of the magnet and his theory of magnetic attraction show the same concern to provide "clear" explanations. In his response to the Aristotelian Pierre de Cazrée[135] and in his treatment of the magnet in the *Syntagma*,[136] Gassendi reviewed the choices of explanation of magnetic activity that were available. To state that magnetic effects are achieved "naturally" (*sponte naturae*), he wrote, is to explain nothing; explanations that rely on a soul in the magnet or the iron or in both are deemed unacceptable by Cazrée himself, and Gassendi ruled out the Aristotelian explanations on the grounds that the theory of forms alone is inadequate to explain the behaviour of magnet and iron; all versions of the theory of action-at-a-distance were unacceptable; the theory that a migratory quality not inhering in a substance should arouse the iron in some way is judged inadequate because it attempts to explain the phenomena by external causality alone, apart from the absurdity of the notion of qualities being emitted which do not inhere in anything bodily. Gassendi devoted a whole chapter in the *Syntagma*[137] to recent observations of magnetic phenomena, and though his description is heavily laden with theory his purpose was to provide an explanation that would fit the observations and his own requirements for a satisfactory explanation as adequately and accurately as possible. His conclusion was that a substantial corporeal emission from the magnet was necessary. He wrote:

> The power of the magnet that is emitted to the iron is a material stream of corpuscles arrayed in a way that causes them to produce a change in the corpuscles of the iron [which results in the iron being drawn to the magnet].[138]

At the same time Gassendi maintained that there was in the magnet something analogous to the life and soul of plants which gave it a power analogous to the power of sensation, thus explaining the 'animal-like' phenomenon of attraction.[139]

Gassendi was prepared to support Cazrée's ridicule of the corpuscular explanation of attraction: the little grappling hooks, tiny drag-chains, claws and minuscule arms that combine into a kind of rod or tight chain.[140] The mechanism may sound ridiculous to Cazrée, but Gassendi stood by it not as certain and indubitable truth, but as "trifles" which were the best that can be offered given our natural incapacity for knowledge of such things. Indeed, Gassendi took pride in his explanation, in the fact that he was seeking to present a better explanation; as he wrote to Cazrée:

> You will dismiss my explanation saying that I go to a lot of trouble to maintain my view that heavy bodies do not fall by their own natural movement but are pulled down by the Earth by means of corpuscles that are diffused all about and attached to them. But of course I do so, most learned and religious Sir, in order that I might not at any stage be overtaken by a fog while I am engaged in searching out natural causes; so, though I walk in thickest darkness I shall not tremble at anything, nor leave any stone unturned, nor any pathway untried, to reach some ray of light, be it only a faint glimmer.[141]

### Obscurity vanquished

In 1637, when he was writing the second chapter of his treatise on causality in MS Tours 709, Gassendi had noted that, in investigating the internal

causes as it was his competence and obligation to do, the natural
philosopher was scrutinizing the secrets of the natural world. He wrote:

> The chief difficulty lies with the internal causes. Those who
> investigate these causes are correctly said to examine the
> secrets of nature.[142]

Gassendi made the confident claim that, in his writings concerning
Aristotelian forms, concerning the generation and growth of plants, stones,
metals and snowflakes, and concerning magnetic phenomena, his
Epicureanism with its theory of corporeal causes provided explanations
which were more satisfactory than explanations that rely on incorporeal
causes. One might well contend that, especially when one takes into account
the magnitude of the challenge in scrutinizing the hidden causes, he did not
succeed in explaining the phenomena any more satisfactorily by his theory
of corporeal causality than others had done with theories of incorporeal
causality, that he would seem to have done little more than re-write, using
materialist terminology, the explanations deriving from theories which
invoked incorporeal causes, and present his version as though it were
essentially different from those which he had re-written. His corpuscles
were just as elusive and beyond the reach of observation as Aristotelian
forms and *species* and other incorporeal causes, yet he believed that he had
offered a more intelligible alternative to the obscurity he found in
Aristotelianism and the mystical obfuscation he found in Hermetic
philosophy. Gassendi's confidence was founded on the "clear", that is the
uncomplicatedly material, nature of the atoms, for he believed that he had
removed a spurious aura of mystery from explanations of natural
phenomena. He was postulating an invisible mechanism involving objects
too small to be perceived by the senses, an entirely acceptable and 'modern'
type of explanation in the seventeenth century.[143]

In context, Gassendi's general designation "obscure" thus referred to
many features that he judged to be defects in the Aristotelian and other
philosophical traditions, while his division of all philosophical traditions
into "clear" and "obscure" expressed the difference that he perceived
between the kind of philosophy he was engaged upon and the diverse forms
of rationalist and/or occult philosophy which he categorised as "obscure":
classical Platonism and Pythagoreanism, their Renaissance Hermetic,
Orphic, Zoroastrian and Cabbalist versions with all their numerological,
astrological, magical and alchemical works, and Aristotelianism both
ancient and modern. It was all a matter of degree: the "absurdities" of the
Rosicrucian Robert Fludd might be more exotic, but in Gassendi's
assessment the Aristotelians were guilty of the same basic obscurity, the
result of defective methods and mistaken goals.

Gassendi's criticism was directed in the first place against obscure,
ambiguous or enigmatic language, whether it be the language of ignorance,

or of a dogmatic presumption to know which masked ignorance, or whether it was affected out of a pretext to be speaking of deep and arcane things.[144] Above all, it was the lack of concern in the obscure traditions to relate terms to things in the universe, to make theory correspond to the realitites of nature that provoked Gassendi's criticism. The acid test of clarity in doctrines and theories for Gassendi was their dependence on the natural world actually observed, their truth to nature. The Aristotelians and other philosophers of the obscure tradition discussed natures, essences, principles and relationships as though they were describing realities and undestanding them, whereas they were wasting their time and that of their students with chimaeras; they attributed meaning and relevance to their discourse without any attempt to make a critical examination of what they were saying in the light of the phenomena; they acted as though it was sufficient to use a word such as "form" in order to speak intelligibly, without ever asking the question whether such things as forms really exist. Such presumptuous obscurity inhibited further investigation and progress in understanding, causing it to be generally believed that everything that could be known was already known.

The mixing of matter and spirit was another characteristic that Gassendi found in philosophies of the obscure tradition. He judged the Aristotelians and Rosicrucians to be at different points on the one spectrum in that they both mingled the material and the immaterial in an unwarranted and inappropriate manner. Gassendi saw his corpuscular theory as achieving a radical elimination of spiritual causes and immaterial actions-at-a-distance, the World Soul and all other theories that tempt philosophers to 'mystical' and/or heretical explanations and magical practices. Gassendi would have fully approved of Robert Boyle's statement in *The sceptical chymist* (1661), "that principles ought to be like diamonds, as well very clear as perfectly solid".[145]

Another characteristic of the clear tradition of philosophy in Gassendi's mind was, somewhat paradoxically, its empirical and hypothetical approach to the study of nature, with its repeated affirmation of ignorance, while an unfounded presumption to attain true and certain knowledge was the hallmark that Gassendi discovered in the obscure philosophies. True knowledge of nature, in Gassendi's mind, is arrived at by investigation of the world using our senses and by reasoning from the signs presented to the senses. We are not given other ways to know nature; we have not been given superhuman insight that would allow us to penetrate to the true natures of things. Consequently, theories and doctrines in the clear tradition are presented as provisional, as expressing some degree of verisimilitude that could well be improved upon in the light of further observation. They do not claim to be other than human attempts to explain things and events in nature as they have been observed. It is in the obscure philosophies, on the other hand, that doctrines are presented dogmatically as complete and final accounts that cannot be improved upon, leading mortals in the more extreme cases to all kinds of rationalist and pseudo-mystical delusions and temptations to magical practices.

Hence, Gassendi's anti-Aristotelianism and pro-Epicureanism are appropriately situated in the context of the comprehensive intellectual movement of the seventeenth century that led to the confrontation of two traditions, the occult and the empirical. New standards of explanation in natural philosophy were being set in conscious opposition to the arbitrary rationalism of much Renaissance neo-Platonism and neo-Pythagoreanism. Gassendi judged that basic Aristotelian concepts and explanations did not meet these new standards and concluded that Aristotelianism was to be rejected on essentially the same grounds as the more extreme rationalist philosophies of nature. Gassendi made it his mission to demonstrate how Epicureanism could meet those standards with its simple, "clear", non-spiritualist explanations in terms of atoms and empty space, and to promote the progress of the observational sciences by convincing his contemporaries to abandon the "obscure" philosophy of Aristotle and rely on the "clear" philosophy of Epicurus.

## CONCLUSION

One feature of Gassendi's philosophical work which has become very clear through the examination of the manuscripts and published works is the homogeneity of the development of his mature Epicurean philosophy from the philosopical doctrines and presuppositions which he accepted in his lectures as a professor of Aristotelian philosophy at Aix-en-Provence, as they have been recorded in the *Exercitationes*. In fact, the posthumously published *Syntagma philosophicum* must be regarded essentially as a much more complete and effective achievement of Gassendi's original project, outlined in the preface to the *Exercitationes*.[1]

Failure to understand clearly the evolutionary link between his first and last publications has made it possible for a common misinterpretation of the significance of Gassendi's work to become widespread. For it has sometimes been claimed that Gassendi was an apologist for the mechanical philosophy who made Epicureanism acceptable to nervous Christians. E.J. Dijksterhuis has described Gassendi's work in that manner. He wrote:

> The atomic theory of Democritus and Epicurus, which from its birth had offended many people by its anti-religious character and which therefore, particularly in the Christian world, had never been able to lead more than an underground existence, met with a striking change of fortune in the first half of the seventeenth century. A Catholic priest [Pierre Gassendi] of great scientific reputation and unsuspected [*sic*] orthodoxy was fascinated by it and regarded it as his life-work to introduce it into Western thought in a theologically acceptable form. He succeeded in this, and consequently this theory, which in the twenties of the century had still been looked upon as a mischief bordering on heresy, rose in a short time to the rank of a respectable theory, of which no Christian scientist need be ashamed.[2]

My objection to this interpretation is that it does not correspond to Gassendi's own goals. Gassendi regarded it as his life's work to remove Aristotelianism from its position of dominance as the generally accepted and even 'official' philosophy, and to have Epicureanism accepted in its

stead. There is little evidence to support the view that Gassendi was hard-
pressed to overcome theological objections and prejudices against
Epicureanism. There were theological objections to Epicureanism,
certainly, and part of Gassendi's program was to remove the cause for such
objections from the version of the philosophy which he advocated, and so
he made a few obvious efforts to harmonise Epicureanism with Christian
doctrine. But they were no more than perfunctory gestures: he was not
seriously concerned about the alleged atheism and materialism of Epicurean
atomism, nor, I claim, did he become so in the course of his intellectual
career. He did no more than flatly contradict the supposedly 'disreputable'
aspects of the Epicurean system and complemented his presentation of it
with doctrines from Thomistic Aristotelianism and voluntarist theology.
Consequently, it is incorrect to claim, as does the traditional text-book
account, that Gassendi made it his life-work to restore Epicureanism from
the stigma of heresy.

   He outlined the goal of his life-work himself: to promote Epicureanism
as a philosophy to take the place of Aristotelianism. As a fundamental step
towards the realisation of that goal he set out to make Epicureanism
acceptable as a Christian philosophy, just as that other ancient pagan
philosophy, Aristotelianism, had been made acceptable in the fourteenth
century. The reason for attempting to do this was that he considered
Epicureanism to be a philosophy more suitable for the needs of the
seventeenth century, both for supporting the faith and for enabling
philosophers to participate in and contribute to the progress of the new
experimental and observational sciences.

   Although on several occasions Gassendi declared his allegiance to
religious authority and professed his readiness to submit to its judgment on
what he wrote,[3] he did not seriously anticipate that the Church authorities
would find anything to censure in his work. So, as we have seen, when it
became necessary, he scrupulously removed all pro-Copernican passages to
avoid such an eventuality. And he showed complete confidence in his own
orthodoxy, even, at times, stressing the paramount importance of being
orthodox.[4] Thus one can only conclude that, in making it his life-work to
promote Epicureanism to take the place of Aristotelianism, Gassendi was
not aware that he might be advocating a philosophy that could be
considered dangerous or shocking. Epicureanism was not looked upon in
the seventeenth century as an especially offensive philosophy.

   Thus the interpretation of Gassendi as the philosopher who somehow
made Epicureanism respectable is quite wide of the mark. A different
interpretation needs to be formulated, and I have presented an alternative
in the preceding pages, which alternative I shall now proceed to outline in
summary form.

   Gassendi's anti-Aristotelianism determined the trajectory of his
philosophy. Together with many other seventeenth-century natural
philosophers, but more single-mindedly than most, he struggled to break

the dominance of Aristotelianism, to free natural philosophy from what he felt to be the yoke of the scholastic tradition, which he claimed was hindering progress in knowledge of the natural world. He began his philosophical career from within the scholastic camp, as it were, first as a student and later as a teacher of Aristotelian philosophy in Aix-en-Provence. He will be seen to have been reacting against what, through his extra-curricular reading of the classical and humanist authors, he had come to consider as the bane of his youth.

The best weapon that Gassendi found for his fight against Aristotelianism was scepticism, and for that reason he was a sceptic. His scepticism was a legacy of Renaissance anti-Aristotelianism: it was inspired by the popular, but theologically suspect, writings of Pierre Charron, and was specifically anti-Aristotelian, following the example and relying heavily on the methods of Ramus and Gianfrancesco Pico della Mirandola.

As an anti-Aristotelian, Gassendi was also a student of Galilean Copernicanism. Galileo embodied for Gassendi all the promise of the new empirical approach to the study of the natural world: if men of learning would all move out of the closed peripatetic Schools with their useless disputations and their idle discussions about things that do not even exist, and if they would all imitate Galileo and apply their ingenuity to exact observation of the world of nature as it presents itself to their senses, if they would learn to read the book of nature instead of their unprofitable Aristotelian commentaries, Gassendi was convinced that they, too, would discover mysteries hitherto unrevealed to the human race. Gassendi thus applauded Galileo's discoveries and writings not only for the spectacular confirmation of the Copernican hypothesis that they provided, but also because of the new methods for examining the heavens and the behaviour of falling bodies that Galileo had used. At the same time Gassendi was very pleased to be able to use some of Galileo's discoveries as seemingly irrefutable arguments against particular points of Aristotelian doctrine. Subsequently, and as a consequence of the ecclesiastical condemnation of Galileo and the Copernican theory Gassendi found that Copernican anti-Aristotelian arguments had lost their impact. Reluctantly he accepted the geocentric compromise theory of Tycho Brahe, his own previous arguments against geocentrism notwithstanding: although he rarely deployed his scepticism to other than anti-Aristotelian ends, he relied on it to support him through the intellectual crisis which he experienced following the condemnation. Gassendi submitted to the judgment of the Roman authorities and taught the hypothesis of Tycho Brahe with enthusiasm, at the same time noting that the judgment, though authoritative, was not an article of faith. (The fact that he even mentioned this latter point is an indication that he might not have managed to "enslave" his intellect in accepting the judgment of the Holy Office as he had resolved to do.) But no allowances were made in the seventeenth century for even private dissent from authoritative Church teachings.[5] Had he not abandoned his early Copernican beliefs and adopted the more respectable and fashionable hypothesis of Tycho Brahe he would have run the risk of attracting unwanted attention from the custodians of orthodoxy, he would have encountered much more personal unpleasantness in his dealings with Aristotelians like Pierre de Cazrée, and he would have been at the mercy of eccentric anti-Copernicans like Jean-Baptiste Morin. And after all, Copernicanism was not central to Gassendi's philosophy; his project of substituting Epicureanism for Aristotelianism continued to advance, after some re-writing of his manuscripts for the *Syntagma*, in spite of the disrepute into which Galileo's discoveries and writings had fallen.

In pursuit of his goal of presenting a version of Epicurean atomism that would be found acceptable as a sustitute for Aristotelian philosophy, Gassendi extensively re-wrote many of the major features of Aristotelian doctrine, particularly those relating to the physical world. In fact, Gassendi's philosophy is an anti-Aristotelian version of Epicureanism. He presented, for instance, an account of the Epicurean theory of space as a substitute for the Aristotelian doctrine of place; the Epicurean theory of atoms in opposition to the Aristotelian theory of prime matter; the Epicurean theory of modes of matter to replace the Aristotelian theory of accidents and qualities. In his account of cognition Epicurean atomism provided the physical theory to explain natural phenomena such as light and vision, and the processes by which information concerning objects in the natural world was obtained by the mind, while Epicurean canonic provided the rules that the intellect should follow in its investigation of the objects of the natural world by means of the signs perceived by the senses. Also anti-Aristotelian was Gassendi's Epicurean empiricism, and his rejection of the Aristotelian standard for the philosopher's accounts of natural phenomena: *viz.*, knowledge of essences or inner natures of things and certain knowledge of how events or properties proceed as effects from their causally-effective essences. Gassendi's alternative was a form of scepticism: the goal of the philosopher should be understood as the less ambitious knowedge of appearances, and "verisimilitude" or truth-seeming was as much as one can expect of explanations concerning the natural world. Gassendi advocated this Epicurean empiricism especially because it stimulated open-ended research into nature; explanations that were no more than probable promoted further enquiry, whereas the Aristotelianism of the Schools forestalled it, according to Gassendi's account, by their dogmatically asserted 'true' explanations. Gassendi's scepticism, therefore, was predominently an anti-Aristotelian stratagem, and should not be seen as an anti-sceptical, "mitigated" scepticism calculated to overcome a seventeenth-century 'sceptical crisis': he advocated the more sceptical Epicurean empiricism as an alternative to the Aristotelian *scientia*.

Gassendi's anti-Aristotelianism was inspired above all by his enthusiasm for the new empirical methods in natural philosophy and the insistence in the developing sciences that theory should be tailored to correspond to observations. He found that Aristotelianism deserved to be rejected for essentially the same reasons as the more extreme rationalist and visionary neo-Platonic, neo-Pythagorean, Orphic, Zoroastrian, Hermetic and Cabbalist systems of doctrine: it resorted to arbitrary, sterile explanations based on "obscure" immaterial causes.

Gassendi's incorporation of the Epicurean philosophical system into his anti-Aristotelian project was pragmatic and eclectic. He adopted it in his natural philosophy as a theoretical explanation of the hidden mysteries of nature, an explanation that should be presented not as the truth of what lies beyond our senses but as verisimilitude, a likely explanation that is truer than all others. Gassendi was too much the anti-Aristotelian sceptic to allow himself to be trapped into ultimate commitment to even the fundamentals of Epicureanism. His pragmatic use of Epicureanism is also apparent in the way he was able to reject with ease all aspects of the pagan philosophical system that conflicted with Christianity. He did not take from Epicurean philosophy principles that played a leading role in his explanations at what for him was the *most* fundamental level of reality, the level of Creation, Design and Providence: his voluntarist theology provided such principles when necessary, while Epicureanism provided no more than *a posteriori* hypotheses to fit facts known by observation.

It is in the manner just outlined, therefore, that I consider Gassendi's life-work should be understood. If one were to attempt to explain in a few words what kind of philosopher he was, one would have to say that he could not be described as a particularly original philosopher. It is quite easy, for instance, to find sources on which he was heavily dependent for almost every philosophical position he adopted and every doctrine he formulated. His usual practice was to incorporate other people's explanations into his writings adding corpuscles to the theory where they seemed to be required. Hence the content of his philosophy does not seem to yield evidence of a creative and original genius at work. Perhaps one should not be surprised at such a lack of originality in a philosopher whose chief formative influences were scholastic Aristotelianism and Renaissance Humanism, for both these traditions prized the thought and doctrines of the past above all else, and positively discouraged originality. Gassendi *can* be described, on the other hand, as an essentially polemical philosopher. For him, a doctrine or a point of view was rarely a simple statement of how things were in nature. It was often, and usually more importantly, a statement of how things were *not*.

Our study of Gassendi's life-work in the light of his aims has given some insight into the seventeenth-century intellectual climate and has helped complete our picture of the environment in which the prominent figures of that period worked. The difference between Gassendi and Mersenne in their perceptions of the alleged dangers to Christianity in the spread of scepticism is illuminating: while Mersenne reacted against scepticism or Pyrrhonism as a threat to Christian faith, Gassendi did not share his alarm at all. Thus even these two Catholic priests who shared a close bond of friendship differed considerably in their attitude on this matter of considerable importance for both of them. Thus, the more we study this period the more we learn that it is hazardous to generalise about the nature, origins, and even the existence of a "general crisis" in the seventeenth century.

Galileo's carelessness in bringing down upon himself the condemnation of 1633 becomes more intelligible when one notes Gassendi's prior enthusiastic support for the great man's discoveries and writings and his subsequent total surprise at the action of the Roman authorities. The warning given to Galileo in 1616 had long been a dead letter, and there were any number of good scholars who before 1633 saw no conflict between the Christian faith and the Copernican hypothesis.

Gassendi was born of a peasant family, but because he aspired to enter the ranks of the clergy, and because he was gifted, he received a Church education which also allowed him entry into the community of humanist scholars, which community was already anti-Aristotelian and interested in the developing empirical sciences. Gassendi may be seen as a type of the informed and religiously committed French Catholic intellectual of the early seventeenth century, who had received the kind of education which the Church favoured, but who was, nevertheless, free to follow his own inclinations in philosophy as long as they did not come into obvious conflict with ecclesiastical authority. The fact, therefore, that he should so quickly have broken out of the Aristotelian mould, and that he should have done so in such a radical fashion, is an indication of the extent to which Aristotelianism was dependent for its survival on the support of the Church establishment. Further, the fact that, despite his rupture with Aristotelianism and his support of Copernicanism in public lectures and in the *Exercitationes*, and in part because of these stands, Gassendi enjoyed a good reputation and had good relations with local authorities, both religious and civil, indicate that the intellectual milieu, at least in Provence, was relaxed to the point of *insouciance* in the face of the decline of Aristotelianism.

Indeed, if Gassendi is to be looked upon as a typical scholar of his day, Aristotelianism should have been doomed to lose support altogether; the state of philosophical education in the college of Aix-en-Provence while Gassendi held the chair of philosophy certainly did not augur well for its future, and Gassendi's attitude reflected that of the educated public of the region. But Church authority was coming to the rescue: when the Counter-Reformation movement reached Aix-en-Provence Gassendi lost his teaching post to the Jesuits who were providing the new style of scholastic ministerial training considered appropriate for the needs of the modern Catholic Church. Though there were some hurt feelings at the time Gassendi seems not to have born any grudges, nor is there any reason to believe that his anti-Aristotelianism was further stimulated by his virtual sacking, though he must have been disappointed to see that the philosophical component in the curriculum at the college under the Jesuits was to be unambiguously Aristotelian. Henceforward, Aristotelianism was to survive especially in the Counter-Reformation seminaries, institutions for the education of candidates for the Catholic Priesthood, where it continued to be the prescribed philosophy for another three whole centuries, the prescription only being dropped by Vatican Council II (1962-1965).[6] It would have been a disappointment for Gassendi that his efforts to win men over to a "truer and better philosophy" received so little response from his own Catholic Christian community, and he would have been astounded at the way Aristotelianism was bolstered by Church authority long after it had ceased to be an effective component of Western civilisation.

If Gassendi was a prophet who went unhonoured in his own country, he did not suffer the ultimate indignity of being treated with indifference: in neo-scholastic manuals of philosophy for use in seminaries he is still to be found listed among the "adversaries" to particular theses, together with brief explanations of his doctrines - even in the twentieth century.[7] The Aristotelians never forgot him!

# NOTES

## Introduction

1   On the reform of seminaries decreed by the Council of Trent (1543-1563) and the role of the Jesuits in the post-Conciliar reform of Catholic education, cf. R. Mandrou: 1978, *From humanism to science 1480-1700*, Penguin, Harmondsworth, pp.154-160; also H.O. Evennett: 1968, *The spirit of the Counter-Reformation*, Cambridge University Press, Cambridge, pp.78-79, 114.

2   "Les pères Jesuites, s'introduisant dans la ville et s'emparant tout aussitot de Collège, il [Gassendi] fut contraint d'achever son cours ... dans le quartier de St Ivan, Monsieur Bergamon son ami, pour lors chanoine d'Aix ... lui donna une grande sale [sic] chez lui pour cet effect." *Mémoire touchant la naissance, vie et moeurs de P. Gassendi (revu par un membre de sa famille)*, conserved in the Bibliothèque Nationale, *Fonds français*, MS 12270, and attributed to Antoine de la Potherie with revisions by Gassendi's nephew in B. Rochot (Ed.): 1944, *Lettres familières à François Luillier pendant l'hiver 1632-1633*, J. Vrin, Paris, p.xv.

3   "Real philosophy has almost slipped from men's hands and is now lodged in obscurity and silence with very few." "Germana illa pene elapsa ex hominum manibus in umbra et silentio apud perpaucos hospitatur." (P. Gassendi: 1658, *Opera omnia*, 6 vols., Lyon, *VI*, p.30.)

4   Cf. Gassendi's letter to J.-B. Van Helmont of 9.7.1629, in P. Gassendi, *Opera omnia*, *VI*, pp.19b-24a. One should note, however, that Gassendi posed the arguments against the eating of meat in his letter as part of a Pyrrhonnist disputation. Nevertheless, apparently upon the basis of this letter, the tradition has been preserved that Gassendi was a vegetarian. Cf. J. Bougerel: 1737, *Vie de Pierre Gassendi*, J. Vincent, Paris, pp.45-57; also B. Rochot, "La vie, le caractère et la formation intellectuelle," in B. Rochot *(et al.)*: 1955, *Pierre Gassendi 1692-1655, sa vie et son oeuvre* (Centre International de Synthèse), Paris, pp.9-54, espc. p.16.

5   For a fuller account of Gassendi's life history, cf. H. Jones: 1981, *Pierre Gassendi 1592-1655. An intellectual biography*, B. De Graaf,

Nieuwkoop; also the introduction in H. Jones: 1981, *Pierre Gassendi's Institutio logica (1658)*, Van Gorcum, Assen.

6  P. Gassendi: 1624, *Exercitationum paradoxicarum adversus Aristoteleos libri septem. In quibus praecipua totius peripateticae doctrinae fundamenta excutiuntur: opiniones verae aut novae, aut ex vetustioribus obsoletae stabiliuntur. Authore Petro Gassendo ...,* P. Verderii, Grenoble.

7  P. Gassendi, *Opera omnia, III*, pp.149a-210b.

8  P. Tamizey de Larroque (Ed.): 1888-1898, *Lettres de Peiresc,* 7 vols., Paris, *IV*, pp.178-181.

9  Cf. *ibid., III*, p.133; *IV*, pp.203-204.

10  P. Gassendi: 1649, *Animadversiones in decimum librum Diogenis Laertii, qui est de vita, moribus placitisque Epicuri*, G. Barbier, Lyon. The translation and notes are published in P. Gassendi, *Opera omnia, VI*, pp.1-166. Concerning the work of translation itself, cf. Gassendi's letter to Peiresc of 11.9.1629, given in P. Tamizey de Larroque, *Lettres de Peiresc, IV*, pp.217-218.

11  *Ibid, IV*, pp.250-252.

12  P. Gassendi: 1647, *De vita et moribus Epicuri libri octo*, G. Barbier, Lyon; P. Gassendi, *Opera omnia, V*, pp.167-236.

13  Indications of the progress of Gassendi's work in writing the manuscripts are found in MS Carpentras 1832, f.205, P. Tamizey de Larroque, *Lettres de Peiresc, IV*, pp.172-173, P. Gassendi, *Opera omnia, V*, p.116, MS Tours 709, f. 268v, and elsewhere. Cf. also René Pintard: 1943, *La Mothe le Vayer, Gassendi - Guy Patin. Etudes de bibliographie et de critique suivie de textes inédits de Guy Patin*, Boivin, Paris, Ch. 3 ("Des manuscrits de Gassendi à l'oeuvre imprimée: la genèse du Syntagma philosophicum"); also O.R. Bloch: 1971, *La philosophie de Gassendi. Nominalisme, matérialisme et métaphysique*, Nijhoff, The Hague, pp.xxix-xxx.

14  P. Gassendi, *Philosophiae Epicuri syntagma*, in P. Gassendi, *Opera omnia, III*, pp.1-94. This is the only known published version of this work.

15  To be precise, MS Tours 706 begins with the heading "Syntagmatis philosophici pars logica". Earlier, Gassendi had described his writings

on Epicurean philosophy as "commentaries", cf. P. Tamizey de Larroque, *Lettres de Peiresc*, *IV*, p.402, pp.414-415. For an account of the fortunes of the manuscripts of Gassendi, cf. P. Meyer: 1883, "Les manuscrits du Connetable de Lesdiguieres", in *Romania*, *12*, pp.336-342.

16    P. Gassendi, *Commentarii de rebus caelestibus*, in P. Gassendi, *Opera omnia*, *IV*, pp.75-498.

17    P. Gassendi: 1630, *Epistolica exercitatio, in qua principia philosophiae Roberti Fluddi, medici, reteguntur, et ad recentes illius libros adversus R.P.F. Marinum Mersennum ... respondetur ...*, S. Cramoisy, Paris; P. Gassendi, *Opera omnia*, *III*, pp.213-267.

18    P. Gassendi: 1630, *Parhelia, sive soles quatuor qui circa verum apparuerunt Romae, die xx mensis martii anno 1629, et de eisdem Petri Gassendi ad Henricum Renerium epistola*, A. Vitray, Paris; P.Gassendi, *Opera omnia*, *III*, pp.651-662.

19    P. Gassendi: 1632, *Mercurius in sole visus et Venus inviso Parisiis anno 1631 ... Epistolae duae, cum observatis quibusdam aliis*, S. Cramoisy, Paris; P. Gassendi, *Opera omnia*, *IV*, pp.499-504.

20    Cf. M.H. Carré (Trans.): 1937, *Edward, Lord Herbert of Cherbury, De veritate*, J.W. Arrowsmith, Bristol, introduction; Peter Gay: 1968, *Deism, an anthology*, Van Nostrand, Princeton, p.29.

21    P. Gassendi, *Opera omnia*, *III*, pp.411-419.

22    P. Gassendi: 1642, *De apparente magnitudine solis humilis et sublimis epistolae quatuor, in quibus complura physica opticaque problemata proponuntur et explicantur*, L. de Heuqueville, Paris; P. Gassendi, *Opera omnia*, *III*, pp.420-477.

23    P. Gassendi: 1641, *Viri illustris Nicolai Claudii Fabricii de Peiresc Senatoris Aquisextiensis vita*, S. Cramoisy, Paris; P. Gassendi, *Opera omnia*, *V*, pp.237-358.

24    Cf. P. Gassendi, *Opera omnia*, *V*, pp.359-360.

25    P. Gassendi: 1642, *De motu impresso a motore translato epistolae duae, in quibus aliquot praecipuae, tum de motu universe, tum speciatim de motu terrae attributo, difficultates explicentur*, L. de Heuqueville, Paris.

26  P. Gassendi, *Epistolae tres de motu impresso a motore translato*, in P. Gassendi, *Opera omnia, III*, pp.478-563.

27  P. Gassendi: 1646, *De proportione qua gravia accidentia accelerantur epistolae tres, quibus ad totidem epistolas R.P. Petri Cazraei ... respondetur*, L. de Heuqueville, Paris; P. Gassendi, *Opera omnia, III*, pp.564-650.

28  "Amicitiae jure" (P. Gassendi, *Opera omnia, III*, p.273a, p.271).

29  P. Gassendi, "Objectiones quintae. Eximio viro Renato Cartesio P. Gassendus S.a, et responsio authoris ad quintas objectiones", in R. Descartes, *Oeuvres de Descartes* (1897-1913, C. Adam and P. Tannery (Eds.), 12 vols., L. Cerf, Paris), *VII*, pp.256-391; P. Gassendi: 1644, *Disquisitio metaphysica, seu dubitationes et instantiae adversus Renati Cartesii metaphysicam et responsa*, J. Blaeu, Amsterdam; P. Gassendi, *Opera omnia, III*, pp.269-410.

30  P. Gassendi: 1645, *Oratio inauguralis habita in Regio Parisiensi Collegio die novembris 23*, L. de Heuqueville, Paris, 1645; P. Gassendi, *Opera omnia, IV*, pp.66-73.

31  P. Gassendi: 1647, *Institutio astronomica iuxta hypotheseis tam veterum quam Copernici et Tychonis Brahei ...*, L. de Heuqueville, Paris; P. Gassendi, *Opera omnia, IV*, pp.1-65.

32  "Historia non mala coeptae instaurari astronomiae, a Peurbachio ad Tychonem usque." (P. Gassendi, *Opera omnia, V*, p.518.)

33  P. Gassendi: 1654, *Tychonis Brahei vita ... Accessit Nicolai Copernici, Georgii Peurbachii et Joannis Regiomontani, astronomorum celebrium, vita*, M. Dupuis, Paris; P. Gassendi, *Opera omnia, IV*, pp.363-516.

34  T. Gregory: 1961, *Scetticismo ed empirismo. Studio su Gassendi*, Editori Laterza, Bari.

35  O.R. Bloch: 1971, *La philosophie de Gassendi. Nominalisme, matérialisme et métaphysique* (Archives internationales d'histoire des idees, 38), Martinus Nijhoff, The Hague.

36  *Idem*, p.3.

37  P. Gassendi, *Syntagma philosophicum*, in P. Gassendi, *Opera omnia, I* and *II*.

38   P.-Félix Thomas: 1889, *La philosophie de Gassendi*, F. Alcan, Paris.

39   T. Gregory, *Scetticismo ed empirismo*, p.8.

40   G. Sortais: 1922, *La philosophie moderne depuis Bacon jusqu'à Leibniz*, P. Lethielleux, Paris.

41   G.S. Brett: 1908, *The philosophy of Gassendi*, Macmillan and Co., London.

42   P. Pendzig: 1908, *Pierre Gassendis Metaphysik und ihr Verhaltnis zur scholastischen Philosophie*, P. Hanstein, Bonn. Cf. the criticism of this study in T. Gregory, *Scetticismo ed empirismo*, pp.10-11.

43   B. Rochot *et al.*: 1955, *Pierre Gassendi 1592-1655, sa vie et son oeuvre* (Centre International de Synthèse), Paris.

44   B. Rochot *et al.*: 1957, *Actes du Congrès du Tricentenaire de Pierre Gassendi (4-7 août, 1955)*, Digne.

45   F.X. Kiefl: 1893, *Pierre Gassendis Erkenntnisstheorie* (Dissertation presented at the University of Fulda).

46   H. Berr, *An jure inter scepticos Gassendus numeratus fuerit*, Paris, 1898. It was Berr who first discussed the "systematic postulate".

47   G. Hess: 1930, *Pierre Gassendi - Der französische Späthumanismus und das Problem von Wissen und Glauben*, W. Gronau, Leipzig.

48   R. Pintard: 1943, *Le libertinage érudit dans la première moitié du XVIIe siècle*, Boivin, Paris; cf. espc. pp.ix-x.

49   R. Pintard: 1948, "Modernisme, humanisme, libertinage - petite suite sur le 'cas Gassendi'", in *Revue d'histoire littéraire de la France*, 48, pp.1-52.

50   Cf. espc. R.H. Popkin: 1965, "The high road to Pyrrhonism", in *American philosophical quarterly*, 2, pp.18-32; R.H. Popkin: 1968, "Scepticism, theology and the scientific revolution in the seventeenth century", in I. Lakatos and A.E. Musgrave (Eds.): 1968, *Problems in the philosophy of science*, North-Holland Publishing Co., Amsterdam, pp.1-28; R.H. Popkin: 1964, *The history of scepticism from Erasmus to Descartes*, revised edition, Harper and Row, New York.

51 T.K. Rabb: 1975, *The struggle for stability in early modern Europe*, Oxford University Press, New York, p.vii.

52 Cf. *infra* Ch. 4.

53 B. Rochot: 1944, *Les travaux de Gassendi sur Epicure et sur l'atomisme 1619-1658*, J. Vrin, Paris.

54 B. Rochot (Ed.): 1944, *Pierre Gassendi. Lettres familiàres ç Franèois Luillier pendant l'hiver 1632-1633* ..., J. Vrin, Paris.

55 B. Rochot (Ed.): 1959, *Pierre Gassendi. Dissertations en forme de paradoxes contre les Aristotéliciens ... Livres I et II* ..., J. Vrin, Paris.

56 B. Rochot (Ed.): 1962, *Pierre Gassendi. Disquisitio metaphysica, seu dubitationes et instantiae adversus Renati Cartesii metaphysicam et responsa* ..., J. Vrin, Paris.

57 B. Rochot: 1955, "Pierre Gassendi. La vie, le caractère et la formation intellectuelle", in B. Rochot *et al.*: 1955, *Pierre Gassendi, sa vie et son oeuvre*, pp.9-58.

58 B. Rochot: 1957, "Gassendi et les mathématiques", in *Revue d'histoire des sciences*, *10*, pp.69-77.

59 B. Rochot: 1955, "Gassendi et la 'logique' de Descartes", in *Revue philosophique de la France et de l'Etranger*, 1955, pp.300-308.

60 B. Rochot: 1952, "Beekman, Gassendi et le principe d'inertie", in *Archives internationales d'histoire des sciences*, *5*, pp.282-289.

61 B. Rochot: 1964, "Gassendi et l'expérience", in 1964, *Mélanges Alexandre Koyré*, 2 vols., Paris, *II*, pp.411-422.

62 B. Rochot: 1956, "Sur les notions de temps et d'espace chez quelques auteurs du XVIIe siècle, notamment Gassendi et Barrow", in *Revue d'histoire des sciences*, *9*, pp.97-104.

63 Cf. the *Proemium* to the *Pars physica* of Gassendi's *Syntagma philosophicum*, in P. Gassendi, *Opera omnia*, *I*, p.126a-b.

64 P. Humbert: 1931, "La première carte de la lune", in *Revue des questions scientifiques*, *100*, pp.193-204; 1934, "Un manuscrit inédit de Gassendi", in *Revue des questions scientifiques*, *106*, pp.5-11; 1936, *L'oeuvre astronomique de Gassendi* (Actualités scientifiques et

industrielles, No. 378), Paris; 1940, "Une lettre inédit de Gassendi", in *Ciel et terre*, *56*, pp.14-17; 1947, "Les observations astronomiques de Gassendi à Digne", in *Sciences*, *74*, pp.336-349; 1952, *L'astronomie en France au 17e siecle*, Paris; 1950, "A propos du passage de Mercure 1631", in *Revue d'histoire des sciences*, *3*, pp.27-31; 1953, *Philosophes et savants*, Paris, pp.79-107.

65 A.G. Debus: 1963, "Pierre Gassendi and his 'scientific expedition' of 1640", in *Archives internationales d'histoire des sciences*, *16*, pp.129-142.

66 P. Ariotti: 1972, "From the top to the foot of a mast on a moving ship", in *Annals of science*, *28*, pp.191-203; P. Ariotti: 1972, "Aspects of the conception and development of the pendulum in the seventeenth century", in *Archive for history of exact sciences*, *8*, pp.329-410.

67 P. Pav: 1966, "Gassendi's statement of the principle of inertia", in *Isis*, *57*, pp.24-34.

68 J. Clark: 1963, "Pierre Gassendi and the physics of Galileo", in *Isis*, *54*, pp.352-370.

69 "Chi volesse contraporre queste soluzioni, come se ciascuna dovesse necessariamente escludere l'altra, dimenticherebbe una delle principali caratteristiche dell'autore e dell'epoca, che è nella consapevolezza dei limiti di ogni sapere umano e quindi della possibilità della coesistenza di soluzioni diverse.' (T. Gregory, *Scetticismo ed empirismo*, p.249.)

70 O. Bloch, *La philosophie de Gassendi*, p.xvi.

71 *Idem*, p.76.

72 *Idem*, pp.156-157.

73 O. Bloch: 1973, "Gassendi and the transition from the middle ages to the classical era", in *Yale French studies*, *49*, pp.43-45.

74 R. Tack: 1974, *Untersuchungen zum philosophie und wissenschaftsbegriff bei Pierre Gassendi (1592-1655)*, A. Hain, Meisenheim am Glan.

75 W. Detel: 1978, *"Scientia rerum natura occultarum." Methodologische studien zur physik Pierre Gassendis*, de Gruyter, Berlin.

76  H. Jones: 1981, *Pierre Gassendi 1592-1655. An intellectual biography*, B. De Graaf, Nieuwkoop; cf. also, H. Jones: 1981, *Pierre Gassendi's Institutio logica (1658)*, Van Gorcum, Assen.

77  L.T. Sarasohn: 1982, "The ethical and political philosophy of Pierre Gassendi", in *Journal of the history of philosophy*, 20, pp.239-260; 1985, "Motion and morality: Pierre Gassendi, Thomas Hobbes and the mechanical world-view", in *Journal of the history of ideas*, 46, pp.363-379.

78  M.J. Osler: 1983, "Providence and divine will in Gassendi's views on scientific knowledge", in *Journal of the history of ideas*, 44, pp.549-560; cf. also her subsequent article, 1985, "Eternal truths and the laws of nature: the theological foundations of Descartes' philosophy of nature", in *Journal of the history of ideas*, 46, pp.349-362.

79  W. Charleton: 1654, *Physiologia Epicuro-Gassendo-Charltoniana: or, A fabrick of science natural, upon the hypothesis of atoms, founded by Epicurus, repaired by P. Gassendus, augmented by W. Charlton. Pt I*, T. Heath, London, 1654.

80  F. Bernier: 1678, *Abregé de la philosophie de Gassendi*, 7 vols., Anisson et Posuel, Lyon.

81  Cf. J. Bougerel, *Vie de Pierre Gassendi*, Paris, 1737, pp.358, 362-368.

## Chapter 1

1   "Nunquam satis laudari digne poterit philosophia: cui qui pareat, omne tempus aetatis sine molestia possit degere" (Cicero, *De senectute* (Loeb classical library edition), I.2.); P. Gassendi, *Opera omnia, III*, p.99.

2   Cf. Gassendi's letter to Henri du Faur de Pibrac, a prominent public figure, later President of the Parlement of Provence, son of Guy du Faur de Pibrac: P. Gassendi, *Opera omnia, VI*, p.2.

3   P. Gassendi, *Opera omnia, III*, p.99.

4   "Verum mihi animos adiecit, timoremque omnem depulit et Vivis, et mei Charonii lectio, ex qua visus sum non iniuria suspicari sectam illam non esse penitus probandam, quod probaretur quamplurimis. Sed

et vires accrevere ex Ramo praesertim, ac Mirandulo: quorum idcirco mentionem facio, quod ingenuum semper duxerim profiteri per quos profecissem." (P. Gassendi, *Opera omnia, III*, p.99.)

5    Cf. B. Rochot: 1955, "La vie, le caractère et la formation intellectuelle", in B. Rochot *et al*.: 1955, *Pierre Gassendi 1592-1655, sa vie et son oeuvre* (Centre International de Synthèse), Paris, pp.9-54, espc. p.16; also R. Lenoble: 1971, *Mersenne ou la naissance du mécanisme*, 2nd Edition, J. Vrin, Paris, p.410.

6    P. Gassendi, *Opera omnia, III*, pp.99-106a; *VI*, p.30.

7    *Idem, III*, p.106a-b.

8    *Idem, III*, pp.107a-108a.

9    "Per mathematicas scimus, si quid scimus." (*Idem, III*, p.107a.) This statement was a criticism of the Aristotelians. It is not to be concluded from it that Gassendi was himself a mathematician in any sense, for he was not. Cf. B. Rochot: 1957, "Gassendi et les mathématiques", in *Revue d'histoire des sciences, 10*, pp.69-78. Gassendi was doing no more than repeat what he had read in the writings of Vives, Ramus and Mersenne; cf. P. Dear: 1984, "Marin Mersenne and the probabilistic roots of 'mitigated scepticism'", in *Journal of the history of philosophy, 22*, pp.173-205.

10   P. Gassendi, *Opera omnia, III*, p.107b.

11   "Uno verbo de hac rerum natura nihil perviderunt: quando suas scholas ingressi, aliam naturam ingressi sunt cum hac exteriori minime congruentem." (*Idem, III*, p.108a.)

12   See H.O. Evennett: 1968, *The spirit of the Counter-Reformation*, Cambridge University Press, Cambridge, pp.78-79, 84-86; also Robert Mandrou: 1978, *From humanism to science 1480-1700*, Penguin, Harmondsworth, pp.156-159.

13   See Ignatius of Loyola: 1558-1599, *The constitution of the Society of Jesus, IV*, Ch.13; Father Aquaviva S.J.: 1599, *Ratio studiorum*; George E. Ganss S.J. (Ed.): 1970, *Saint Ignatius of Loyola. The constitution of the Society of Jesus*, St. Louis, pp.215ff. Ganss claims: "One great merit of the *Ratio* of 1599 is that it produced a unity of procedure throughout the far-flung hundreds of Jesuit schools in Europe and the Americas. That procedural unity was greater than would be desirable or possible today; but it was a significant advantage and achievement

amid the educational disorganisation of the 1500's and 1600's." (*Idem*, p.216, note 4.)

14    Ignatius, *Constitution, IV*, ch. 14.3; Aquaviva, *Ratio studiorum*, ch. 3 ("De studio philosophiae").

15    For example, two text-books issued by faculty members of the Collegio Romano: Benedetto Pereira: 1576, *De communibus omnium rerum naturalium principiis et affectionibus libri quindecim*, Rome; and Francisco de Toledo: 1585, *Commentaria, una cum quaestionibus in octo libros Aristotelis 'de Physica* ..., Cologne; also the text-books of the Jesuits of Coimbra, for example: Conimbricenses: 1602, *Problemata quae in ... physicis* ..., Moguntiae, 1601; and *Commentariorum ... in octo libros physicorum* ..., Cologne. These text-books were used very widely in Jesuit schools.

16    Cf. A.C. Crombie: 1977, "Mathematics and Platonism in the sixteenth-century Italian universities and in Jesuit educational policy", in *ΠΡΙΣΜΑΤΑ* , *Festschrift für Willy Hartner*, Wiesbaden, pp.63-94.

17    Cf. E.A. Fellmann, "Fabri, Honoré", *Dictionary of scientific biography, IV*, pp.505-507.

18    It was true of all sixteenth and early seventeenth-century scholastic texts that I have consulted (see bibliography). Charles B. Schmitt has written as follows: "... even a casual reading of the Aristotelian commentaries of the period [late sixteenth and early seventeenth centuries] reveals a peculiar reluctance to quote authors other than the school tradition ... the Aristotelian commentary had changed remarkably little over a period of several centuries, considering how much philosophical water had passed under the bridge since the beginning of the humanist criticism of the schools ... All in all, the school philosophy was considerably more traditionally oriented - both in form and content - than were the other philosophical movements which emerged in the course of the fifteenth and sixteenth centuries." (Charles B. Schmitt: 1964, "Who read Gianfrancesco Pico della Mirandola?", in *Studies in the Renaissance, II*, pp.125-126.) Paul Dibon, in his interesting work (1954), *La philosophie néerlandaise au siècle d'or.* Tome I, *L'enseignement philosophique dans les universités à l'époque précartésienne ( 1576-1650)*, L'Institut Français d'Amsterdam, Amsterdam, has painted a different picture of scholastic teaching as it was conducted in Holland. Dibon has given a number of examples of Peripatetic philosophers teaching in scholastic institutions who were adapting their teaching in order to reflect the new intellectual movements. This was especially true in Leyden, he claimed, in the

cases of Daniel Voetius, Cornelius Valerius and Jaccheus. This detail is of particular interest, since Gassendi visited Leyden in 1629 and later sent outlines of his Epicurean project to scholars of the Academy (cf. *infra*, Chs. 2, 3).

19  P. Gassendi, *Opera omnia, III*, p.99, 100.

20  Gassendi had a theory that the chyle passed through the choledoch duct, and had debated this theory with a certain Professor Merindol of Marseilles. He was forced to abandon it when the *De lacteis venis* of Gasparo Aselli was published in 1627. Cf. Gassendi's letter to Peiresc of 16.5.1628 (P. Tamizey de Larroque (Ed.), *Lettres de Peiresc, IV*, pp.186-189; also Georges Martin-Charpenel: 1957, "Gassendi physiologiste", in B. Rochot *et al.*: 1957, *Actes du Congrès du Tricentenaire de Pierre Gassendi (4-5 août, 1955)*, Digne, pp.207-215).

21  P. Gassendi, *Opera omnia, III*, p.102.

22  *Idem, IV*, p.76.

23  *Idem, III*, p.102. Cf. the letter of Gassendi to Peiresc of 28.2.1629, in which he referred to the dissections of Payan that he had witnessed at an earlier time, in P. Tamizey de Larroque (Eds.), *Lettres de Peiresc, IV*, pp.203-209; also Martin-Charpenel: (1957), "Gassendi physiologiste".

24  "Postquam enim pervidere licuit quantis Naturae Genius ab humano ingenio dissideret intervallis, quid aliud potui, quam existimare effectorum naturalium intimas causas prorsus fugere humanam perspicaciam? Miserescere proinde, ac pudere coepit me levitatis et arrogantiae Dogmaticorum Philosophorum, qui et glorientur se arripuisse, et tam severe profiteantur naturalium rerum scientiam." (P. Gassendi, *Opera omnia, III*, p.99.)

25  "Enitendum duxi, quantum in me esset, retundere huius tantae credulitatis aciem, probaturus num simul quidpiam ex turgida illa Aristoteleorum praesumptione detraherem." (*Idem, III*, p.100.) There seems to be a verbal echo of Vives who complained that the Aristotelian subtleties "break and blunt the spearhead of the intelligence" ("frangunt ingenii aciem ac retundunt") (J.L. Vives, *Opera omnia*, 1782, Gregorio Majansio (Ed.): *Joannis Ludovici Vivis Valentini opera omnia*, 8 vols., B. Monfort, Valencia, *VI*, p.352).

26  *Supra*, p.15.

27 Cf. *supra*, p.15; Sextus Empiricus, *Outlines of Pyrrhonism* (Loeb classical library edition), I.190,200.

28 "Nullum veriorem hoc sapiente Christianum fore puto." (J. Vives, *Opera omnia, III*, p.17.) Concerning the ethical writings of Vives, cf. Carlos G. Norena: 1970, *Juan Luis Vives*, Martinus Nijhoff, The Hague, Ch.10.

29 For an account of the storm and for a spirited defence of Pierre Charron that goes against the standard censorious view, cf. the study of Charron by a latter-day kinsman, Jean Daniel Charron: 1960, *The "wisdom" of Pierre Charron. An original and orthodox code of morality*, University of North Carolina Press, Chapel Hill.

30 P. Charron: 1601, *De la sagesse livres trois*, S. Millanges, Bordeaux.

31 See the objections of those whom Charron called *"esprits faibles"*, and others, as they are listed in 1606, *Traicté de sagesse*, D. Le Clerc, Paris, pp.224-225, and in the preface to the second and all subsequent editions of the *Sagesse*. The objections which Charron took most note of were the claim that he was a Pelagian heretic and the objections against his Pyrrhonism on the grounds of its alleged danger for the faith.

32 P. Charron: 1606, *Traicté de sagesse, composé par Pierre Charron, Parisien*, D. Le Clerc, Paris.

33 *Idem.*, ch. 2, par.9; ch. 4, par.2,3; ch. 7,*etc.*

34 "Infame escrivain, cynique et brutal s'il en fut jamais" (P.F. Garasse S.J.: 1625, *La somme théologique des véritez capitales de la réligion chrestienne*, S. Chappelet, Paris, p.665). Garasse was himself subsequently condemned by the Sorbonne; cf. Richard H. Popkin: 1968, *The history of scepticism from Erasmus to Descartes*, revised edition, Harper and Row, New York, pp.114-118.

35 Charron replied in *Traicté de sagesse*, ch. 2, par.9; ch. 4, pars.2,3.

36 Sextus Empiricus, *Outlines of Pyrrhonism*, I.190, 200.

37 *Idem.*, I.8, 10, 196, 205.

38 *Idem*, I.8, 10, 12, 17, 28-30.

39   J. Vives, *Opera omnia, VI*, pp.23-24; cf. C.G. Norena, *Juan Luis Vives*, pp.248-249.

40   "Philosophia tota opinionibus et conjecturis verisimilitudinis est innixa" (J. Vives, *Opera omnia, VI*, p.417).

41   P. Charron, *Traicté de sagesse*, p.224.

42   "Ces sont choses opposites" (P. Charron, *Traicté de sagesse*, p.225).

43   "Pulchre porro me admones authorem hunc mecum in solitudinem ducam ... Charronio vero quis sanior iudex?" (Letter of 8.4.1621, P. Gassendi, *Opera omnia, VI*, pp.1-2.)

44   Gianfrancesco Pico della Mirandola: 1520, *Examen vanitatis doctrinae gentium, et veritatis Christianae disciplinae distinctum in libris sex, quorum tres omnem philosophorum sectam universim, reliqui Aristoteleam et Aristotelis armis particulatim impugnant, ubicumque autem Christiana et asseritur, et celebratur disciplina*, Mirandola.

45   "I came to the conclusion that it was much better and much more useful to reduce all the dogmas of the philosophers to uncertainty, than to reconcile them with one another as my uncle wished to do." "Mihi autem venit in mentem consentaneum magis esse, et utile magis, incerta reddere philosophorum dogmata, quam conciliare, ut patrinus volebat." (Preface written by Gianfrancesco Pico to his edition of his uncle's works entitled: Giovanni Pico della Mirandola: 1572-1573, *Opera omnia Joannis Pici, Mirandulae Concordiaeque comitis ...*, 2 vols., Basileae, *II*, p.738.)

46   "Quid restat praeterea ut non ipsa gentium doctrina et vana, et incerta prorsus iudicetur." (G.F. Pico della Mirandola, *Idem*, preface.)

47   *Idem, II*, pp.812-815; pp.718-719. Ramus also supported this view; cf. Reijer Hooykaas: 1958, *Humanisme, science et réforme: Pierre de la Ramée (1515-1572)*, E.J. Brill, Leyden, pp.9.ff.

48   This conclusion has been arrived at after a certain amount of discussion among the scholars. Fortunat Strowski argued in his work *Montaigne*, F. Alcan, Paris (1906), that the *Examen vanitatis* had a very considerable influence on later thinkers. The opposite view was taken insofar as it concerned the relationship of Pico's work with that of Montaigne, in the work of Pierre de Villey: 1908, *Les sources de l'évolution des essais de Montaigne*, Fondation Thiers, Paris, *II*, p.166, pp.324-325. In more recent times both R.H. Popkin, *History of*

*scepticism*, pp.19-22, and Charles B. Schmitt: 1964, "Who read Gianfrancesco Pico della Mirandola?" in *Studies in the renaissance, II*, pp.105-132, and in 1967, *Gianfrancesco Pico della Mirandola (1469-1533)*, Martinus Nijhoff, The Hague, have been in general agreement that the influence of Pico was not great, but that the *Examen vanitatis* was of some importance as a source-book for the anti-Aristotelians in the sixteenth and early seventeenth centuries.

49    C.B. Schmitt: 1964, pp.128-129.

50    Charles B. Schmitt: 1972, *Cicero scepticus: a study of the 'Academica' in the Renaissance*, Martinus Nijhoff, The Hague, ch. 4.

51    "Aristotelis philosophiam, orbis terrarum pene totam et solam philosophiam esse" (preface to Bks IX and X of 1556, *Animadversionum Aristotelicarum libri XX*, A. Wechelum, Paris). For complaints of Ramus against the Aristotelian commentators, see the same preface, also Bk. II, p.67, Bk. III, p.97; cf. also Hooykaas, *Humanisme, science et réforme*, p.13.

52    C.B. Schmitt, *Cicero scepticus*, p.89.

53    Cf. C.B. Schmitt, *Cicero scepticus*, p.12.

54    Sextus Empiricus: 1562, *Sexti philosophi Pyrrhoniarum hypotypwsewn [sic] ... interprete Henrico Stephano*, M. Juvenum, Paris; Sextus Empiricus: 1569, *Adversus mathematicos, Gentiano Herveto Aurelio interprete...*, M. Juvenum, Paris. Cf. R.H. Popkin, *History of scepticism*, pp.68-69.

55    "Quanto usui autem esse possit Sexti Empirici commentarius ad tuenda Christianae religionis dogmata adversus externos Philosophos, pulchre docet Franciscus Picus Mirandulanus in eo libro quo Christianam tueter philosophiam adversus dogmata externorum Philosophorum." (Preface of Gentian Hervet to his translation of Sextus Empiricus: 1569, *Adversus mathematicos*, as quoted by C.B. Schmitt (1964), p.114.)

56    See Charles B. Schmitt: 1967, *Gianfrancesco Pico della Mirandola (1469-1533) and his critique of Aristotle*, Martinus Nijhoff, The Hague, pp.172-174. Another author who might very possibly have drawn Gassendi's attention to Pico was Giovanni Battista Bernardi, author of a dictionary of philosophical quotations entitled *Seminarium totius philosophiae* ... (1582-1585); cf. C.B. Schmitt, *Idem*, pp.170-171.

57    P. Gassendi, *Opera omnia, III*, pp.99-100.

58   Cf. the account of Pyrrhonic doubt given by Sextus Empiricus: *"Chapter XXVI of the expressions "I am non-apprehensive" and "I apprehend not".* Both the expressions "I am non-apprehensive" and "I apprehend not" are indicative of a personal state of mind, in which the sceptic, for the time being, avoids affirming or denying any non-evident matter of enquiry, as is obvious from what we have said above concerning the other expressions.' (Sextus Empiricus, *Outlines of Pyrrhonism*, I.201.) The Pyrrhonist's manner of proceeding has been described as follows: "The Academician takes active part in philosophical discussion, maintaining a definite position, a standpoint; the sceptic in the sense of Sextus [i.e. the Pyrrhonist] has no position ... Although he throws arguments into the discussion, he takes no part in it. Although he confronts the dogmatist with counterarguments, he does so without accepting any of them as true or valid." (Arne Naess: 1968, *Scepticism*, Routledge and Kegan Paul, London, p.4.) Cf. P. Gassendi, *Opera omnia, I, p*, 13b.

59   "Quantis Naturae Genius ab humano ingenio dissideret intervallis" (P. Gassendi, *Opera omnia, III*, p.99).

60   "Aristoteles  ...  adolescentes  in  thesi,  non  ad  hunc  morem philosophorum tenuitur disserendi: sed ad copiam rhetorum in utramque partem, ut ornatius et uberius dici posset, exercuit." (P. Gassendi, *Opera omnia, III*, p.100) Gassendi referred to Cicero, probably *De oratore* (Loeb classical library edition), I, xi. 49-54, as his authority.

61   "Tam indigna opera" (P. Gassendi, *Opera omnia, III*, p.101).

62   "Sed utcumque se res habeat: seu dogmatice quid defendo, seu sceptico more quid experior: et, seu profero quidpiam verum, seu quidpiam dico probabile ..." (P. Gassendi, *Opera omnia, III*, p.101.)

63   Cf. A. Naess, *Scepticism*, p.2ff.

64   "Paradoxa mea publice disputata sunt apud celeberrimos illos totius Provinciae consessus ..." (P. Gassendi, *Opera omnia, I*, p.98.)

65   Sextus Empiricus, *Outlines of Pyrrhonism*, I.1.

66   "At vero nostrates philosophi, quorum princeps idem, philosophorum omnium facile sapientissimus, Aristoteles Stagyrites fuit." (J. Vives, *Opera omnia, III*, p.18.)

67  "Nullum videtur fuisse ingenium Aristotelico praestantius." (*Idem, III*, p.25.)

68  "Nugatoria et praepostera doctrina valde ineptum, nec ulla fere parte Aristoteleum ..." (P. Ramus: 1556, *Animadversionum Aristotelicarum libri XX* ..., Bk. 3, p.97.)

69  'Detrahant a Grammatica omnia definitionum partitionumque lumina: pro exemplis elegantibus misceant abecedaria figmenta." (*Idem*, Bk. 2, p.67.)

70  *Idem*, preface to Bks. 9 and 10. Cf. R. Hooykaas, *Humanisme, science et réforme*, p.13ff.

71  P. Gassendi, *Opera omnia, III*, p.101.

## Chapter 2

1  Cf. Galileo Galilei *et al.* (1960, Stillman Drake and C.D. O'Malley, Trans.), *The controversy on the comets of 1618: Galileo Galilei, Horatio Grassi, Mario Guiducci, Johann Kepler*, University of Pennsylvania Press, Philadelphia.

2  Tycho Brahe: 1588, *De mundi aetherii recentioribus phaenomenis liber secundus qui est de illustri stella caudata ab elapso fere triente Novembris anni 1577 usque in finem Januarii sequentis conspecta*, Uraniburg, in Tycho Brahe, *Tychonis Brahe Dani opera omnia* (1913-1929, I.L.E. Dreyer (Ed.)), 15 vols., Copenhagen, *IV*, pp.1-377.

3  Tycho Brahe, *De mundi aetherii recentioribus phaenomenis*, pp.82-83; Aristotle, *Meteorologica* 344a5-345a10. For a description of Tycho's methods for determining parallax, cf. J.L.E. Dreyer: 1890, *Tycho Brahe. A picture of scientific life and work in the sixteenth century* (1963, Dover Publications, New York), pp.165-166.

4  P. Gassendi, *Opera omnia, IV*, p.78; cf. Gassendi's other references to Tycho's observations of comets, *e.g.* P. Gassendi, *idem, IV*, p.702b; also Gassendi's preface to his biography of Tycho Brahe, P. Gassendi: 1654, *Tychonis Brahei, equitis Dani, astronomorum coriphaei, vita* ..., in P. Gassendi, *idem, V*, pp.363-496.

5    "Quo loco cometas traiicio per aetherea spatia, illosque statuo non
     minus perpetuos, quam sidera perpetuo conspicua." (P. Gassendi,
     *Opera omnia, III*, p.102.)

6    "Cum videamus ergo ubique difficultates occurrere, planius est ut
     nihil definiamus, contentique simus heic animi gratia narrare
     historiam cometae illius qui ut nuperus exstitit sic visus nobis primus
     fuit et, coniiciendo solum, attexere quid ex collatione ipsius cum
     caeteris dicere quis quadam cum specie verisimilitudinis possit." (P.
     Gassendi, *Opera omnia, II*, p.704b.)

7    P. Gassendi, *Opera omnia, VI*, pp.4a–6a.

8    Galileo Galilei: 1623, *Il saggiatore nel quale con bilancia esquisita e
     giusta si ponderano le cose contenute nella libra astronomica e
     filosofica di Lotario Sarsi Sigesano scritto in forma di lettera ...*, G.
     Mascardi, Rome.

9    Lothario Sarsi ( = Orazio Grassi): 1619, *Libra astronomica ac
     philosophica, qua Galilei Galilei opiniones de cometis a Mario Guiducio
     in Florentina academia expositae, atque in lucem nuper editae,
     examinantur a Lothario Sarsio ...*, Perugia, in S. Drake and C.D.
     O'Malley (Eds.), *The controversy on the comets*, pp.67–132. (N.B. The
     Galileo scholar, Stillman Drake, renders Orazio Grassi as Horatio
     Grassi.)

10   Galileo Galilei, *Il saggiatore*, Chs. 8, 9; S. Drake and C.D. O'Malley
     (Eds.), *The controversy on the comets*, pp.82ff; cf. W.R. Shea: 1972,
     *Galileo's intellectual revolution*, Macmillan Press, London, ch. 4, "The
     challenge of the comets".

11   There were still quite a number of people in the seventeenth century
     arguing the traditional Aristotelian position that comets were sub-
     lunar, atmospheric phenomena; cf. Lothario Sarsi ( = Orazio Grassi) in
     S. Drake and C.D. O'Malley, *The controversy on the comets*, p.73;
     Gassendi commented in similar manner in his biography of Tycho
     Brahe, cf. P. Gassendi, *Opera omnia, V*, p.163; cf. also *I*, p.703a; *V*,
     p.417a–b.

12   P. Gassendi, *Opera omnia, II*, p.702b.

13   P. Gassendi, *Opera omnia, II*, pp.600b–601a; Aristotle *Metaphysics*
     1073b1–1074a17.

14 "Ac mille nugas commenti sunt, quibus insomnis suffulcirent: videlicet soliditatem, realitatemque sphaerarum caelestium, canales, quos astra trajiciant ..." (P. Gassendi, *Opera omnia, III*, p.107b: cf. also *I*, pp.597b-602b (MS Tours 710, ff.621v-623r).)

15 Tycho Brahe, *De mundi aetherii recentioribus phaenomenis*, in *Opera omnia, IV*, p.159.

16 Cf. E. Rosen: 1985, "Dissolution of the solid celestial spheres", in *Journal of the history of ideas, 46*, pp. 13-31; Rosen takes issue with N.M. Swerdlow: 1976, "*Pseudodoxia Copernicana*", in *Archives internationales d'histoire des sciences, 26*, pp.108-158; he is also critical of W. H. Donahue: 1981, *The dissolution of the celestial spheres 1595-1650*, Arno Press, New York; cf. also, W.H. Donahue: 1975, "The solid planetary spheres in post-Copernican natural philosophy", in R.S. Westman (Ed.): 1975, *The Copernican achievement*, University of California Press, Berkeley, pp.244-275. Nicholas Jardine comments on the discussion in his article: 1982, "The significance of the Copernican orbs", in *Journal for the history of astronomy, 3*, pp.168-194.

17 Aristotle, *De caelo* 269b29-31; *Metaphysics* 1073a34-35; 1073b5-8; 1074a35-36.

18 P. Gassendi, *opera omnia* , *I*, p.518b. Of course, Gassendi was able to base his argument on recorded appearances of Novae and, after 1626, on his own observations of sunspots, but the evidence of comets was always especially impressive if for no other reason than that comets arouse intense public interest. Cf. P. Gassendi, *Opera omnia, IV*, p.99; *I*, pp.517b-518b.

19 "... et stellis fixis et soli comparatur quies: Terrae vero, quasi uni ex planetis, conciliatur motus ..." (P. Gassendi, *Opera omnia, III*, p.102.)

20 "Inprimis ergo, mi Galilee, velim sic tibi persuasum habeas, me tanta cum animi voluptate amplexari Coperniceam illam tuam in astronomia sententiam, ut exinde videar mei probe iuris factus, cum soluta, et libera mens vagatur per immensa spatia, effractis nempe vulgaris mundi sustematisque repagulis." (Letter to Galileo of 20.7.1625, in P. Gassendi, *Opera omnia, VI*, p.4b.)

21 "Mihi certe nihil est antiquius quam colere summam sapientiam ac eruditionem tuam. Ex quo enim tempore tuus ille caelestium interpres tam incognita generi humano patefecit mysteria, dici non potest quo tacito cultu memet tibi devoverim." (*Idem*, p.4a.)

22  Galileo Galilei: 1610, *Siderius nuncius, magna ... spectacula pandens ... quae a Galileo Galileo ... sunt observata in lunae facie ... apprime vero in quatuor planetis circa Jovis stellam disparibus intervallis ... quos ... novissime author deprehendit primus atque medicea sidera nuncupandos decrevit*, T. Baglionum, Venice.

23  Galileo Galilei: 1613, *Istoria e dimostrazioni intorno alle macchie solari e loro accidenti comprese in tre lettere scritte all'illustrissimo signor Marco Velseri Linceo da signor Galileo Galilei Linceo*, G. Mascardi, Rome.

24  "... foelicitatis ingenii tui laudator perpetuus, quocumque ducas sim sequuturus ... Perge tu, admirande vir, sublimeis curas agitare, dignas maiestate naturae, dignas te ipso, dignas iis qui avebunt te imitari." (Letter to Galileo of 1.3.1632, in P. Gassendi, *Opera omnia*, *VI*, pp.45b-46a.)

25  Galileo Galilei: 1632, *Dialogo di Galileo Galilei Linceo ... dove ne i congressi di quattro giornate si discorre sopra i due massimi sistemi del mondo Tolemaico, e Copernicano; proponendo indeterminatamente le ragioni filosofiche e naturali tanto per l'una, quanto per l'altra parte*, G.B. Landini, Florence.

26  Cf. letter to Galileo of 20.7.1625 already quoted, in P. Gassendi, *Opera omnia*, *VI*, p.4a-b.

27  "... quam grate acceperim librum, quam iucunde percurrerim. Equidem tanta sum affectus inter legendum voluptate ut etiam-num, quoties mente repeto mirifice movear." (Letter to Galileo of 1.11.1632, in P. Gassendi, *Opera omnia*, *VI*, p.53b.)

28  "Dicerem plura, sed si perspectus tibi utcumque meus est genius, divinabis plane nihil esse in tuis ratiociniis quod summopere mihi non arrideat." (P. Gassendi, *Opera omnia*, *VI*, p.53b.)

29  "... de observatis solaribus maculis emittere nihil in animo est, nisi quod iuxta principia tua conducere videbitur ad impugnandam Aristotelismum, adhortandumque homines ad aliquam verisimiliorem sanioremque philosophiam." (Letter to Galileo of 20.7.1625, in P. Gassendi, *Opera omnia*, *VI*, p.5a.)

30  Cf. Pierre Humbert: 1936, *L'Oeuvre astronomique de Gassendi* (Actualités scientifiques et industrielles 378), Paris, p.4.

31 Cf. letter to Galileo of 1.3.1632. Referring to the copy of his account of the observation of the transit of Mercury (P. Gassendi: 1632, *Mercurius in sole visus et Venus invisa Parisiis anno 1631 ... Epistolae duae, cum observatis quibusdam aliis*, S. Cramoisy, Paris) which he enclosed with his letter, Gassendi wrote to Galileo:

> "Receive this as a work which belongs to you, since whatever is a result of your discoveries must be sent back to you." "Tu ut debitum excipe, cum referendum ad te sit quidquid debetur tuis inventis." (P. Gassendi, *Opera omnia*, *VI*, p.45a.)

32 Johann Kepler: 1630, *Admonitio ad astronomos, rerumque coelestium studiosos, de raris mirisque anni 1631 phaenomenis Veneris puta et Mercurii in solem incursu, excerpta ex ephemeride anni 1631 e certo authoris consilio huic praemissa ...*, Frankfurt.

33 Cf. letter to Peiresc of 21.7.1629 (P. Tamizey de Larroque (Ed.), *Lettres de Peiresc*, *IV*, pp.198-202).

34 Christoph Scheiner: 1630, *Rosa ursina, sive sol ex admirando facularum et macularum phoenomeno varius ... libris quatuor mobilis ostensus*, Bracciani; Carolus Malapertius: 1633, *Austriaca sidera heliocyclia, astronomicis hypothesibus illigata, opera R. P. Caroli Malapertii ...*, Duaci.

35 P. Tamizey de Larroque (Ed.), *Lettres de Peiresc*, *IV*, p.201.

36 The list reads: Rheticus, Maestlin, Gilbert, Lansberg, Schickard, Hortensius, Bouillaud, and above all, Kepler and Galileo. Cf. P. Gassendi, *Opera omnia*, *I*, p.620a (cf. MS Tours 710, f.629v). Philip of Lansberg was a friend of Isaac Beeckman, and no doubt it was Beeckman who made Gassendi aware of his lost opportunity in not visiting Lansberg while Gassendi was at Middelbourg. Gassendi made reference to Lansberg on several occasions: P. Gassendi, *Opera omnia*, *IV*, pp.502b-503a; *I*, p.565a.

37 "... le meilleur philosophe que j'aye encore rencontré". (P. Tamizey de Larroque, *Opera omnia*, *IV*, p.201.)

38 Cf. J.A. Schuster: 1977, *Descartes and the scientific revolution 1618-1634. An interpretation* (Ph.D. dissertation presented to the faculty of Princeton University), pp.23ff.

39  C. de Waard (Ed.): 1939, *Journal tenu par Isaac Beeckman de 1604 à 1634* ..., 4 vols., La Haye, *I*, pp.123-124.

40  S. Marolois: 1628, *Oeuvres mathematicques ... traictant de la géométrie et fortification ... corrigées* ..., G.J. Caesius, Amsterdam.

41  "... tous ces gens la sont pour le mouvement de la terre." (letter to Peiresc of 21.7.1629, *Lettres de Peiresc, IV*. p.201.)

42  Cf. P. Duhem: 1629, *To save the phenomena. An essay on the idea of physical theory from Plato to Galileo* (E. Doland and C. Maschler (Transl.)), University of Chicago Press, Chicago, Ch. 7.

43  Gassendi's use of the term "opinion" is discussed in Ch. 4, *infra*.

44  "Antiquorum omnium rationes et hypotheses apparere nugas et insomnia mera, quando cum invento tuo comparatur.' (Letter to Galileo of 1.11.1632, in P. Gassendi, *Opera omnia, VI*, p.54a.)

45  Letter to Peiresc of 28.4.1631, enclosure, *Lettres de Peiresc, IV*, pp.250-252.

46  P. Gassendi, *Syntagma philosophicum, pars secunda, quae est physica*, in P. Gassendi, *Opera omnia, I*, p. 125 - *II*, p.658.

47  Cf. P. Duhem, *To save the phenomena*, pp.92ff, bearing in mind Edward Rosen's criticism of the sweeping nature of Duhem's historical account of the reifying of the hypotheses of the celestial spheres; cf. E. Rosen: 1985, "Dissolution of the solid celestial spheres", in *Journal of the history of ideas, 46*, pp.13-31.

48  Galileo Galilei, *Le opere di Galileo Galilei* (1890-1909, Edizione Nazionale sotto gli auspicii di sua Maestà il re d'Italia), 20 vols. in 21, G. Barbera, Florence, *XIX*, pp.402-407.

49  "Ex amplis nuper a Galileo epistolis rescivi ipsum brevi Romae, quo citatus est, adfuturum. Id miratus sum, quoniam nihil non approbatum edidit; sed nostrum non est nosse haec momenta." (Letter of Gassendi to Campanella of 8.5.1633 in P. Gassendi, *Opera omnia, VI*, p.56b.) Neither the letter here referred to nor any of the other letters written by Galileo to Gassendi have been traced.

50  "Magna mea tenet expectatio (o magnum aevi nostri Decus) quid rerum tibi contigerit. Tametsi enim rumore crebro nescio quid divulgatum est, haud fido nihilominus donec res fuerit plane

perspecta." (Letter of Gassendi to Galileo of 19.1.1634, in P. Gassendi, *Opera omnia, VI*, p.66b.)

51   Cf. *infra*, pp.42-43.

52   Galileo Galilei, *Opere, XIX*, pp.321, 322.

53   "A propos de Mr Diodati je suy bien aise de la faveur que vous luy faites en envoyant vostre Foscarin. Il sera bon neantmoins de l'avertir qu'il prenne garde que Bernegger ne face point mention que vous le luy avez envoye. Escrivant a Mr Diodati je lui diray a tout hazard ce que peut estre il ne scait pas, c'est que le dit Foscarin avec Galilei avoient este censurez des je ne scay quelle annee, me souvenant d'en avoir veu la censure dans le commentaire du pere Mercenne sur la Genese; ce ne sera pas pour l'empescher de faire ce qu'il voudra faire, mais afin qu'il soit adverty du tout." (Letter to Peiresc of 11.2.1634, in *Lettres de Peiresc, IV*, pp.458-459.)

54   P.A. Foscarini: 1615, *Lettera del R. Padre Maestro Paolo Antonio Foscarini, Carmelitano, sopra l'opinione de' Pittagorici e del Copernico della mobilità della terra e stabilità del sole, e il nuovo Pittagorico sistema del mondo*, L. Scoriggio, Napoli.

55   Cf. Galileo Galilei, *Opere, XIX*, pp.322-323.

56   Cf. *infra* p.46.

57   Jean-Baptiste Morin (1583-1656) was an astrologer and Hermeticist, and a champion of anti-Copernicanism. He was a life-long irritant for Gassendi. He criticised Morin's astrological writings for their alleged absurdities and contradictions (cf. P. Gassendi, *Opera omnia, I*, pp.726b-727a; also the letter of Gassendi to Galtier of 9.6.1631, in C. de Waard (Ed.): 1945-1972, *Correspondence du P. Marin Mersenne, Religieux Minime*, 12 vols., Centre National de la Recherche Scientifique, Paris, *III*, pp.173-179). Gassendi sharply rebuked Morin for calling Kepler a "wholly Earth-bound, fibrous philosopher", (*terrestrem, fibratumque admodum philosophum*), when referring to Kepler's theory of gravitational attraction (cf. letter of Gassendi to Galtier of 9.7.1631, in de Waard, *idem, III*, p.174). The public exchanges continued between Gassendi and Morin after Morin's attack on Gassendi's writings on motion in 1642 (cf. *infra*.), becoming increasingly bitter, and Morin eventually widened the scope of his attack on Gassendi's work to embrace his Epicurean philosophy as a whole (cf. J.-B. Morin: 1650, *Dissertatio ... de atomis et vacuo contra P. Gassendi Philosophiam Epicuream*, Paris). Despite their different

outlooks, Morin and Gassendi were both former pupils of the one master, Joseph Galtier; cf. letter of Gassendi to Galtier of 9.7.1631, in *Correspondence de Mersenne, III*, p.173, note 1.

58 Gassendi acknowledged Morin's presence in his inaugural oration, cf. P. Gassendi: 1645, "Oratio inauguralis habita in Regio Parisiensi Collegio, anno 1645, die Novembris 23", in P. Gassendi, *Opera omnia, IV*, p.72b.

59 J.-B. Morin: 1631, *Famosi et antiqui problematis de telluris motu, vel quiete, hactenus optata solutio*, Paris.

60 P. Gassendi: 1642, *De motu impresso a motore translato epistolae duae, in quibus aliquot paraecipuae, tum de motu universe, tum speciatim de motu terrae attributo, difficultates explicantur*, L. de Heuqueville, Paris.

61 Cf. J.-B. Morin: 1643, *Alae telluris fractae cum physica demonstratione, quod opinio copernicana de telluris motu sit falsa, et novo conceptu de oceani fluxu atque refluxu, adversus clarissimi viri Petri Gassendi libellum de motu impresso a motore translato ...*, Paris.

62 Pierre de Cazrée: 1645, *Physica demonstratio, qua ratio, mensura, modus ac potentia accelerationis motus in naturali descensu gravium determinatur adversus nuper excogitatum a Galileo Galilei, ... de eodem motu pseudo-scientiam ...*, J. Du Breuil, Paris.

63 "Non exigis, ut repetam fecisse me id, non ut telluri assererem motum, sed ut veritatis amore, innuerem quietem ipsius firmiore ratione esse stabiliendum." (P. Gassendi, *Opera omnia, III*, p.519a.) Cf. also, Allen G. Debus: 1963, "Pierre Gassendi and his 'scientific expedition' of 1640", in *Archives internationales d'histoire des sciences, 16*, pp.129-142.

64 Cf. Joseph T. Clark: 1963, "Pierre Gassendi and the physics of Galileo", in *Isis, 54*, pp.352-370.

65 P. Gassendi: 1643, *De motu impresso a motore translato epistola III in librum a viro cl. Ioanne Morino, Regio Matheseos Professore, conscriptus est adversus duas priores epistolas, et inscriptus 'Alae telluris fractae'*. (Cf. P. Gassendi, *Opera omnia, III*, pp.521b-563b.)

66 P. Gassendi, *De proportione qua gravia accidentia accelerantur epistolae tres, quibus ad totidem epistolas R.P. Petri Cazrei ... respondetur*, L. de Heuqueville, Paris.

67    S. Drake (Ed.), *Discoveries and opinions of Galileo*, pp.173-216.

68    "... non de consistentia in eodem loco, sed de constantia in sui
      compositione, incorruptioneve secundum se totam (quasi fiant quidem
      in partibus eius, ac superficialibus praesertim, generationum,
      corruptionumque vicissitudines continentes, sed ipsa tamen interim
      secundum se totam eadem constanter perseveret." (P. Gassendi, *Opera
      omnia, I*, p,630a; cf. MS Tours 710, f.652v.) Cf. also P. Gassendi,
      *Opera omnia, II*, pp.9a-10b (cf. MS Tours 707, gg.863v-865v); *III*,
      p.519a-b; *IV*, p.60a.

69    "... quod ea loco secus explicentur a viris, quorum, ut constat, tanta est
      in Ecclesia auctoritas, ea propter ipsa ab illis sto, et hac occasione
      facere captivum intellectum non erubesco." (P. Gassendi, *Opera
      omnia, III*, p.519b.)

70    P. Gassendi, *Opera omnia, III*, p.641b.

71    "... illorum iudicium habendum praeiudicium sit, quod non possit apud
      fideleis non esse maximi momenti." (P. Gassendi, *Opera omnia, III*,
      p.519b. Cf. *I*, p. 630a (cf. MS Tours 710, f.653r-v), *IV*, p.60b. It is
      noteworthy that Gassendi's interpretation of the force of the sentence
      against Galileo was identical with that expressed by the Jesuit Father
      Riccioli in his *Almagestum novum astronomiam veterum novamque
      complectens* (1651), p.162; cf. Jerome J. Langford: 1966, *Galileo,
      science and the Church*, Desclee Co., New York, p.156.

72    P. Gassendi, *Opera omnia, III*, p. 641b; Cf *I*, p.617b.

73    Cf. the title of the *Dialogo* itself.

74    Cf. MS Tours 710, ff.620v-627v.

75    "Adnotari praeterea potest duas esse quasi capitaleis de dispositione
      mundi opiniones, aliam vulgarem, et ab Aristotele praesertim
      defensam, quae terram statuit in centro mundi; aliam abhorrentem a
      sensu, ac olim praecipue a Platone, Pythagoricisque et nuper a
      Copernico, sequacibusque propugnatam, quae solem in centro
      constituit." (MS Tours 709, f.442r.) In the *Syntagma* version Gassendi
      attributed the heliocentric theory to Plato "in his old age" ("iam
      senescentis") (cf. P. Gassendi, *Opera omnia, I*, p.148a). He was almost
      certainly referring to the *Timaeus* of Plato, in which the theories of
      the World Body and the World Soul were expounded (especially Plato,
      *Timaeus* 31B-37C; cf. the edition of F.M. Cornford: 1937, *Plato's*

*cosmology. The Timaeus of Plato*, London, pp.43-97). The soul at the centre of the world, as described in *Timaeus* 34B, was identified with the Sun, source of vital generation through its heat and light, in Neoplatonic and Hermetic writings, and in Copernican theory.

76    P. Gassendi, *Opera omnia, I*, pp. 147a-149a; cf. also *IV*, p.62b.

77    1. De caeli siderumque substantia; 2. de varietate, positione et intervallis siderum; 3. de magnitudine et figura siderum; 4. de motu corporum caelestium. (Enclosure with a letter of Gassendi to Peiresc of 28.4.1631, in *Lettres de Peiresc, IV*, pp.250-252.)

78    That was the point of his journey to the Low Countries; also cf *infra*, Ch. 3.

79    "probabiliore, aut perspicua magis" (MS Tours 710, f.627r; P. Gassendi, *Opera omnia, I*, p.617b.

80    P. Gassendi, *Opera omnia, I*, pp.615b-630b; MS Tours 710, f.624v-653v.

81    Compare, *e.g.*, MS Tours 710, f.653r-v with the corresponding passage in the *Syntagma* version (P. Gassendi, *Opera omnia, I*, p.630a). In the *Syntagma* version Gassendi found it advisable to moderate further the pro-Copernican tenor of the passage.

82    The story of Descartes' hesitations about publishing *Le monde* has some parallels with Gassendi's cautious manoeuvres. Descartes suppressed his original treatise following the condemnation of Galileo and presented a revised version in the *Principia* in 1644; cf. R. Descartes, *Le monde, ou Traité de la lumière* (1979, M.S. Mahoney (Trans.), Abaris Books, Inc., New York), Introduction.

     The first version of Gassendi's *Pars logica* is also missing, presumably destroyed along with the first version of the *Pars physica* with which it would have been collected together. There would have been little reason to preserve the *Pars logica*, since Gassendi went on to write three further versions of the logic. One is preserved in MS Carpentras 1832, ff.205r-256r (1634). Another was described by Gassendi in a long series of letters to Louis of Valois in 1642 (cf. P. Gassendi, *Opera omnia, VI*, pp.138-154). The final version (post 1649) was published in the *Syntagma* (cf. P. Gassendi, *Opera omnia, I*, pp.31-124). Cf. also, H. Jones: 1981, *Pierre Gassendi's Institutio logica (1658), a critical edition with translation and introduction*, Van Gorcum, Assen.

83 "... piu ingegnoso ... non pero ... verace, e concludente ..." (Galileo Galilei, *Opere*, pp.457-458.)

84 Cf. Ludovico Geymonat: 1965, *Galileo Galilei. A biography and inquiry into his philosophy of science*, (Trans. S. Drake), McGraw-Hill, New York, p.127; also Jerome J. Langford, *Galileo, science and the Church*, pp.128-129.

85 "... quantumcumque enim coniecturae tuae sint verisimillimae, non sunt tibi tamen plusquam coniecturae." (P. Gassendi, *Opera omnia, VI*, p.54a.)

86 Olivier Bloch in his work *La philosophie de Gassendi*, pp.80-109, has described Gassendi's scepticism as a "constant" in his philosophy. In this chapter I have presented a picture of Gassendi as being rather selective in his scepticism, and I have argued that his scepticism tended to wax and wane. It does not seem possible to describe Gassendi's attitude to Galileo's Copernicanism as being a sceptical one before 1634, while his attitude became markedly sceptical after that date.

87 Sextus Empiricus, *Outlines of Pyrrhonism* (Loeb Classical Library Edition), I,1.

88 "Quippe quotiescumque aliquid causam habere multiplicem potest, variisque modis contingere, tum causas modosque scepticorum more inter se opponit." (P. Gassendi, *Opera omnia, I*, pp.13b-14a.)

89 Gassendi's translation reads:"Quod si quis unum quidem modum retineat, alium vero, tametsi aeque apparentibus consonum, repudiet, is perspicue ab omni vera de rebus naturalibus philosophandi ratione deflectit, delabiturque ad fabulas." (P. Gassendi, *Opera omnia, I*, p.14a.) This is a good translation of the original in Diogenes Laertius: "ὅταν δέ τις τὸ μὲν ἀπολίπῃ, τὸ δὲ ἐκβάλῃ ὁμοίως τρόπον σύμφωνον ὃν τῷ φαινομένῳ, δῆλον ὅτι καὶ ἐκ παντὸς ἐκπίπτει φυσιολογήματος, ἐπὶ δὲ τὸν μῦθον καταρρᾷ" D. Laertius, *De clarorum philosophorum vitis, dogmatibus et apothegmatibus libri decem, X* (1973, G. Arrighetti (Ed.), *Epicuro opere*, Turin), 10.87.

90 P. Gassendi, *Opera omnia, I*, p.14a; D. Laertius, *De clarorum philosophorum vitis*, 1,34.4; 2,38.6, 50.9; 4,127.6; 1,21.9; 2,78.6, 80.9; 3, 87.11, 88.10, 90.2, 93.3, 94.6, *etc.*

91 MS Carpentras 1832, f.236r.

92  P. Gassendi, *Opera omnia*, *I*, p.13b.

93  Cf. J.M. Rist: 1972, *Epicurus. An introduction*, Cambridge University Press, Cambridge, p.17.

94  *Ibid.*, pp.32-37. Mental perception was an inner sensation for Epicurus, since the mind was understood as being moved in the same way as the other senses.

95  "Videlicet expensis variis de mundi extremo opinionibus, pervidet quidem omneis non-nulla probabilitate fulciri, at nullam esse quae persuadeatur indubitatis rationibus; atque idcirco sua unicuique verisimilitudine relicta, assensum modeste continere maluit, quam de re posita tam procul, tamque incomperta oculis mortalium quicquam fidenter asseverare." (P. Gassendi, *Opera omnia*, *I*, p.152a (cf. MS Tours 709, f.444).)

96  "Simili modo, qui contendet illud esse immobile, quomodo evincet ipsum non moveri, ac potissimum cum videamus quae corpora in illo sunt, ab ortu in occasum ferri? Et qui contendit mobile esse, quomodo evincet non esse immobile; ac potissimum cum, tametsi astra appareant moveri in occasum, tam id possit contingere translatione nostri in ortum, quam apparet nobis e nave moveri portum versus navim; quamvis certum sit portum quiescere, et navim versus ipsum moveri?" (P. Gassendi, *Opera omnia*, *I*, p.152a (cf. MS Tours 709, f.444).) Cf. also P. Gassendi, *Opera omnia*, *I*, p.513a-b (cf. MS Tours 710, f.588r-v), *I*. p.583a (cf. MS Tours 7120, f.612v). Gassendi did not attribute the same weight to Galileo's arguments for the Copernican system as he had done previously.

97  See the decree in Galileo Galilei, *Opere*, *XIX*, pp.402-406.

98  "... tametsi opinio de motu terrae probari videatur quibusdam verisimilibus argumentis, nulla est tamen demonstratio quae illam esse veram convincat; adeo ut exprobrari non possit opinioni oppositae quod demonstrationibus careat, certitudineque ab ipso vincatur." (P. Gassendi, *Opera omnia*, *I*, p.630a (MS Tours 710, f.653v).)

99  P. Gassendi: 1647, *Institutio astronomica iuxta hypotheseis tam veterum quam Copernici et Tychonis Brahei ...*, L. de Heuqueville, Paris.

100 "Adeo proinde, ut quibus tueri Coperniceam hypothesis religio est, Braheana praesto occurrat, quae verisimillima omnium sit." (P. Gassendi, *Opera omnia*, *I*, p.630a.)

101 "Denique solemne iam esse, ut cum hypothesis Ptolemaica, et qua praesertim constat ex solidis orbibus, Mercuriumque ac Venerem infra Solem detinet, defendi commode non possit; Copernicea vero ob motum Terrae attributum, qui repugnans Sacrae Scripturae videatur, soleat refugi, neque ulla alia supersit quae salvandis phaenomenis aeque ac Tychonica idonea sit; ideo ipsa sit quam amplecti passim ac tueri iuvet." (P. Gassendi, *Opera omnia, I*, p.615a.)

102 P. Gassendi: 1654, *Tychonis Brahei, vita* ..., cf. P. Gassendi, *Opera omnia, V*, pp.363-496.

103 I cannot trace the comparison in Kepler's published works.

104 P. Gassendi, *Opera omnia, V*, p.384.

105 As quoted from L. Sarsi (=O. Grassi), in S. Drake and C.D. O'Malley (Eds), *The controversy on the comets*, p.71.

## Chapter 3

1   Cf. C-A. Fusil: 1926, "Montaigne et Lucrèce", in *Revue du seizième siècle, 13*, pp.256-281.

2   Cf. C.-A. Fusil: 1928, "La renaissance de Lucrèce au XVIe siècle", in *Revue du seizième siècle, 15*, pp.134-150.

3   Gassendi indicated the date of completion of the work in letters to Peiresc written 1.1.1634 and 13.1.1634; cf. *Lettres de Peiresc, IV*, pp.406, 414-415.

4   P. Gassendi, *De vita et moribus Epicuri libri octo*, G. Barbier, Lyon, 1647.

5   Gassendi's Epicurean ethics has recently been studied by Louise Sarasohn; cf. L.T. Sarasohn: 1979, *The influence of Epicurean philosophy on seventeenth century ethical and political thought: the moral philosophy of Pierre Gassendi* (Ph.D. dissertation presented to the University of California); 1982, "The ethical and political philosophy of Pierre Gassendi", in *Journal of the history of philosophy, 20*, pp.239-260; 1985, "Motion and morality: Pierre

Gassendi, Thomas Hobbes and the mechanical world-view", in *Journal of the history of ideas*, *46*, pp.363-379.

6      "Restituitur Epicurus in philosophorum chorum." (P. Gassendi, *Opera omnia*, Bk. VII, ch. 7.)

7      "Cum Epicurus infamis fuisset habitus tota illa pene saeculorum serie, qua literae bonae sepultae jacuerunt, vix tamen libros humaniores, pulvere excusso, rediisse in manus ante duo fere saecula, quam omnes pene eruditi symbolum pro eo contulerunt." (P. Gassendi, *Opera omnia*, *V*, p.224a.) Gassendi's words here have a remarkably similar ring to the following passage from the writings of Louis Le Roy, professor of Greek at the Collège Royal, Paris, from 1572: "During the reign of Tamberlan the restoration of [ancient] languages and all the disciplines commenced ... [Petrarch] opened the closed rooms of the libraries and cleared off the dust and filth that had gathered on the good books of ancient authors." ("Durant le règne de Tamberlan commença la restitution des langues et de toutes disciplines ...[Petrarche] ouvrant les librairies pieca fermées, et ostant la pouldre et ordure de dessus les bons livres des autheurs anciens." (French version as quoted in D.P. Walker: 1972, *The ancient theology: studies in Christian Platonism from the fifteenth to the eighteenth century*, London, p.77, note 3.)

8      F. Filelfo: 1480, *Epistolae Francisci Philelphi*, Venice, Bk. 8, ch. 7., and F. Filelfo: 1552, *De morali disciplina libri quinque* ..., Venice, opening paragraph.

9      Alexander ab Alexandro, 1532, *Genialium dierum libri sex* ..., Paris, Bk. III, ch. 11;

10     Ludovicus Caelius Richerius, Rhodiginus, *Lectionum antiquarum, libri XXX*, Basle, Bk. XIII, ch. 25.

11     Raphael Maffejus of Volterra, R. Volaterrani: 1506, *Commentariorum urbanorum*, Rome, Bk. XV.

12     Gianfrancesco Pico della Mirandola. G.-F. Pico della Mirandola: 1520, *Examen vanitatis doctrinae gentium, et veritatis Christianae disciplinae distinctum in libris sex, quorum tres omnem philosophorum sectam universim, reliqui Aristoteleam et Aristotelis armis particulatim impugnant, ubicumque autem Christiana et asseritur, et celebratur disciplina*, Mirandola, 1520, Bk. I, ch. 2.

13     Andreas Arnaudus: 1609, *Ioci (Epistolae, etc.)* ..., Paris, pp.215ff.

14 Marcellus Palingenii stellati: 1552, *Zodiacus vitae, hoc est de hominis vita, studio ac moribus optime instituendis libri XII* ..., Basileae; Gassendi quoted from the section of the poem that concerned Gemini.

15 Letter of 25.4.1626 in *Lettres de Peiresc, IV*, pp.178-181.

16 "Ce à quoy je m'occupe maintenant, c'est de traduire le Xe livre de Laërce qui est tout d'Epicure rempli de tant de [fautes] qu' [il n'] est pas presque recognoissable en tous les lieux les plus importants. J'ay devant moy diverses traductions, notes et manuscripts et conferant le tout avec la petite cognoissance que j'ay de la philosophie de cet homme, je tasche d'en faire une traduction à ma mode, et que je puisse debiter quand j'employeray l'authorité de Laërce." (Letter of Gassendi to Peiresc of 11.9.1629, in *Lettres de Peiresc, IV*, pp.217-218.)

17 1563, *Titi Lucretii Cari. De rerum natura libri sex. A Dionysio Lambino ... locis innumerabilibus ex auctoritate quinque codicum manu scriptorum emendati, atque in antiquum ac nativum statum fere restituti, et praeterea brevibus, et perquam utilibus commentariis illustrati*, Parisiis et Lugduni.

18 Cf. C.-A. Fusil (1926), p.141; P. de Villey: 1933, *Les sources et l'évolution des essais de Montaigne*, 2 vols., Fondation Thiers, Paris, *I*, p.188; S.J. Dick: 1982, *Plurality of worlds. The origins of the extraterrestrial life debate from Democritus to Kant*, Cambridge University Press, p.46.

19 I am grateful to Dr. Harold W. Jones of the University of Bradford for this piece of information.

20 Cf. letter of Gassendi to Peiresc of 28.2.1633 in *Lettres de Peiresc, IV*, p.402; also letter of Gassendi to Peiresc of 13.1.1634, *idem*, pp.414-415.

21 "Nosti iam quandam a me collocatam Epicuro operam, illam interdum retexere soleo, dum exploro et alia. Meditor nempe, et comparo celebriora quaedam placita antiquorum philosophorum; ac omneis cum suspiciam, singulorum opiniones sic enitor expendere, ut si in cuiusvis transfunderes genium ..." (Letter of Gassendi to Jacob Golius, Professor of Leyden, of 8.3.1630, in P. Gassendi, *Opera omnia, VI*, p.32b).

22 MS Tours 709, Bks XVIII, XVIX; P. Gassendi, *Opera omnia*, *I*, pp.338a–457b. Cf. *infra* pp.58–59.

23 Cf. *infra*, *e.g.*, pp.118ff.

24 Gassendi may thus be cited in support of an affirmative reply to the question in the title of the article by P. Barker and B.R. Goldstein: 1984, "Is seventeenth-century physics indebted to the Stoics?" in *Centaurus*, *27*, pp.148–164.

25 F. Luillier was a public figure, an Administrator of Public Finances (Mitre des Comptes), and a member of the Parlement of Metz. He was a friend and admirer of scholars and a frequenter of scholarly academies in Paris. Gassendi and Luillier became firm friends; cf. B. Rochot (Ed.): 1944, *Pierre Gassendi, lettres familières à François Luillier pendant l'hiver 1632–1633*, J. Vrin, Paris.

26 P. Gassendi, *Opera omnia*, *V*, p.171.

27 "Prisci Patres invicti fuere maxime adversus Aristotelem eiusque philosophiam, sectamque exosam habuerunt; ubi vero etiam philosophi fuere qui dedere nomen sacrae fidei, coepere graviores errores seponi, et quod superest, philosophia ita religioni fuit accommodata, ut illi non amplius suspecta, sed quasi ancillans subserviensque evaserit. Quod dico non modo ob Aristoteleam, quae publice etiam foret praelegi, verum etiam ob caeteras, Stoicam quoque ac Epicuream, quarum nulla est quae frugi plurima non contineat, ac adscisci quoque, seclusis confutatisque erroribus, perinde ac Aristotelea, cuius errores oppido graves reiciuntur, non valeat; ut nos certe in hoc negotio affecti comparatique simus, testatum fecimus abunde cum praefati in vitam moresque Epicuri sumus." (P. Gassendi, *Opera omnia*, *VI*, p.5a.)

28 Letter of Gassendi to Galileo of 20.7.1625 (P. Gassendi, *Opera omnia*, *VI*, p.5a).

29 P. Gassendi, *Opera omnia*, *III*, p.102.

30 "Et stellis fixis et Soli comparatur quies. Terrae, vero, quasi uni ex planetis, conciliatur motus." (P. Gassendi, *Opera omnia*, *III*, p.102.)

31 "You will readily see that I have been dreaming a little on this subject if you would be so good as to read the preface of the book which I am sending you. There is a brief passage there in which I promise to treat of these questions in Book IV." "Somniasse quippe me aliquid circa hoc argumentum pervidebis facile, si digneris forte legere quod tribus

dumtaxat verbis in praefatione libelli ad te missi polliceor me quarto libro tractaturum." (Letter of Gassendi to Galileo of 20.7.1625, in P. Gassendi, *Opera omnia*, *VI*, p.4b.)

32   Cf. *supra*, pp.35-36.

33   Cf. Gassendi's letter to Jacob Golius, a scholar who specialised in Arabic astronomy, 8.3.1630 (P. Gassendi, *Opera omnia*, *VI*, p.32b). Furthermore, Gassendi sent an outline of his Epicurean project to Gerard Voss of Leyden soon after returning from his journey, evidently as a sequel to Gassendi's discussions with the scholars of Leyden; cf. the letter of Gassendi to Voss of 14.9.1629 (P. Gassendi, *Opera omnia*, *VI*, p.25).

34   Cf. *supra*, p.35.

35   Cf. J.A. Schuster: 1977, *Descartes and the scientific revolution 1618-1634. An interpretation*, (Ph.D. dissertation presented to the faculty of Princeton University), pp.23, 572ff.

36   Cf. *supra*, pp.36-37.

37   For evidence of the extraordinary influence of Beeckman on Descartes in the latter's early philosophical development, cf. C. Adam and P. Tannery (Eds.): 1897-1913, *Oeuvres de Descartes*, 12 vols., *X*, pp.162-163.

38   "Quae omnia et probavit et cum gaudio et admiratione visus est audire." (C. de Waard (Ed.): 1939, *Journal tenu par Isaac Beeckman de 1604 à 1634* ..., 4 vols., La Haye, *I*, p.123.)

39   "Le meilleur philosophe que j'aye encore recontré." (Letter of Gassendi to Peiresc of 21.7.1629 (Lettres de Peiresc, *IV*, p.201). There seems to be insufficient evidence to allow a very precise estimate of the influence of Beeckman on Gassendi. It is certainly not too much to say that Gassendi was greatly encouraged in his project to restore Epicureanism by his visit to Beeckman; cf. B. Rochot: 1952, "Beeckman, Gassendi et le principe d'inertie", in *Archives internationales d'historie des sciences*, 5, pp.228-229.

40   Galileo Galilei, *Opere*, *XIX*, pp.402-407.

41   Letter of Gassendi to Galileo of 17.11.1636 (P. Gassendi, *Opera omnia*, *VI*, p.92a).

42   Cf. *e.g.*, the introduction which Dominic Soto wrote to his commentary
     on the *Physics* of Aristotle: 1582, *R.P.D. Soto ... super octo libros*
     *physicorum Aristotelis commentaria*, 3a editio, Salamanca.

43   "Ea mihi mens est, ut quoties non modo ad graviora illa capita
     pervenero, sed etiam quoties quidpiam occurret quod videri possit vel
     quam minimum fidei sacrae dissentaneum in Epicuram nervos
     contendam ac eius sententiam quam maximo semper rationis vigore
     potero convellam." (P. Gassendi, *Opera omnia, V*, p.171.)

44   P. Gassendi, *Opera omnia, I*, pp.266a-279b, 280b, 375a, 472a-486b;
     Cf. *III*, p.466.

45   For the doctrines of Aristotle (which are often less than faithfully
     represented in the Aristotelian manuals), see: Aristotle, *Physics*
     194b.9-10 and *Metaphysics* 1029a.24-25 (form); *On generation and*
     *corruption* 330a30 - 331b.39 (generation); *Categories* 8b.25 - 11a.19,
     and *Metaphysics* 1020a.33 - 1020b.25 (qualities). Cf. Ivor Leclerc:
     1972, *The nature of physical existence*, Allen and Unwin, London,
     pp.114-121; A. Mansion: 1946, *Introduction à la physique*
     *Aristotélicienne*, 2me éd., Institut Supérieur de Philosophie, Louvain,
     pp.240-251. The difference between the doctrines of Aristotle and
     those of Gassendi on these subjects are discussed in this and the next
     chapter.

46   "Videri posse atomos pro materiali rerum principio, primave materia
     admitte." (P. Gassendi, *Opera omnia, I*, p.279b.)

47   P. Gassendi, *Opera omnia, I*, p.279b.

48   P. Gassendi, *Opera omnia, I*, pp.229a-282b, especially pp.232a-b,
     259b. Gassendi's chief sources for the doctrine of Epicurus were
     Diogenes Laertius, *De clarorum philosophorum vitis, dogmatibus et*
     *apothegmatibus libri decem, X* (G. Arrighetti (Ed.): 1973, *Epicuro*
     *opere*, G. Einaudi, Turin), 38-39, and Lucretius, *De rerum natura, I*,
     215-264. For Aristotle's doctrine, cf. especially Aristotle *Physics*,
     189b30 -191a23. It is to be noted that Gassendi was not attempting to
     argue that the Aristotelian and Epicurean doctrines of matter were
     equivalent as such: he was rather preparing the ground for his
     assertion that Epicureanism was an adequate substitution for
     Aristotelianism because the former explained in its (better) way what
     the latter attempted to explain. It would appear, therefore, that
     Gassendi did not deserve the criticism of R. Dugas:
           "Why can [the] existence [of atoms] be asserted? First of all,
        because only atoms can satisfy the conditions exacted by Aristotle

of an incorruptible prime matter - a very poor argument indeed for one who did not admit any authority in philosophy." (R. Dugas: 1958, *Mechanics in the seventeenth century. From the scholastic antecedents to classical thought*, (Transl, F. Jacquot), Editions du Griffon, Neuchatel, p.104.

Dugas here accuses Gassendi of feeling obliged to answer a problem posed by Aristotle out of respect for Aristotle's authority. But it is clear that Gassendi considered that there was a need for prime matter, or a permanent substratum through all change, independently of Aristotle's teaching.

49 P. Gassendi, *Opera omnia, I*, pp.232b-234a; cf. MS Tours 709, f.216r-v. Cf. the doctrine of Epicurus in Diogenes Laertius, *De clarorum philosophorum vitis*, 38, and in Lucretius, *De rerum natura, I*, 150.

50 P. Gassendi, *Opera omnia, I*, p.281b; cf. MS Tours 709, f.245v. Epicurus did indeed teach a doctrine of eternal, subsistent matter according to Diogenes Laertius (*De clarorum philosophorum vitis*, 39) and Lucretius (*De rerum natura, I*, 215-219). It was less correct to say that Aristotle taught such a doctrine. Gassendi, like seventeenth-century philosophers generally, it seems (cf. Ivor Leclerc, *The nature of physical existence*, pp.115-117), interpreted Aristotle's concept of matter as a concept of substance.

51 P. Gassendi, *Opera omnia, I*, pp.280a-281b.

52 *Ibid., I*, pp.279a-280b.

53 "Quatenus ut omnia conservat, ita coagit rebus omnibus." (*Ibid., I*, p.280a; cf.*III*, pp.466a-467b.) One finds very similar doctrine in the *Principia philosophica* of Descartes; cf. *Oeuvres de Descartes, IX*, par.83; cf. also Margaret J. Osler: 1979, "Descartes and Charleton on nature and God", in *Journal of the history of ideas, 40*, pp.445-456.

54 P. Gassendi, *Opera omnia, I*, p.282b; Gassendi's allusion was to the third section of the *Pars physica*, idem., *II*, pp. 193-658.

55 Cf. *infra*, pp.94-95; P. Gassendi, *Opera omnia, II*, pp.437bff.

56 P. Gassendi, *Opera omnia, II*, pp.840a-847a; cf. L.T. Sarasohn: 1982, "The ethical and political philosophy of Pierre Gassendi", in *Journal of the history of philosophy, 20*, pp.239-260, also 1985, "Motion and morality: Pierre Gassendi, Thomas Hobbes and the mechanical world-view", in *Journal of the history of ideas*, 1985, *46*, pp.363-379. Cf.

also, Leopold Damrosch, Jr.: 1979, "Hobbes as Reformation theologian: implications of the free-will controversy", in *Journal of the history of ideas*, *40*, pp.339-353.

57  P. Gassendi: 1646, *De proportione qua gravia accidentia accelerantur epistolae tres, quibus ad totidem epistolas R. P. Petri Cazraei ... respondetur*, L. de Heuqueville, Paris, republished in P. Gassendi, *Opera omnia*, *III*, pp.564-650.

58  "Non esse atomorum minus quam Aristoteleae materiae tolerabilem in religione positionem" (P. Gassendi, *Opera omnia*, *III*, p.636a.)

59  "A quality can be defined generically as a mode of a substance." "Potest quidem qualitas universe definiri modus sese habendi substantiae." (*Idem*, *I*, p.372b; cf. MS Tours 709, f.335r.) Gassendi's chief sources for the doctrine of Epicurus on qualities were Diogenes Laertius, (*De clarorum philosophorum vitis*, 54-56), and Lucretius (*De rerum natura*, *II*, 333-477, 730-841).

60  "[A quality is] the condition and state of the commingled principles." "Sive conditionem ac statum quo principia inter se commista se habent." (P. Gassendi, *Opera omnia*, *I*, p.372b.) For the Stoics, physical qualities were generated by the *pneuma*, the all-pervading substratum, or principle; cf. Plutarch, *De Stoicorum repugnantiis* (Loeb classical library edition), 1054b; also S. Sambursky: 1959, *Physics of the Stoics*, Routledge and Kegan Paul, London, pp.1,7.

61  "[A quality is] that in virtue of which a concrete thing is said to be of such a kind." "Omne id a quo res concretae denominantur quales." (P. Gassendi, *Opera omnia*, *I*, p.372b.) Cf. Aristotle, *Categories*, 8b25. Gassendi has here given a hybrid definition, part Aristotelian and part Epicurean: note the intrusion of the Epicurean term "res concretae". Gassendi removed the term when he prepared the *Syntagma* version.

62  Cf. *Opera omnia*, *I*, p.372b. Gassendi appears to have taken this definition from the scholastic text-book of Eustache de Saint-Paul, a Parisian teacher whom both Gassendi and Descartes used as a reference work for Aristotelian doctrine. The text-book was 1609, *Summa philosophiae quadripartita: de rebus dialecticis, moralibus, physicis et metaphysicis, authore Fr Eustachio a Sancto Paulo ...*, C. Chastellain, Paris. The definition of quality given by Eustache was: "A quality ... is described by Aristotle as that by which things are named as to what kind of things they are." "Qualitas ... describitur ab Aristotele, a qua res denominantur quales." (*Idem*, p.117.) Gassendi's use of Eustache's text is well documented by Bernard Rochot in his

edition of the *Exercitationes* (Bernard Rochot (Ed.): 1959, *Pierre Gassendi. Dissertations en forme de paradoxes contre les Aristotéliciens* ..., J. Vrin, Paris). Descartes, for his part, wrote a letter to Mersenne praising Eustache's text for being the best of its kind (letter of Descartes to Mersenne of 11.11.1640, in F. Alquié (Ed.): 1963-1967, *Descartes. Oeuvres philosophiques*, 2 vols.).

63  P. Gassendi, *Opera omnia, I*, p.373a. Cf. Aristotle, *Categories* 1b-2a, where 'quality' is listed as a category, and Aristotle, *Topics* 102a-103b, where 'accident' is listed as one of the predicables. These two doctrines were not altogether mutually consistent. So, Gassendi had to force Aristotle's meaning considerably to present accidents and qualities as one and the same in Aristotle.

64  *Idem, I*, p.373a-b. Scholars agree that Aristotle implied that there was some flexibility in his theory of categories, such that it was possible to place some items in more than one category. It was the medieval scholastics, it is claimed, who treated Aristotle's theory as final, exhaustive and inflexible. (See G.E.M. Anscombe and P.T. Geach: 1973, *Three philosophers*, Basil Blackwell, Oxford, pp.14-19.) Gassendi had declared his preference for the Nominalist interpretation of Aristotelianism in the *Exercitationes* (P. Gassendi, *Opera omnia, III*. p.165), and this fact seems relevant, for the Nominalists viewed the categories as logical constructs rather than real divisions in the natural world. This I take to be implied in the following description of the theory of William of Ockham: "Only substance and form are real, together constituting actual being; all the other categories are the attributes of individual being neither inhering in being nor standing for independent essences of things or forms, but merely describing the different ways in which individual things can be said to exist ..." (Gordon Leff: 1975, *William of Ockham. The metamorphosis of scholastic discourse*, Manchester University Press, Manchester, p.562.)

65  P. Gassendi, *Opera omnia, I*, p.373a; cf. MS Tours 709, ff.278v, 335v.

66  *Idem, I*, pp.374a-375a; MS Tours 709, ff.339v-340v.

67  "Maneat, proinde, quicquid spectatur in corporeis hisce, ac physicis rebus (ipsa anima rationali, quae in homine est, excepta) aut esse substantiam, quae eadem sit materia, et corpus, materialiumve, et corporeorum principiorum aggeries; aut esse qualitatem, quae sit accidens, modusve se habendi eiusdem." (P. Gassendi, *Opera omnia, I*, p.373b; the passage is not found in MS Tours 709.)

68   "Maneat, inquam, et vel ipso quidem Aristotele non abnuente, cum solam substantiam esse proprie ens censuit, accidens autem voluit non tam ens esse, quam entis ens, seu modum se habendi entis." (P. Gassendi, *Operas omnia*, *I*, p.373b; MS Tours 709, f.336v.) Cf. Aristotle, *Metaphysics* 1025a.14-15, 31-33.

69   "De motu et mutatione rerum" (P. Gassendi, *Opera omnia*, *I*, pp.338a-371b).

70   "Quia mutationes omnes terminantur ad qualitates, et insequens liber instituendum est de ipsis qualitatibus." (*Idem*, *I*, p.371b; MS Tours 709, f.334v.)

71   *Idem*, *I*, 338b; MS Tours 709, ff.298v, 300r. Gassendi here gave an incorrect account of Aristotle's doctrine: Aristotle attributed a preferential status to local motion (cf. Aristotle, *Physics* 208a32, 260b22), but he did not reduce all change to local motion as Gassendi claimed. Cf. Leclerc, *The nature of physical existence*, p.112.

72   Cf. Aristotle, *Physics* 225a34; *Metaphysics* 1069b 9-13.

73   P. Gassendi, *Opera omnia*, *I*. pp.362b-364a, a re-written version of MS Tours 709, ff.289v0301v.

74   MS Tours 709, Bk. XIX.

75   P. Gassendi, *Opera omnia*, *I*, pp.375a-457b.

76   Aristotle, *Meteorologica* 378b10 - 390b21.

77   Cf. *e.g.*, P. Gassendi, *Opera omnia*, *I*, p.375a. It should be noted that Gassendi was not consistent in his terminology, or in his explanation of qualities. He consistently treated a number of qualities or accidents as though they were substances, while still referring to them as qualities. (This was particularly the case with the Aristotelian primary qualities, hot and cold, wet and dry.) Thus Gassendi spoke of atoms of heat, cold, fire, light, and also of visible species atoms as being qualities (P. Gassendi, *Opera omnia*, *I*, 401b, *etc.*). He spoke of "real and positive" qualities, by which he meant *active* qualities, as when he asked whether cold is such a quality or whether it is a mere privation of heat, and concluded that it is a real and positive quality, just like heat and "the others" are (*idem*, *I*, 401b; MS Tours 709, f.376v). For Aristotle, to be active was a prerogative of a substance, the source of action being attributed to the substantial form. What is noteworthy about such terminological inconsistency on Gassendi's part is not so

much that he should explain cold and heat in atomist terms, but that he should show no concern about continuing to refer to them as qualities or modes of substances when he understood them as substances in their own right.

78    Cf. *supra*, p.55. Aristotle could at most be said to have upheld a theory of eternal matter in the sense that pure potentiality can be eternal: the question of the existence of eternal, substantial, corporeal matter would seem not to have been a concern for Aristotle.

79    P. Gassendi, *Opera omnia*, *I*, p.162aff. The work of Christianising Aristotelian philosophy in the Middle Ages had required correction of this doctrine; cf. Thomas Aquinas, *Summa theologiae* (Blackfriars edition), 1a, q.46, a. 1,2,3. Cf. Anton Herman Chroust: 1978, "Aristotle's doctrine of the uncreatedness and indestructibility of the universe", in *New scholasticism*, *52*, pp.268-279, for a discussion of the influence of Aristotle's *On philosophy*, a work which now exists only as a fragment but which reinforces the view of Aristotle as the principal and most influential advocate among the ancient philosophers of the eternity of the universe or world.

80    P. Gassendi, *Opera omnia*, *I*, p.162b; MS Tours 709, ff.456rff. Gassendi referred to Aristotle, *Physics* 251aff., also to a place in the *Metaphysics* which is at least difficult to identify, to the first chapters of Aristotle, *De mundo* and *De caelo*, and to the second chapter of Aristotle, *De generatione et corruptione*. Since Aristotle's "world" encompassed both the heavens and the earth (cf. Aristotle, *De mundo* 391b.9-19); Gassendi's use of the term was equivocal in this whole discussion. He found the Epicurean doctrine especially in Lucretius, *Opera omnia*, *V*, 65ff.

81    P. Gassendi, *Opera omnia*, *I*, p.163a.

82    *Idem*, *I*, p.170b. Cf. Chroust (1978), p.268.

83    P. Gassendi, *Opera omnia*, *I*, p.171b; MS Tours 709, f.492r. Lucretius, *De rerum natura*, *V*, 65ff.

84    "Docent igitur potius probatiores interpretes non interiturum in nihilum mundum, sed renovatum solum iri, idque non secundum substantiam, sed secundum qualitates. Hoc est, eandem et caelorum et elementorum remansuram substantiam, sed repurgatam ab omni sorde, et proprietatibus illustriorem factam. Videlicet, cum lunae splendor futurus sit qualis iam est solis, et qui nunc est solis tum futurus sit

septuplo praeclarior." (P. Gassendi, *Opera omnia*, *I*, p.178b; MS Tours 709, f.500v.)

L'abbé Cotin, also an Epicurean, may have been one of these "more approved authors". In 1646, in his work, he linked the question of the non-annihilation of matter with the question of the existence of an All-Wise Providence. Cf. Henri Busson: 1933, *La pensée religieuse française de Charron à Pascal*, J. Vrin, Paris, p.77.

Gassendi explained that he linked the Christian doctrine as interpreted by the more approved authors with the Epicurean doctrine of indestructible atoms eternally capable of recombining.

85   P. Gassendi, *Opera omnia*, *I*, pp.139a-162a; cf. MS Tours 709, ff.443r-456v.

86   *Idem, I*, pp.163aff.; MS Tours 709, ff.464vff. Cf. Lucretius, *De rerum natura*, *V*, 324-331.

87   Aristotle, *Physics* 212a.20; cf. P. Gassendi, *Opera omnia*, *I*, pp.217a 180a.

88   This was a common (Aristotelian) view, Gassendi observed; P. Gassendi, *Opera omnia*, *I*, p.182a.

89   *Idem, I*, 185b; MS Tours 709, ff.193rff.

90   *Idem, I*, pp.216b-220a.

91   Hero of Alexandria (Bennet Woodcroft, Ed.): 1851, *The pneumatics of Hero of Alexandria*, 1971 Facsilile edition, Macdonald and Co., London.

92   Cf. Marie Boas: 1949, "Hero's *Pneumatica*. A study of its transmission and influence", in *Isis*, *40*, pp.38-48.

93   Cf. P. Gassendi, *Opera omnia*, *I*, pp.192b-193a, 197a-b, *etc.*; Hero of Alexandria, *The pneumatics* (Bennett Woodcroft, Ed.), p.2.

94   P. Gassendi, *Opera omnia*, *I*, pp.198ff. Such machines, however, were widely discussed throughout the middle ages, so it is not necessarily a sign of dependence on Hero that Gassendi should also discuss them. Cf. Edward Grant: 1981, *Much ado about nothing. Theories of space and vacuum from the middle ages to the scientific revolution*, Cambridge University Press, Cambridge, pp.80-86.

95   *Idem, I*, p.187a.

96  Cf. Boas, (1949), p.47.

97  MS Tours 709, Bk. XIV, ch. 2; cf. Lucretius, *De rerum natura*, *I*, 329 - 397.

98  "Following Aristotle, the void can be considered in two ways ..." "Etenim hocce inane potest ex Aristotele duobus modis considerari ..." (MS Tours 709, f.194r.)

99  P. Gassendi, *Opera omnia*, pp.196b-203a.

100 MS Tours 709, ff.200r-v. Galileo had accepted the same prinple in the *Discorsi* (G. Galileo: 1638, *Discorsi e dimostrazioni matematiche intorno a due nuove scienze attenenti alla mecanica e i movimenti locali*, Elseviri, Leiden, pp.16-20), which was published in the year following Gassendi's writing of the MS Tours 709 version of his treatise on space.

101 MS Tours 709, f.200r.

102 *Idem*, f.200v.

103 P. Gassendi, *Opera omnia*, *I*, p.197a-b.

104 MS Tours 709, f.199v.

105 P. Gassendi, *Opera omnia*, *I*, pp.197b-202b.

106 *Idem, I*, pp.203b-216b.

107 *Idem, I*, p.197b.

108 MS Tours 709, ff.209vff. Cf. also P. Gassendi, *Opera omnia*, *I*, pp.220a-228b, *III*, pp.131b, 140a, 144b. For Aristotle, place was an accident of bodies (cf. *supra*, p. 11 of Ch 3); time also was ultimately dependent on bodies, being the measure of change (Aristotle, *Physics* 218b21-220a26). Gassendi proclaimed place and space to be identical and to be an independent reality with its own incorporeal dimensions (P. Gassendi, *Opera omnia*, *I*, pp.216b-220a; cf. MS Tours 709,f.204r), while time became likewise an independent reality measureable in itself.

109 " κενὸν καὶ χώραν καὶ ἀναφῆ φύσιν ", "Void or place or intactile nature". (Diogenes Laertius, *De clarorum philosophorum vitis*, 40.1); cf. also

Sextus Empiricus, *Adversus physicos* (Loeb classical library edition), II.2; MS Tours 709, f.193v; P. Gassendi, *Opera omnia, I,* pp.221bff.

110 Sextus Empiricus, *Adversus physicos,* II.219; Diogenes Laertius, *De clarorum philosophorum vitis,* 72.1 - 73.6; P. Gassendi, *Opera omnia, I,* p.221b.

111 Cf. N.R. Hanson: 1958, *Patterns of discovery,* Cambridge University Press, Cambridge, pp.31-49.

112 The date attributed to the treatise by Pintard (R. Pintard: 1943, *La Mothe le Vayer, Gassendi - Guy Patin. Etudes de bibliographie et de critique suivie de textes inédits de Guy Patin,* Boivin, Paris, Ch.3).

113 "Denique, ut locus dimensiones habet permanenteis, quibus corporum longitudo, latitudo ac profunditas congruat: sic tempus habet successivas quibus corporum motus adaequatur." (MS Tours 709, f.210v; P. Gassendi, *Opera omnia, I,* p.224b.)

114 "Atque ex his tandem non videtur tempus esse aliquid a motu dependens, aut illi posterius; sed motu solum indicari, ut mensuratum a mensura." (MS Tours 709, f.211r; P. Gassendi, *Opera omnia, I,* p.225a.)

115 P. Gassendi: 1642, *De motu impresso a motore translato epistolae duae, in quibus aliquot praecipuae, tum de motu universe, tum speciatim de motu terrae attributo, difficultates explicantur,* L. de Heuqueville, Paris, in P. Gassendi, *Opera omnia, III,* pp.478-563.

116 Cf. J.T. Clark: 1963, "Pierre Gassendi and the physics of Galileo", in *Isis, 54,* pp.352-370.

117 Cf. N.R. Hanson, *Patterns of discovery,* pp.31-49.

118 Aristotle, *De caelo* 279a12-13; cf. P. Gassendi, *Opera omnia, I,* pp.141b-142a, 186a.

119 Aristotle, *De caelo* 276a18 - 276b22. Cf. Edward Grant: 1969, "Medieval and seventeenth-century conceptions of an infinite void space beyond the cosmos", in *Isis, 60,* pp.39-60, especially p.39; also Edward Grant, *Much ado about nothing,* pp.105ff.

120 Diogenes Laertius, *De clarorum philosophorum vitis,* 41.10ff; Lucretius, *De rerum natura, I,* 951ff; *II,* 1052-1066. Cf. G.S. Kirk and J.E. Raven: 1957, *The Presocratic philosophers. A critical history with*

*a selection of texts*, Cambridge University Press, Cambridge, pp.409-412; Steven J. Dick: 1982, *Plurality of worlds. The origins of the extraterrestrial life debate from Democritus to Kant*, Cambridge University Press, Cambridge, pp.6-19.

121 Cf. the account given by Simplicius in his commentary on Aristotle's *De Caelo*: 1540, *Simplicii ... commentaria in quatuor libros de celo Aristotelis Guillermo Morbeto interprete*, H. Scotum, Venice, f.44v, Ch. 2, as cited in Edward Grant (1969), p.41 note 13; the theory was also repeatedly mentioned in the writings of Chrysippus according to Plutarch, cf. Plutarch, *Moralia* (Loeb classical library edition), *XIII*. "De Stoicorum repugnantiis", 1054.44. Stoic cosmology was widely adopted in the late sixteenth and early seventeenth centuries through the influence of Francesco Patrizi; cf. F. Patrizi: 1587, *Philosophiae de rerum natura libri duo ... alter de spacio physico, alter de spacio mathematico*, Ferrara; F. Patrizi: 1591, *Nova de universis philosophia in qua aristotelica methodo, non per motum, sed per lucem et lumina, ad primam causam ascenditur, deinde propria Patricii methodo, tota in contemplationem venit divinitas; postremo methodo platonica, rerum universitas, a conditore Deo deducitur ...*, Ferrara. Cf. also, E. Grant, *Much ado about nothing*, pp.199-206.

122 Bernard le Bovier de Fontenelle: 1686, *Entretiens sur la pluralité des mondes*, Paris; cf. J.S. Dick, *Plurality of worlds*, Ch. 5.

123 P. Gassendi, *Opera omnia*, *I*, pp.141a-144b; MS Tours 709, ff.461r-463v; cf. S.J. Dick, *Plurality of worlds*, pp.53-59.

124 P. Gassendi, *Opera omnia*, *I*, pp.139b, 189ff; cf. MS Tours 709, ff.202v-203r. For the medieval discussions, cf. Edward Grant (Ed.): 1974, *A source book of medieval science*, Harvard University Press, Cambridge, Mass., pp.547-554.

125 Cf. article 34 of the condemnation by Bishop Tempier in H. Denifle and E. Chatelain (Eds.): 1889-1897, *Chartularium Universitatis Parisiensis*, Delalain, Paris, 4 vols., *I*, pp.543-555.

126 P. Gassendi, *Opera omnia*, *I*, p.189ff; cf. *idem, I*, p.139b. In Ms Tours 709, f.156v, Gassendi made passing reference only to the doctrine of imaginary space.

127 "This space is ... nothing other than the imaginary spaces that most of the Doctors talk about and accept as real." "Hoc sane ... nihil aliud est quam quae pars maxima Doctorum vocat, admittitque spatia imaginaria." (*Idem, I*, p.189b.) Gassendi referred to St. Augustine, *De*

*civitate Dei*, XI, 5 (P. Gassendi, *Opera omnia*, *I*, p.189b). See also Edward Grant (Ed.), *A source book of medieval science*, p.562.

128  See, for example: Conimbricenses: 1602, *Commentariorum Collegii Conimbricensis Societatis Jesu: In octo libros Physicorum Aristotelis Stagiritae*, Bk. VIII, ch. 10, quaestio 2, article IV.

129  "Non quod non revera seclusaque imaginatione non sint, sed quod eas, quae in ipsis dimensiones spatiales sunt, instar corporearum, quae in corporibus familiare est observare, imaginemur." (P. Gassendi, *Opera omnia*, *I*, p.189b.)

130  "Quare eius dimensiones non iccirco imaginariae dici consueverunt quod fictitiae sint, aut a sola mentis notione pendeant, nec extra intellectum dentur; sed quia imaginamur illas in spatio proportione quadam respondentes realibus ac positivis corporum dimensionibus." (Conimbricenses, *Commentariorum in libros physicorum Aristotelis*, Bk. VII, ch 10, quaestio 2, article IV, col. 519.) Evidence that the doctrine was to be specially identified with the teaching of the Jesuits is to be seen in the following extract from a seventeenth-century Jesuit school note-book: "Is God also present in the imaginary spaces? I reply, "Affirmative". Following which the first among the authors cited in support of the thesis were the Jesuits of Coimbra. (Note-book conserved in the Bibliothèque Nationale, *fonds latin*, MS 11139, f.209r.)

131  The Jesuits, and Gassendi following them, presumably, interpreted Augustine as accepting the theory of imaginary space, whereas even the most casual reading of the passage in the *De civitate Dei* reveals that Augustine was expressing non-acceptance of the theory. (Cf. S. Aurelii Augustine, *De civitate Dei*, XI.5.)

132  Conimbricenses, *Commentariorum in libros physicorum Aristotelis*, Bk. VIII, ch. 10, quaestio 2, article IV; P. Gassendi, *Opera omnia*, *I*, p.189b.

133  P. Gassendi, *Opera omnia*, *I*, pp.190b-191b. Thomas Bradwardine: 1618, *De causa Dei contra Pelagium et de virtute causarum ...*, J. Billium, London, Bk. I, ch. 5, pp.177-180 (as translated in Edward Grant, *A source book of medieval science*, pp.556-560). Gassendi was careful to stress that God was not really extended: he referred to God's "infinity of quasi-extension" ("infinitatem quasi extensionis") (P. Gassendi, *Opera omnia*, *I*, p.191a).

134  Cf. Edward Grant, *A source book of medieval science*, p.559.

135  *Idem*, p.553.

136  *Idem*, p.556.

137  Cf. Diogenes Laertius, *De clarorum philosophorum vitis*, 41.10 - 42.5; also Lucretius, *De rerum natura*, *I*, 329ff.

138  Cf. the condemnation of 1277 (H. Denifle and E. Chatelain (Eds.), *Chartularium Universitatis Parisiensis*, *I*, pp.543-555).

139  Eustache de Saint-Paul: 1609, *Summa philosophiae*.

140  *Idem*, pp.84-85.

141  G. Bruno, *De l'infinito universo e mondi* (Giordano Bruno, *Opere* (1830, A. Wagner, Ed.), 2 vols., Weidmann, Lipsia, *II*, pp.1-104, especially p.37). Cf. A. Koyré: 1957, *From the closed world to the infinite universe*, John Hopkins Press, Baltimore, pp.35-54. Koyré interpreted Bruno's space as "Lucretian" (*idem*, pp.47-54), and I have opted to follow this seemingly correct, though conservative judgment. Frances Yates has argued that Bruno's view of space was Hermetic (cf. Frances Yates: 1964, *Giordano Bruno and the Hermetic tradition*, Routledge and Kegan Paul, London, pp.238ff.), but her judgment has been strongly contradicted (cf. Robert S. Westman: 1977, "Magical reform and astronomical reform: the Yates thesis reconsidered", in Robert S. Westman and J.E. McGuire: 1977, *Hermeticism and the scientific revolution*, University of California Press, Los Angeles, pp.1-91, especially pp.22ff.)

142  "Cognoscimus praeterea hunc mundum, sive substantiae corporeae universitatem, nullos extensionis suae fines habere. Ubicunque enim fines illos esse fingamus, semper ultra ipsos aliqua spatia indefinite extensa non modo imaginamur, sed etiam vere imaginabilia, hoc est, realia esse percipimus; ac proinde, etiam substantiam corpoream indefinite extensam in iis contineri. Quia, ut jam fuse ostensum est, idea ejus extensionis quam in spatio qualicunque concipimus, eadem plane est cum idea substantiae corporeae." (R. Descartes: 1644, *Principia philosophiae*, par. 21, in *Oeuvres de Descartes*, *VIII*, p.52.)

143  Descartes' *Principia* was published in 1644, after Gassendi had written his MS Tours version of the treatise on space in 1637, and before he commenced the *Syntagma* version soon after 1649.

144 Cf. P. Gassendi: 1644, *Disquisitio, seu dubitationes et instantiae adversus Renati Cartesii metaphysicam et responsa*, in P. Gassendi, *Opera omnia, III*, pp.269-410, cf. pp.300bff; cf. also *idem, I*, pp.92aff.

145 *Supra*, note 130.

146 P. Gassendi, *Opera omnia, I*, p.283a; cf. MS Tours 709, f.247r.

147 *Idem, I*, p.274a; MS Tours 709, f.248r.

148 "It seems evident that the efficient cause and cause as such are one and the same thing." "Perspicuum videtur efficiens et caussam synonyma esse." (*Idem, I*, p.283a; MS Tours 709, f.247r.)

149 Gassendi quoted the Stoic Seneca as a supporting authority for the replacement, cf. Seneca, *Epistulae morales ad Lucilium*, Ep. LXV; P. Gassendi, MS Tours 709, f.247r.

150 Cf. *supra*, pp.58ff.

151 P. Gassendi, *Opera omnia, I*, p.338a.

152 O.R. Bloch, *La philosophie de Gassendi*, pp.238ff, espc. pp.354-376, 474-481; cf. *supra*, pp.10-12.

153 L.T. Sarasohn: 1985, "Motion and morality: Pierre Gassendi, Thomas Hobbes and the mechanical world-view" in *Journal of the history of ideas, 46*, pp.363-379, espc. pp.369ff.

154 *Idem, I*, pp.311aff; *III*, p.466.

155 Cicero *De natura deorum* (Loeb classical library edition), II, 87-88, 93, 95. Gassendi's argument from design, and that of Balbus in Cicero's *De natura deorum*, was simply that there was so much evidence of order and design in the universe that it was impossible for a reasonable person who seriously considered the matter to claim that the universe was the product of chance and not the work of an intelligent and purposeful Designer.

156 P. Gassendi, *Opera omnia*, pp.314b-315a.

157 *Idem, I*, p.320a. This is an interesting and somewhat puzzling remark. In the early seventeenth century it would appear that atheism, in the strict sense of unbelief in the existence of God, was considerably on the increase; cf. H. Busson: 1933, *La pensée religieuse française de*

*Charron à Pascal*, J. Vrin, Paris, pp.16ff. But the meaning of the term "atheist" was rather imprecise at that time; thus Mersenne considered Fludd to be an atheist, while Gassendi did not. It is possible that Gassendi, by underestimating the number of atheists that were abroad, was reacting to Mersenne's habit of overestimating it; cf. M. Mersenne: 1623, *Quaestiones celeberrimae in Genesim ... athei et deistae impugnantur ...*, S. Cramoisy, Paris, preface, pp.16ff, 24ff.

158 "The Stoics, Epicureans and others combined theology with physics. Since the task of theology is to contemplate the natures of things, these philosophers considered that the contemplation of the Divine Nature and of the other immortal beings was included, especially since the Divine Nature reveals itself in the creation and government of the universe." "Nam Stoici quidem, Epicurei, et alii Theologicam partem retulerunt ad Physicam, quod cum illius munus sit speculari naturas rerum, existimarint eiusdem esse Naturam Divinam, aliarumque rerum immortalium contemplari, et maxime quidem cum Natura Divina ex fabricatione, gubernationeque naturae rerum innotescat." (P. Gassendi, *Opera omnia, I*, p.27a.)
   "As for theology, Plato considered it as a part of philosophy that is distinct from physics ... but the Stoics and other Epicureans considered it as a part of physics insofar as physics, when investigating the causes of things, acknowledged the divine causes as well, especially the Creative, Conserving and Governing Cause of the universe." "Quod spectat ad Theologiam, Plato quidem illam ut partem a Physica distinctam habuit ... at Stoici, Epicurei alii fecere partem Physicae, prout Physica causas investigans, agnoscit in ipsis divinas, ac potissimum Productricem, Conservatricem, Gubernatricem naturae rerum." (Letter of Gassendi to Count Louis of Valois, 28.3.1642 (*idem, VI*, p.137b). Cf. Diogenes Laertius, *De clarorum philosophorum vitis, X*, 78.1-5.)

159 *Opera omnia, I*, pp.27a-29b.

160 Gassendi employed the term "Royal Way" ("regia via") in his critique of Descartes' *Meditations*, when complaining that the latter had abandoned the Royal Way in his third meditation: "It is not right that you should abandon the Royal Way in which the existence of God is proven from his manifest effects in the universe, in order to prove it by the so-called objective reality of the idea." "Haud jure relinqui regiam viam, qua Dei existentia probatur ex effectibus in Universo manifestis, ut per vocatam objectivam ideae realitatem probetur." (P. Gassendi, *Opera omnia, III*, p.239b.)
   Gassendi's "Royal Way" was the argument from design, a way of 'proving' the existence of God from the evidence of 'manifest design'

in nature. Gassendi's "Way" differed from the "Fifth Way" of Thomas Aquinas. Gassendi cited the design of the end product as evidence of purposive (teleological) action in the universe: since one finds things without intelligence directed to ends, one infers a directing intelligence outside them. (Cf. Thomas Aquinas, *Summa theologiae* (Blackfriars edition), 1a, q.2, a.3, together with commentary in Appendix 1 (p.173) and Appendix 10 (pp.206-208).)

161 Cf. *e.g.*, P. Gassendi, *Opera omnia, I*, pp.144a-b, 151a-b, 154a-155a, 163a.

162 Marin Mersenne: 1625, *La verité des sciences contre les sceptiques ou pyrrhoniens*, T. Du Bray, Paris.

163 P. Gassendi, *Opera omnia, I*, pp.133b-134a.

164 P. Gassendi, MS Tours 709, Bk. XX, ch. 1 (opening words).

165 P. Gassendi, *Opera omnia, I*, pp.133b-134a.

166 Cf. *infra*, ch. 5, in which I argue that Gassendi also achieved results helpful to the ideals of the developing empirical sciences.

167 Cf. P. Gassendi, *Opera omnia, I*, p.27a; *VI*, p.137b.

168 "Scopus Epicuri correctus" (MS Tours 709, Bk. XII, ch. 3); cf. also P. Gassendi, *Opera omnia, VI*, p.155a, 122b; *V*, p.201a-203a.

169 Diogenes Laertius, *De clarorum philosophorum vitis, X*, 78.1-82.9, 85.7-10, 142.10 - 143.7; Lucretius, *De rerum natura*, I, 102-111, 127-131, 146-148.

170 P. Gassendi, *Opera omnia, I*, p.130a; MS Tours 709, f.150v; cf. Seneca, *Naturales quaestiones*, VI, 4.2.

171 P. Gassendi, MS Tours 709, f.150v; cf. P. Gassendi, *Opera omnia, I*, pp.125bff.

172 P. Gassendi, MS Tours 709, f.150v; cf. P. Gassendi, *Opera omnia, I*, p.128b.

173 P. Gassendi, MS Tours 709, ff.150v-152r; cf. P. Gassendi, *Opera omnia, I*, pp.127b-128a (Gassendi added more authorites in the *Syntagma* version).

174 "De principio efficiente, seu de causis rerum" (P. Gassendi, *Opera omnia, I*, p.283).

175 "De caussis, fortuna et fato" (MS Tours 709, ff.247r-255r).

176 "De Deo Authore et Rectore mundi". This treatise is now catalogued as Ashburnham 1239. Together with the *Liber proemialis* of MS Tours 706, it is numbered among the twenty-three articles that disappeared from the Bibliothèque de Tours between 1842 and 1847, and which were sold to Lord Ashburnham in 1847 by Libri (cf. P. Meyer: 1883, "Les manuscrits du Connetable de Lesdiguières", in *Romania, 12*, pp.336-342).

177 "Praeter has caussas agnitum fuisse primam, generalem, divinam" (MS Tours 709, ff,.253r-255r).

178 The material from the *Pars ethica* of the *Animadversiones* comes from pp.1251-1295 of that work: it is now Ch. 2 (that part of the chapter which was not taken over from ff.253v-255r of MS Tours 709), Ch. 3 and Ch. 4 of the *Syntagma* treatise on causality. The material from the *Pars physiologica* of the *Animadversiones* comes from pp.708-750 of that work: it is now Chs. 6 and 7 of the *Syntagma* treatise.

179 Bloch describes and discusses the more significant changes; cf. O.R. Bloch, *La philosophie de Gassendi*, pp.354-376

180 For a helpful discussion of Gassendi's theological voluntarism and its epistemological consequences, cf. Margaret J. Osler: 1983, "Providence and Divine Will in Gassendi's views on scientific knowledge", in *Journal of the history of ideas, 44*, pp.549-560. For a more general treatment of the influence of theology and different forms of theology on the development of modern science, cf. M.B. Foster: 1934, "The Christian doctrine of Creation and the rise of modern natural science", in *Mind, 43*, pp.446-468; M.B. Foster: 1935, "Christian theology and modern science of nature (I)', in *Mind, 44*, pp.439-466; M.B. Foster: 1936, "Christian theology and modern science of nature (II)', in *Mind, 45*, pp.1-27; E.M. Klaaren: 1977, *Religious origins of modern science; belief in Creation in seventeenth-century thought*, Eerdmans, Grand Rapids. Cf. also, J.E.McGuire: 1972, "Boyle's conception of nature", in *Journal of the history of ideas, 33*, pp.523-542.

181 MS Tours 709, ff.251vff; P. Gassendi, *Opera omnia, I*, pp.280a-b, 282b, 311aff, 333a-334a.

182 Cf. *supra*, pp.30-33.

183  P. Gassendi, *Opera omnia*, *I*, p.503a; MS Tours 710, ff.579v-580r.

184  P. Gassendi, *Opera omnia*, *I*, pp.633a-634b, 637b. Aristotle, *Metaphysics* 1073a23-1074b13; Aristotle, *De caelo* 292a10-293a14. Gassendi did concede that the Aristotelians could claim that the soul of the heavenly spheres operated as the physical principle or cause of movement as does the soul in an animal; cf. P. Gassendi, *Opera omnia*, p.634a. He even adopted the Aristotelian terms "form" and "soul" to denote the mechanical principle of motion in his own theory; cf. P. Gassendi, *Opera omnia*, p.638b.

185  "Deterioris fore conditionis corpora caelestia, quam caeteras res naturaleis, veluti ignem, aut lapidem, aut ipsa certe animalia, quae se ipsa movent; neque ut moveant, destinatas per Aristotelem Intelligentias obtinent." (*Idem, I*, p.637b.) Aristotle had held that the heavenly bodies were exceptional in nature because the laws of the superlunary realm were regarded as different from those of the sublunary realm. But this made them exceptional in the sense of being more noble. Gassendi strove to show that Aristotelian theory actually degraded the heavenly bodies, presenting them as lower than the earthly bodies.

186  *Idem, I*, p.638a.

187  "Nativam formam, contexturamve, et constitutionem" (*idem, I*, p.638b).

188  *Idem, I*, p.638a.

189  "Exinde nempe esse potuit non modo circularis motus, sed etiam tenor eius perennis, ob perseverantem compactionem, et texturam globi, perseveranteisque proinde interius circumpulsationis, et circumductionis causas." (*Idem, I*, p.638b.)

190  Cf. P.A. Pav: 1966, "Gassendi's statement of the principle of inertia", in *Isis*, *57*, pp.24-34.

191  P. Gassendi, *Opera omnia*, *I*, pp.343b, 384b; cf. MS Tours 709, ff.306r, 354r.

192  "The motive force in composite objects originates in the atoms." "Vis motrix, quae in unaquaque re concreta est, originem atomis debet." (*Idem, I*, p.384b; cf. MS Tours 709, f.354r.)

193  P. Gassendi: 1642, *De motu impresso a motore translato epistolae duae, in quibus aliquot praecipuae, tum de motu universe, tum speciatim de motu terrae attributo, difficultates explicantur,* L. De Heuqueville, Paris, in P. Gassendi, *Opera omnia, III,* pp.478a–563b, espc. p.489b.

194  "Ipsa nativa atomorum vis, neque dum res ipsae concrete incipiunt criescere, pereat, sed impediatur solummodo; neque dum res moveri incipiunt, gignatur, sed libertatem solum acquirat; ideo dici posse iuxta ante supposita, tantum impetus perseverare constanter in rebus, quantum ad usque initio fuit. Ex quo efficitur, ut quia, quantum una atomus in aliam impacta ipsam impellit, tantum ab ipsa repellitur, sicque impetus neque increscit, neque decrescit; sed ob factam compensationem idem semper manet, et motus idem perseverat, donec per spatium liberum, ac sine resistentia fit." (*Idem, I,* p.343b; MS Tours 709, f.306r-v.)

195  "Eapropter res quoque concretae, dum se invicem pellunt ac repellunt intelligi possint ita a se invicem pate, ut seu paribus viribus occurrant, parum utrimque motum retineant, seu imparibus, ea sit compensatio, qua in simul acceptis tantumdem motus perseveret." (*Idem, I,* p.343b.)

196  "Omnem impressum motum ex se indelibilem esse." (*Idem, I,* p.357b; MS Tours 709, f.325r.)

197  "Vis seu impulsio naturae ex una parte universi in aliam absque ullo termino." (MS Tours 709, f.185r.) Cf. Lucretius, *De rerum natura* I, 1074–1080.

198  "Vigore quoque ingenito, seu interna illa energia ... quaque illas cieri per inane (sic voluit) ut, cum inane sit infinitum et centro omni careat, nunquam cessaturae ab illo suo motu, ut sibi naturali sint, sed in omne aevum in eo perstiturae, nisi aliae aut atomi, aut concretiones occurrerint, a quibus aliorsim flectantur." (P. Gassendi, *Opera omnia, I,* p.276b; cf. MS Tours 709, f.192v.)

199  Cf. the comments of A. Koyré on this aspect of Gassendi's expression of the principle of inertia. (A. Koyré: 1939, *Etudes Galiléennes,* 3 vols. (Actualités scientifiques et industrielles 852-854), Paris, *III,* pp.144–157.) Koyré was impressed by the fact that Gassendi appeared to eliminate the concept of *impetus,* but he was mistaken. Gassendi did not refer to his Epicurean theory in his letters *De motu impresso a motore translato;* had he done so he would have referred to the theory as we have described it.

200  P. Gassendi, *Opera omnia*, *I*, pp.274a-276a; cf. MS Tours 709, ff.189r-191v. Gassendi was echoing the teaching of Epicurus as presented by Lucretius (cf. Lucretius, *De rerum natura*, II, 217ff), maintaining that, since Lucretius did not leave room for a theory of a natural centre of the world, he did not accept such a theory.

201  "De rebus naturae universe" (P. Gassendi, *Opera omnia*, *I*, pp.125-494). In the version of MS Tours 709 this heading is not given, and as a consequence the link between micro-level and macro-level theory is not made so clear.

202  "Ut motum atomorum ... ita in rebus concretis ..." (*Idem, I*, p.344b).

203  "Quod spectat vero ad motus rectos ... sive elementa sint, sive mista ..." (*Idem, p.345a*). This extrapolation has been called "the analogy of nature" (cf. J.E. McGuire: 1970, "Atoms and the 'analogy of nature'; Newton's third rule of philosophising", in *Studies in history and philosophy of science*, *I*, pp.3-58). It was an elaboration of Epicurean atomism that was original in Gassendi's exposition.

204  "Nativam formam, contexturamve, et constitutionem" (P. Gassendi, *Opera omnia*, *I*, p.638b).

205  *Idem, I*, p.638a.

206  "Exinde nempe esse potuit non modo circularis motus, sed etiam tenor eius perennis, ob perseverantem compactionem, et texturam globi, perseveranteisque   proinde   interius   circumpulsationis,   et circumductionis causas." (*Idem, I*, p.638b.) It is highly probable that Gassendi was indebted to Isaac Beeckman for this explanation of the circularity of the motion of the heavenly bodies; cf. I. Beeckman, *Journal tenu par Isaac Beeckman de 1604 à 1634* (1939, C. de Waard (Ed.)), 4 vols., La Haye, *I*, p.253, entry dating between 23rd November and 26th December, 1618; cf. A. Gabbey: 1980, "Force and inertia in the seventeenth century: Descartes and Newton", in S. Gaukroger (Ed.): 1980, *Descartes. Philosophy, mathematics and physics*, Harvester Press, Brighton, pp.230-320, espc. p.243.

207  P. Gassendi, *Opera omnia*, *I*, p.638a.

208  "In regard to the principles of movement in the Aristotelian theory, especially those that are described by contemporary Aristotelians, one must not deny that God could make use of some such Agents, but there are no convincing reasons to believe that he does." "Quod ad motores vero aristoteleos, maximeque quales a nostris describuntur,

attinet; negandum quidem quoque non est, quin Deus uti aliquibus huiuscemodi Administris possit; at quod sane utatur, nihil est, quod convincat." (*Idem, I*, p.637a).

209  "Addendum profecto est internam illam contexturam ... ex atomis ... Deum ter-Maximum habuisse Authorem, ut et ipsa principia quibus impetus non cessaturus fuit impressus; adeo ut, si iam sidera isto, non alio modo moveantur, id debeant Authori naturae, qui ita initio constituerit, qui motum ita incipere, ita constare voluerit." (*Idem, I*, p.638b.) This passage is an addition to Gassendi's manuscripts for the *Syntagma* version. Gassendi's concern to relate all nature to God the First Cause was a permanent feature of his natural philosophy, according to my earlier argument (*supra*, pp.70-76), thus he simply achieved more fully his original aims in this passage.

210  *supra*, p.53.

211  *E.g.* MS Tours 710, ff.624v-653v; P. Gassendi, *Opera omnia*, pp.615b-630b. The *Syntagma* version in this instance is made to accord with the decision of the Roman authorities especially by the addition of the following sentence on p.630a:

> "Consequently, for those whose religion bars the Copernican hypothesis, the hypothesis of Tycho Brahe comes to the rescue, and this is the most plausible of all the hypotheses."
> "Adeo proinde, ut quibus tueri Coperniceam hypothesis religio est, Braheana praesto occurrat, quae verisimillima omnium sit."

Cf. *supra*, pp.37-47.

212  Copernicanism was condemned by the Roman authorities on June 22nd, 1633; cf. Galileo Galilei, *Opere, XIX*, pp.402-407.

213  "De rebus terrenis", *idem, II*, pp.9a-658b; the passage referred to is found in *idem, II*, p.9a.

214  That is the date attributed to MS Tours 707, the only version we have of this section; cf. R. Pintard: 1943, *La Mothe le Vayer, Gassendi - Guy Patin. Etudes de bibliographie et de critique suivie de textes inédits de Guy Patin*, Boivin, Paris, pp.39-40.

215  Lucretius, *De rerum natura*, V, 449-451. Lucretius referred to the formation of the world by an agglomeration of heavy Earth particles; lighter particles were squeezed out to form sea, stars, sun, moon and

the walls of the world. According to Epicurus and Lucretius, however, there was an infinite number of these "worlds" in the universe, a doctrine which Gassendi rejected in favour of the Stoic cosmology. Gassendi did not insist, and in fact he would have realised that he would have found it difficult to sustain this interpretation of the doctrine of Epicurus in the light of the seemingly conflicting Epicurean doctrine of an infinity of worlds. Gassendi had himself declared that the doctrine of Epicurus of a plurality of worlds was against faith and reason (P. Gassendi, *Opera omnia, I*, pp.140a-141b).

## Chapter 4

1    Cf. *supra*, Ch. 1.

2    P. Gassendi, *Opera omnia, I*, p.13b; Gassendi was making allusion to the division of philosophical systems into "Dogmatic", "Academic" and "Sceptic" made by Sextus Empiricus in his *Outlines of Pyrrhonism* (Loeb classical library edition), I, 1.3-4.

3    Cf. David Fate Norton: 1980, "The myth of 'British Empiricism'", in *History of European ideas, I*, pp.331-344; Norton claims that Gassendi was the "seminal" figure in seventeenth and eighteenth-century empiricism, and the most likely candidate for the title Founder of Modern Empiricism. Admirers of Gassendi have made such claims in the past; cf. G. Coirault, "Gassendi et non Locke créateur de la doctrine sensualiste moderne sur la génération des idées", in B. Rochot et al.: 1957, *Actes du Congrès du Tricentenaire de Pierre Gassendi (4-7août, 1955)*, Digne, pp.69-94.

4    Cf. R.I. Aaron: 1937, *John Locke*, Oxford University Press, London, p.31; O.R. Bloch, *La philosophie de Gassendi*, pp.133-134; R.W. Kroll: 1984, "The question of Locke's relation to Gassendi", in *Journal of the history of ideas, 1984, 45*, pp.339-359). J. Locke: 1694 (second edition), *An essay concerning human understanding* (1924, A.S. Pringle-Pattison (Ed.), Clarendon Press, Oxford).

5    P. Gassendi, *Syntagma philosophicum*, in P. Gassendi, *Opera omnia, I - II*.

6    Letter of Gassendi to Peiresc of 28.4.1631, enclosure, *Lettres de Peiresc, IV*, pp.250-252.

7    MS Carpentras 1832, ff.205r-256r. Gassendi composed this version immediately after completing the manuscript of *De vita et moribus Epicuri libri octo* in 1634; cf. R. Pintard: 1943, *La Mothe le Vayer, Gassendi - Guy Patin. Etudes de bibliographie et de critique suivie de textes inédits de Guy Patin*, Boivin, Paris, Ch. 3 ("Des manuscrits de Gassendi à l'oeuvre imprimèe: la genèse du Syntagma philosophicum"); also O.R. Bloch, *La philosophie de Gassendi*, pp.xix-xxx.

8    Cf. the numerous letters to Louis of Valois that are bound in chronological sequence with other letters in Latin of Gassendi's correspondence in P. Gassendi, *Opera omnia, VI*, pp.95-324; the letters relevant to Gassendi's logic are found especially between pp.138-154.

9    P. Gassendi, *Opera omnia, I*, pp.31-124.

10   Letter of Gassendi to Peiresc of 28.4.1631, enclosure, *Lettres de Peiresc, IV*, p.250. For Gassendi's exposition of the term "Canonic", MS Carpentras 1832, ff.204r-206v.

11   According to Epicurus, the senses were the first, irrefutable criterion or canon of truth. They never erred since they did no more than receive the sensible species which were presented to them. The possibility of error occurred when opinion was involved, and there was no opinion involved in the operation of the senses. The "anticipation" was an "apprehension", a "true appearance or idea", or a "universal idea" (*e.g.* of a man) which remained in the perceiver as the result of a sense perception. The mind judged new apprehensions against the "anticipation" as a criterion or standard and thus came to recognise other objects of perception; *e.g.* apprehensions of men fitted the "anticipation" of a man. Cf. Diogenes Laertius, *De clarorum philosophorum vitis* (1973, G. Arrighetti (Ed.), *Epicuro opere*, G. Einaudi, Turin), 31-34.

12   Epicurus referred to two "passions": pleasure and pain. Pleasure was considered to be according to nature. With these two passions as criteria, judgments could be made concerning what was to be chosen (*viz.* what gave pleasure) and what was to be avoided (*viz.* what gave pain). Cf. *idem*, 34.

13   "De canonica dialecticae substituta". (Ms Carpentras 1832, f.205r.)

14 *Idem*, f.219r; P. Gassendi, *Opera omnia*, *I*, p.52b. Gassendi was repeating the classical interpretation; cf. D. Laertius, *De clarorum philosophorum vitis*, 1, 31.5-6.

15 P. Gassendi: 1624, *Exercitationes paradoxicae adversus Aristoteleos, in quibus praecipua totius Peripateticae doctrinae atque dialecticae fundamenta excutiuntur* ..., Bk. 2, in P. Gassendi, *Opera omnia*, *III*, pp.149a-210b. MS Carpentras 1832, f.219v. Gassendi explained that he referred to the art of disputation as practised by the "dialecticians" (P. Gassendi, *Opera omnia*, *III*, p.149a). He used the terms "dialectic" and "dialectician" in a pejorative sense.

16 MS Carpentras 1832, f.219v; cf. also P. Gassendi, *Opera omnia*, *VI*, p.144a, where Gassendi wrote: "Epicurus had repudiated the study of dialectic ... not for any false teaching, but because it was concerned with utterly useless and laborious questions." "Epicurus repudiaverit dialecticae studium ... non ut praecepta falsa tradentem, sed ut inutilissima et operosissima congruentem."

17 Gassendi wrote: "There is no end to the precepts that they invent and tangle up." "Neque unquam confingendorum intricandorumque praeceptorum finis est." (P. Gassendi, *Opera omnia*, *III*, p.149a.)

18 P. Gassendi, *Opera omnia*, *III*, p.109b.

19 *Idem*, *III*, pp.156a-157a.

20 *Idem*, *III*, pp.149b-157a.

21 "[Dialectica aristotelica] naturam ergo non aperit, sed solum perinde facit ac ille qui inventionem thesauri pollicitus, quaere, inquit, ubi delitescat et illud invenies?" (*Idem*, *III*, p.150a.)

22 "Paucos canonas, quibus intellectus in veri disquisitione adiutaretur." (*Idem*, *I*, p.52b.)

23 "Ars bene cogitandi." (*Idem*, *I*, p.32b.)

24 "De arte intellectus dicendum heic est, quae sane non ipsa versatur in rebus in quibus verum disquiritur; talis enim physica potius, seu scientia naturalis est, sed in eo tamen occupatur ut regulas tradat quibus intellectus dum rerum naturam contemplatur, dirigi possit." (*Idem*, *I*, p.31a.)

25  "Physica nimirum, caeteraeque scientiae ita ex professo circa suam
    quaequae materiam occupantur utquid in ea sit verum perscrutentur;
    logica vero singulis praeit quamdamque veluti facem praefert,
    quatenus praecepta generalia tradit, regulasque omnibus communeis
    quibus si utantur a veri inquirendi via non aberrent, aut ubi
    aberraverint, tum sui erroris admoneantur tum rectiorem viam
    instituant." (*Idem, I*, p.86b.)

26  Aristotle, *Analytica posteriora, passim*; cf. C.-G, Granger: 1976, *La
    théorie aristotélicienne de la science*, Aubier Montaigne, Paris, pp.97-
    106.

27  P. Gassendi, *Opera omnia, II*, p.371a-b.

28  Cf. A.C. Crombie: 1967, "The mechanistic hypothesis and the
    scientific study of vision: some optical ideas as a background to the
    invention of the microscope", in S. Bradbury and G. L'E. Turner
    (Eds.): 1967, *Historical aspects of microscopy*, Royal Microscopical
    Society, London, especially pp.11-12. For an account of Descartes'
    discussion of these processes, cf. J.A. Schuster: 1980, "Descartes'
    *Mathesis universalis*: 1619-28", in Stephen Gaukroger (Ed.): 1980,
    *Descartes. Philosophy, mathematics and physics*, Harvester Press,
    Brighton, pp.41-96.

29  Cf. Aristotle, *De anima*, III, 431a.1 - 431b.19; cf. also Thomas
    Aquinas, *Summa theologiae* (Blackfriars edition), 1a, qu.84-88.

30  P. Gassendi: 1642, *De apparente magnitudine solis humilis et sublimis
    epistolae quatuor, in quibus complura physica opticaque problemata
    proponuntur et explicantur*, L. de Heuqueville, Paris; cf. P. Gassendi,
    *Opera omnia, III*, pp.420-477.

31  Galileo Galilei, *Opere X, XI, XIII, XIV, XVI, XVII*, and especially
    *XVIII*.

32  Cf. P. Gassendi, *Opera omnia, III*, p.422a.

33  F. Liceti: 1640-1650, *De quaesitis per epistolas a claris viris responsa
    ...*, Bologna and Udina.

34  P. Gassendi, *Opera omnia, III*, pp.422-448.

35  "τὸ δὲ μέγεθος ἡλίου τε καὶ τῶν λοιπῶν ἄστρων κατὰ μὲν τὸ πρὸς ἡμᾶς τηλικοῦτον
    ἐστιν ἡλίκον φαίνεται ... κατὰ δὲ τὸ καθ'αὑτὸ ἤτοι μεῖζον τοῦ ὁρωμένου ἢ μικρῷ

ἔλαττον ἢ τηλικοῦτον"    (D. Laertius, *De clarorum philosophorum vitis*, 3, 91.1-2, 5-6).

36   Lucretius, *De rerum natura* (Loeb classical library edition), *IV*, 324-331, 353-363. Cf. J.M. Rist: 1972, *Epicurus, an introduction*, Cambridge University Press, Cambridge, p.21.

37   Cf. the note in the Arrighetti edition, *Epicuro opere* (G. Arrighetti Ed.), pp.526-528.

38   D. Laertius, *De clarorum philosophorum vitis*, 1, 33.1-10; cf. J.M. Rist, *Epicurus*, Ch. 2, especially pp.32-37.

39   P. Gassendi, *Opera omnia*, *I*, p.572b; *VI*, p.148b. Letter of Gassendi to Peiresc of 24.4.1626, *Lettres de Peiresc*, *IV*, p.179. Cicero, *De natura deorum* (Loeb classical library edition), I, 69ff.

40   P. Gassendi, *Opera omnia*, *III*, pp.420-422; cf. MS Tours 710, ff.606v-607v; P. Gassendi, *Opera omnia*, *I*, pp.572a-573b.

41   T. Brahe, *Opera omnia*, *V*, p.183.

42   J. Kepler: 1604, *Ad vitellionem paralipomena, quibus astronomiae pars optica traditur; potissimum de artificiosa observatione et aestimatione diametrorum deliquiorumque solis et lunae ...*, Marnium et Aubrii, Frankfurt, pp.335-360; cf. David C. Lindberg: 1976, *Theories of vision from Al-Kindi to Kepler*, University of Chicago Press, Chicago, p.187, also Stephen M. Straker: 1970, *Kepler's optics. A study in the development of seventeenth-century natural philosophy* (Ph.D. dissertation presented to the University of Indiana), p.390.

43   P. Gassendi, *Opera omnia*, *III*, pp.420-421.

44   *Idem, III*, pp.420a-422b; J. Kepler, *Ad Vitellionem paralipomena*, pp.158ff.

45   Cf. letters of Peiresc to Du Puy of 15.4.1634 and 15.5.1634 in *Lettres de Peiresc*, *III*, pp.75ff, 103ff.

46   Cf. letter of Peiresc to du Puy of 9.5.1634, *Idem, III*, pp.97-101.

47   "Videndi functionem fieri debere in ea parte potissimum in qua recipi valeant et contineri species omnium visibilium imaginesque omnium colorum." (P. Gassendi, *Opera omnia*, *III*, p.424b.) Aristotelians considered that the crystalline humour was the place of vision because

it was considered to be 'immaterial' and thus able to receive the 'immaterial' species. The theories of the late thirteenth-century treatises on optics supported their doctrine; cf. John Peckham, *Perspectiva communis* (1970, D.C. Lindberg (Ed.), *John Pecham and the science of optics: Perspectiva communis*, University of Wisconsin Press, Madison, 1970), I, 37.

48 "Potissimum albam dilutam ... suffuso rubore, vel caerulo." "It is a dilute white ... with a reddish or bluish tinge." (J. Kepler, *Ad Vitellionem paralipomena*, p.166.) Cf. Lindberg, *Theories of vision from Al-Kindi to Kepler*, p.191.

49 P. Gassendi, *Opera omnia, III*, p.424b.

50 Plater wrote: "The principal organ of vision, namely the optic nerve dilated into the grey hemispherical retina after it enters the eye ..." (As cited in A.C. Crombie: 1967, "The mechanistic hypothesis and the scientific study of vision: some optical ideas as a background to the invention of the microscope", in S. Bradbury and G. L'E. Turner (Eds.): 1967, *Historical aspects of microscopy*, Royal Microscopical Society, London, p.49.). Kepler had relied on the writings of Plater for his knowledge of the anatomy of the eye; cf. J. Kepler, *Ad Vitellionem paralipomena*, p.159.

51 P. Gassendi, *Opera omnia, III*, pp.424b-425a.

52 Cf. Lindberg, *Theories of vision from Al-Kindi to Kepler*, pp.202ff.

53 P. Gassendi, *Opera omnia, III*, p.425a.

54 Cf. J. Pecham, *Perspectiva communis*, I, 33.

55 MS Tours 708, ff.1263r-1276r; P. Gassendi, *Opera omnia, II*, pp.369a-382b.

56 P. Gassendi, *Opera omnia, II*, p.369a; cf. O.R. Bloch, *La philosophie de Gassendi*, pp.6-29.

57 Letter of Galileo to Liceti of January, 1641, in G. Galilei, *Opere*, *XVIII*, p.295.

58 P. Gassendi, *Opera omnia, III*, p.423a. For Gassendi's reliance on experiment to commend his theory at the expense of the Aristotelian theory, cf. *idem, III*, pp.429b-432b, 422a.

59   Lucretius, *De rerum natura*, *IV*, 715ff.; cf. J.M. Rist, *Epicurus*, p.26ff.

60   Cf. A.C. Crombie (1976), pp.11-12.

61   R. Descartes, *Le monde ou le traité de l'homme*, in C. Adam and P. Tannery (Eds.): 1897-1910, *Oeuvres de Descartes*, 12 vols., Paris, *XI*, pp.3-215.

62   "*Philosophicum* hoc *Syntagma*, hoc est eorum quae in philosophia praecipua habentur, coordinationem ..." "This *Philosophical Syntagma*, that is, this systematic treatment of the main things in philosophy ..." (P. Gassendi, *Opera omnia*, *I*, p.29b.) Gassendi first used the title "*Syntagma*" in 1649 when he published his *Philosophiae Epicuri syntagma* (P. Gassendi, *Opera omnia*, *III*, p.1-94). In that year he began to work on the final draft of his manuscripts which was published as the *Syntagma philosophicum*.

63   Concerning the dates of Gassendi's manuscripts, cf. R. Pintard: 1943, *La Mothe le Vayer, Gassendi - Guy Patin. Etudes de bibliographie et de critique suivie de textes inédits de Guy Patin*, Boivin, Paris, ch. 3, "Des manuscrits de Gassendi à l'oeuvre imprimée: la genèse du 'Syntagma philosophicum'", pp.32-46; cf. especially pp.39-40.

64   P. Gassendi, *Opera omnia*, *II*, p.335a. Cf. Galen, *On the usefulness of the parts of the body*, περὶ χρέας μορίων, *De usu partium* (1968, M.T. May translation, 2 vols., Cornell University Press, New York), 9.8 (II, 22-28).

65   A. du Laurens: 1599, *Historia anatomica humani corporis et singularum eius partium multis controversiis et observationibus novis illustrata*, Frankfurt. Gassendi would probably have used the later edition: A. du Laurens: 1603, *Opera anatomica in quinque libros divisa*, Lyon.

66   A. du Laurens, *Opera anatomica*, p.620.

67   Letter of Descartes to Mersenne of 22.7.1633, in C. de Waard (Ed.): 1945-1972, *Correspondence du P. Marin Mersenne, Religieux Minime*, 12 vols., Paris, *III*, pp.457-460. The treatise was published in Paris much later, in 1644; R. Descartes: 1644, *L'homme de René Descartes et un traitté de la formation du foetus du mesme auteur* ..., C. Angol, Paris. For Descartes' description of the structure of the nerves, cf. C. Adam and P. Tannery, *Oeuvres de Descartes*, *XI*, pp.132-138.

68   "Dum sensus externi obiecta sua percipiunt, motionem quandam fieri, tum in externo ipso sensorio in quod aut species aut qualitas rei

sensibilis incurrit, tum propagatione quadam per nervos facta in intimo cerebro, qua parte nervi desinunt, aut originem potius habent. Nempe turgescentes spiritibus nervi concipi possunt quasi radiorum spirituosorum manipuli; adeo ut cum quivis spirituosus radium intentus sit ex cerebro ad externum usque sensorium, idcirco premi, urgerive in ipso externo sensorio tantillum non valeat, quin resulta quodam ipsum cerebrum e quo usque tenditur feriat." (P. Gassendi, *Opera omnia, II*, p.403b.)

69   Cf. Thomas Aquinas, *Summa theologiae* (Blackfriars edition), 1a, q.77, a. 2, 5, 8; 1a, q.79, a. 1, 4, 8, 10; 1a, q.84, a. 1.

70   *Idem.*

71   "[Anima rationalis] merito iure et substantia et substantialis forma censetur." (P. Gassendi, *Opera omnia, I*, p.466b.)

72   "Esse animam rationalem substantiam incorpoream a Deo creatam et in corpus infusam, formam tanquam informantem." (*Idem, II*, p.440a.)

73   *Idem, II*, p.438a; cf. Thomas Aquinas, *Summa Theologiae*, 1a, q.76, a. 1.

74   P. Gassendi, *Opera omnia, II*, pp.425a-446b; Thomas Aquinas, *Summa theologiae*, 1a, qq. 75, 76, 77, 79.

75   P. Gassendi, *Opera omnia, II*, p.451a.

76   *Idem, II*, pp.446b-454b, especially pp.450b-451a.

77   "Species pictura non est, ... neque spectatur per se, neque aliud est quam ratio cognoscendi aliud, id nempe a quo est impressa, eo modo quo etiam ea species quae imprimitur oculo non videtur ipsa sed est solum ratio videndi eam rem a qua est emissa." (*Idem, II*, p.405b.)

78   "Dum phantasia percellitur, ipsi coagat intellectus. Itaque non potest quidem intellectus, cum sit incorporeus, corporea specie, spiritibusve ... percelli; verum, quo momento phantasia perculsa ... ipsam rem quasi inspicit ... eodem momento intellectus ob intimam sui praesentiam cohaesionemque cum phantasia, rem eandem contuetur." (*Idem, II*, p.450a.)

79   Thomas Aquinas, *Summa theologiae*, 1a, q.84, art. 7.

80   *Idem*, 1a, q.85, art. 2.

81   P. Gassendi, *Opera omnia, II*, p.441a.

82   *Idem, I*, p.93a-b, *II*, pp.458b-459a, *III*, pp.159b-160a.

83   *Idem, I*, pp.93a-95b, *III*, pp.159b-160a.

84   "ἐν τοίνυν τῷ Κανόνι λέγων ἐστιν ὁ᾽ Ἐπίκουρος κριτήρια τῆς ἀληθείας ἔιναι τὰς
     αἰσθήσεις καὶ προλήψεις καὶ τὰ πάθη· οἱ δ᾽Ἐπικούειοι καὶ τὰς φανταστικὰς
     ἐπιβολὰς τῆς διανοίας" "In his *Canonic* Epicurus said that the criteria of
     truth are the sensations, preconceptions and passions. The [Stoic]
     Epicureans added also the notions which are produced by the
     voluntary action of the mind." (D. Laertius, *De clarorum
     philosophorum vitis*, I, 31.8-10; note the Italian translation in the
     Arrighetti edition.) Cf. J.M. Rist, *Epicurus*, pp.26ff.

85   D. Laertius, *De clarorum philosophorum vitis*, 1, 33.1-10; cf. J.M. Rist,
     *Epicurus*, Ch. 2, especially pp.32-37.

86   P. Gassendi, *Opera omnia, I*, pp.99a-106b.

87   Cf. J.M. Rist, *Epicurus*, pp.26ff.

88   "Non debet nos vero imprimis morari quod praeter omnem
     proportionem sit, ut intellectus, facultas incorporea, phantasmate,
     specie incorporea [correctly: "corporea"] immediate utatur. Nempe hoc
     minore proportione non fit, quam quod vulgo admittunt incorpoream
     animam iungi immediate corpori, et corporeis membris ad movendum
     uti." (P. Gassendi, *Opera omnia, II*, p.449a.)

89   "Quod nulla sit scientia, et maxime Aristotelea." (P. Gassendi, *Opera
     omnia, III*, pp.192a-210b.)

90   "Fontem, radicem, principium et causam huiuscemodi proprietatum
     ..." (*Idem, II*, p.463a; cf. *II*, p.285a.)

91   *Idem, II*, p.456a, 463b.

92   *Idem, II*, p.456b; cf. *idem, II*, p.333a. Gassendi was referring to the
     Epicurean theory of images as thin films given off from objects: D.
     Laertius, *De clarorum philosophorum vitis*, 1, 49; cf. J.M. Rist,
     *Epicurus*, pp.83ff.

93   "Deducamus ... seu veluti subodoremur" (P. Gassendi, *Opera omnia,
     II*, p.463a).

94   *Idem, II*, p.463a.

95   Aristotle, *Analytica posteriora* 71b8-38.

96   P. Gassendi, *Opera omnia, III*, p.192a-b.

97   P. Gassendi, *Opera omnia*, I, p. 796.

98   Cf. Charles B. Schmitt: 1967, *Gianfrancesco Pico della Mirandola (1469-1533) and his critique of Aristotle*, The Hague, pp.175ff.

99   P. Gassendi, *Opera omnia I*, p.73a; cf. Sextus Empiricus, *Outlines of Pyrrhonism* (Loeb classical library edition), I, 19-20.

100  "Verisimilitudo". Cf. P. Gassendi, *Opera omnia*, *I*, p.132b, where Gassendi quoted Plato, *Timaeus* 29c-d to support his view that science is of the "truth-seeming". Cf. the edition of F.M. Cornford: 1937, *Plato's cosmology. The Timaeus of Plato*, Kegan Paul and Co., London, p.23, where the translation is "a likely story". Cf. also, P. Gassendi, *Opera omnia*, *VI*, pp.146a, 148a, 152b. See the discussion of the term in I. Hacking: 1975, *The emergence of probability. A philosophical study of early ideas about probability, induction and statistical inference*, Cambridge University Press, London, 1975, pp.33ff.

101  Plato, *Republic*, 514a1-518d1.

102  "Iucundissimum quippe est crassiorem illam caliginem et tenebras quasi nocturnas sic excutere depellereque ex animo ut nisi ipsummet veritatis iubar quasi splendidissimum solem contueri nobis concedatur, at versari tamen quasi in aurora verisimilitudinis liceat, ac nisi habeamus perspectas causas quae penitus certae indubiaeque sint, taleis nanciscamur quae habeant speciem aliquam probabilitatis." (P. Gassendi, *Opera omnia*, *I*, p.286b; cf. *I*, p.132a.)

103  *Idem, I*, p.283a.

104  *Idem, III*, p.413b.

105  *Idem, I*, p.79b.

106  *Idem, II*, p.463b.

107 Cf. D. Laertius, *De clarorum philosophorum vitis*, 3, 87.9; also Epicurus, *Deperditorum librorum reliquiae* (G. Arrighetti: 1973, *Epicuro opere*, G. Einaudi, Turin), 29,16.5; 31,9.8 ...

108 Sextus Empiricus, *Outlines of Pyrrhonism*, II, 97-133. Cf. Aristotle, *Analytica priora*, II, 27, 70a7. Cf. G.-G. Granger, *La théorie aristotélicienne de la science*, pp.166-170.

109 D. Laertius, *De clarorum philosophorum vitis*, 1, 31.3; P. Gassendi, *Opera omnia*, *VI*, p.147b.

110 Cf. J.M. Rist, *Epicurus*, p.28.

111 P. Gassendi, *Opera omnia*, *I*, pp.80b-81b.

112 P. Gassendi, *Opera omnia*, *I*, pp.80b-81b. The arguments were not strictly deductive even though Gassendi intended them to be, in view of his claim that legitimate inductive arguments were implicitly deductive; cf. *idem, I*, p.113a-b.

113 *Idem, I*, pp.81b-82a.

114 "Evidentia" was Gassendi's translation of the Greek term " ἐπιμαρτύρησις " as found in D. Laertius, *De clarorum philosophorum vitis*, I, 34.2-3, cf. P. Gassendi, *Opera omnia*, *V*, pp.12-13.

115 "Evidentia est ea sensus apparentia quae in controversiam vocari non potest, quae fidem ex seipsa habet qua probabilius nihil est." (P. Gassendi, *Opera omnia*, *VI*, p.150a.)

116 P. Gassendi, *Opera omnia*, *VI*, p.150a.

117 D. Laertius, *De clarorum philosophorum vitis*, I, 34.2-3. Cf. also Plato, *Theaitetos* (Everyman library edition), 197-210, where a discussion is presented concerning whether true belief (true opinion) can be true knowledge.

118 P. Gassendi, *Opera omnia*, *III*, p.192a.

119 Cf. the treatise on the intellect which dates from late 1644 or early 1645 (*idem, II*, pp.461-468), and the treatise on logic (*idem, I*, p.99b).

120 Aristotle, *Analytica posteriora* 71b8-38.

121 P. Gassendi, *Opera omnia*, *II*, pp.461b, 464a.

122 *Idem, II*, p.462a. Gassendi maintained that there was other knowledge of things of the natural world apart from discursive or demonstrative knowledge. He seemed to be also claiming that knowledge of particulars was scientific.

123 P. Gassendi, *Opera omnia, II*, pp.457b-459a.

124 Concerning "crisis theories" as applied to the seventeenth century, cf. T.K. Rabb: 1975, *The struggle for stability in early modern Europe*, Oxford University Press, New York.

125 R.H. Popkin: 1968, *The history of scepticism from Erasmus to Descartes*, revised edition, Harper and Row, New York, especially Chs. 5,7.

126 R.H. Popkin, *History of scepticism*, pp.132ff.

127 Thus Popkin wrote: "By and large, the revival of Greek scepticism seems to have had great influence on the intellectual controversies of the early 17th century. Its first and main impact was upon theology, probably because the key issue in dispute, the rule of faith, set up a form of the classical Pyrrhonian problem of the criterion. Also, the fideism involved in the 'nouveau Pyrrhonisme', served as an ideal defense for those who employed the sceptical gambits in the religious controversies of the time. As the science of Aristotle began to lose its authority, and competing scientific and pseudo-scientific theories arose, another area for the application of Pyrrhonian arguments came to the fore. In this latter area, the development of the kind of sceptical crisis that had already appeared in theology, was to occur. The 'nouveau Pyrrhonisme' was to envelop all the human sciences and philosophy in a complete sceptical crisis, out of which modern philosophy, and the scientific outlook finally emerged." (R.H. Popkin, *History of scepticism*, pp.87-88; cf. also pp.82-83.) Popkin's theory has been elegantly summarised by Z.S. Schiffman, thus: "The revival of Greek Pyrrhonism fueled the fires of doubt ignited by the Reformation"; cf. Z.S. Schiffman: 1984, "Montaigne and the rise of skepticism in Early Modern Europe", in *Journal of the history of ideas, 45*, pp.499-516.

128 R.H. Popkin, *History of scepticism*, p.151.

129 *Idem*, p.112.

130 "Media quaedam via inter Scepticos ... et Dogmaticos videtur tenenda." "It seems that one should take a middle course between that of the Sceptics and that of the Dogmatists." (P. Gassendi, *Opera omnia, I*, p.79b.)

131 R.H. Popkin, *History of scepticism*, p.148.

132 *Idem*, p.151.

133 Cf., *e.g.*, P. Marin Mersenne: 1625, *La vérité des sciences contre les septiques* [sic] *ou pyrrhoniens* ..., T. Du Bray, Paris. Cf. also, A.C.Crombie: 1975, "Marin Mersenne (1588-1648) and the seventeenth-century problem of scientific acceptability", in *Physis, 17*, pp.186-204.

134 Cf. *e.g.*, R. Descartes: 1641, *Meditationes de prima philosophia, in qua Dei existentia et animae immortalitas demonstratur*, M. Soly, Paris. Cf. also J.A. Schuster: 1980, "Descartes' *Mathesis universalis*: 1619-28", in Stephen Gaukroger (Ed.): 1980, *Descartes. Philosophy, mathematics and physics*, Harvester Press, Brighton, 1980, pp.41-96.

135 For a study which emphasises Descartes' methodological and anti-sceptical aspirations, and the distinction between the two, together with the relatively greater significance of the former by comparison with the latter, cf. J.A. Schuster (1980).

136 P. Gassendi, *Opera omnia, I*, p.13b.

137 MS Carpentras 1832, ff.228r-235v; P. Gassendi, *Opera omnia, I*, pp.79b-86a.

138 Cf. R.H. Popkin, *History of scepticism*, p.112.

## Chapter 5

1 "Verisimiliorem sanioremque philosophiam" (Letter to Galileo of 20.7.1625, in P. Gassendi, *Opera omnia, VI*, p.5a.

2 Cf. letter of Sir Charles Cavendish to John Pell of 10.10.1644: "Mr Hobbes writes Gassendes his philosophie is not yet printed but he hath reade it, and that it is as big as Aristotle's philosophie, but much truer

and excellent Latin." (J.O. Halliwell: 1841, *A collection of letters illustrative of the progress of science in England from the reign of Queen Elizabeth to that of Charles the Second*, Historical Society of Science, London, p.85.)

3   Robert Fludd was a London medical practitioner whose name was linked with the secret Rosicrucian Fraternity, so that he was often accepted as a spokesman for the Fraternity. Fludd was criticised by Kepler in the *Harmonices mundi* (1619), and the controversy between Kepler and Fludd continued until 1623. Following the publication of Marin Mersenne's *Quaestiones celeberrimae in Genesim* (1623), Fludd attacked the author in his *Sophiae cum moria certamen* (1629). Gassendi's critique of Fludd (cf. *infra*) was a response, on Mersenne's behalf, to the latter work of Fludd in which the author had complained that Mersenne made too much of pagan philosophy to the neglect of the philosophy of Moses, *i.e.* the philosophy of the *Hermetica* and the Cabbala. (Cf. A.G. Debus: 1965, *The English Paracelsians*, Oldbourne, London; A.G. Debus: 1975, "The chemical debates of the seventeenth century: the reaction of Robert Fludd and Jean Baptiste van Helmont", in M.L. Righini Bonelli and W.R. Shea (Eds.): 1975 (second edition), *Reason, experiment and mysticism in the scientific revolution*, Macmillan, London, pp.19-47; R. Lenoble: 1971, *Mersenne ou la naissance du mécanisme*, Paris, pp.27ff.; J. Godwin: 1979, *Robert Fludd, Hermetic philosopher and surveyor of two worlds*, Thames and Hudson, London.) Fludd often referred to his philosophy as "the true philosophy"; cf. W.H. Huffman and R.A. Seelinger, Jr.: 1978, "Robert Fludd's 'Declaratio brevis' to James I", in *Ambix, 25*, pp.69-92, espc. p.82; R.S. Westman: 1984, "Nature art and psyche: Jung, Pauli and the Kepler-Fludd polemic", in B. Vickers: 1984, *Occult and scientific mentalities in the Renaissance*, Cambridge University Press, Cambridge, pp.177-229, espc. p.194.

4   P. Gassendi, *Opera omnia, II*, p.463a-b; also O.R. Bloch: 1971, *La philosophie de Gassendi. Nominalisme, matérialisme et métaphysique*, Martinus Nijhoff, La Haye, pp.466-472.

5   P. Gassendi, *Opera omnia*, pp.1-30. This *Liber proemialis de philosophia universe* is of uncertain date. The discoloured condition of the manuscript, and the character of the handwriting, indicate that it was written at a date rather earlier than the rest of MS Tours 706, which is the manuscript of the *Syntagma* version.

6   Ch.1, *Quid philosophia sit?* Ch.2, *De fine philosophiae.*

7    Ch.6, *Quam variae apud Graecos fuerint philosophandi rationes, et sectae.*

8    Ch.9, *Philosophiae partitio.*

9    P. Gassendi, *Opera omnia, I*, pp.14a-16a.

10   *Idem, I*, p.14a-b.

11   P. Gassendi, *Opera omnia, I*, p.15a.

12   "Sapientem nihil quod sapiat fabulam ultro fingere sed rebus veris potius haerere; nihilque adeo impedimenti ad sapientiam inducere." (*Idem, I*, pp.14b-15a.) Gassendi gave no reference to indicate where this 'saying' may be found in the works of Epicurus. He exempted from his criticism of "fables" those fables which he considered to be accommodated to the understanding of ordinary people, giving as an example the fables of Aesop; cf. *idem, I*, p.15a.

13   "Idem porro licet dicere de iis qui ea quae docent symbolis, griphis, aenigmatibus contegunt, quatenus illi pari modo ex re seria ludicram faciunt, ac eo ipso ore quo volunt videri verum declarare tenebras offundunt quibus obscuretur. Idem proinde etiam de iisqui aliunde genus dicendi obscurum affectant; certe, ut nihil aliud improbandum sit, approbari saltem non potest iactura eius temporis quod coniiciendo, haerendo, versando, interpretando consumitur, quodque foret satius progressui uberius tentando impendi." (*Idem, I*, p.15a.)

14   Cf. letter of Gassendi to Peiresc of 2.12.1628 in C. de Waard (Ed.): 1945-1972, *Correspondence du P. Marin Mersenne, Religieux Minime*, 12 vols., Paris, 1945-1972, *II*, p.148.

15   P. Gassendi: 1630, *Epistolica exercitatio, in qua principia philosophiae Roberti Fluddi, medici, reteguntur, et ad recentes illius libros adversus R.P.F. Marinum Mersennum ... respondetur ...*, S. Cramoisy, Paris, in P. Gassendi, *Opera omnia, III*, pp.213-267. The term "Hermeticism" refers to a mystical approach to nature that was popular in the Renaissance, especially in the sixteenth century. Hermeticism had a speculative philosophy as its basis, and embraced a wide variety of practical applications in the fields of astrology, alchemy and other occult sciences; it was characterised by an animist and magical view of nature. The literary sources of Hermeticism were especially the *Corpus Hermeticum* and the *Asclepius*, written, according to a tradition that dated from the fourth century, by a certain Egyptian priest named Hermes Trismegistus who lived shortly after the time of Moses. (Cf.

W. Scott (Ed.): 1924, *Hermetica. The ancient Greek and Latin writings which contain religious and philosophic teachings ascribed to Hermes Trismegistus*, Clarendon Press, Oxford.) The writings of Hermes Trismegistus, therefore, were reputed to transmit the ancient Egyptian wisdom, the Divine revelation to the Gentiles, which prophetically foreshadowed Christianity in a more obscure manner than the literature of the Chosen People. It was also reputed to have been a source of Platonic wisdom; consequently, Renaissance neo-Platonism was deeply affected by Hermeticism. Marsilio Ficino (1433-1499) translated the Greek text of the Hermetic literature into Latin in the fifteenth century, and his translation was very influential thereafter until the early seventeenth century. The mysteries of the Jewish Cabbala, occult expressions of the doctrines of the Jewish religion coloured by Parsi, Zoroastrian, neo-Platonic, neo-Pythagorean, Christian, Gnostic and Muslim influences, were linked with the Hermetic tradition especially through the works of Giovanni Pico della Mirandola (uncle of Gianfrancesco). It was demonstrated by Isaac Casaubon in 1614 that the *Hermetica* were written in post-Christian times, so their neo-Platonic features derived from direct association with neo-Platonic philosophy; they were not the intellectual antecedents of Plato's own philosophy, as was previously supposed.

16  M. Mersenne: 1632, *Quaestiones celeberrimae in Genesim* ..., S. Cramoisy, Paris, cols.569-572; cf. cols.714-718. Cf. P. Gassendi, *Opera omnia, III*, p.215.

17  "Ego illum neque cacomagum habeo neque prorsus atheon credo. Suspicor tamen ipsum non modo a nostra religione dissentire, ut propterea haereticus, hoc est ἑτερόδοξος appellari nobis debeat; verum ea quoque de Deo opinari quae si vera fuerint, videri peiora atheismo possint. Etenim quod atheos non sit, vel ex eo patet quod perpetuo Divinam naturam aliquam decantat, et Scripturae sacrae testimonia non aliquoties sed passim usurpat. Deum admittit, a quo vult fieri, foveri, agi, gubernari omnia ... Verum quod naturam Divinam suo illo modo intelligat; quod compositionis ipsius cum Spiritu illo exposito Author sit; quod tale Compositum Christum seu Messiam faciat; quod angelos et animas ipsius esse particulas velit, caeteraque similia quae ex hucusque dictis sequuntur: cum haec sunt religione sacrae plane heterogenea, a quis non putet ipsius sententiam atheismo ipso periculosiorem? Hac sane ratione Plutarchus non obscure innuit satius longe esse Deum negare, quam de ipso superstitiose seu aliter sentire quam sit." (P. Gassendi, *Opera omnia, III*, pp.240b-241a; cf. *idem*, pp.259ff.)

18    "The absurdity and impiety are both astonishing." "Mira etenim hinc absurditatis, illinc impietatis species." (*Idem*, p.262a.)

19    "Nulla ratione excusari potest prophanus abusus, quo dum isti puris impura permiscent, Scripturam sacram, Fidei mysteria, Religionis ritus pessundant, et nihil tam sanctam non violent, modo ad Alchymiam traducant." (*Idem*, p.253a.)

20    *Idem*, pp.221b, 236a.

21    *Idem*, pp.236b-237b, 226b.

22    Gassendi wrote: "While you [Mersenne] pursue an open philosophy which deals with things perceptible, he philosophises as if he wishes to hide himself all the time, spreading an inky cloud under which he might escape the hook." "Cum philosophiam enim apertam, et sensibilem ipse prosequaris, ille tamen sic philosophatur, ut velit semper delitescere, attramentum offundendo, sub quo hamum effugiat." (*Idem*, p.213.)

23    *Idem*, p.231b.

24    "His division for the Monochord is purely arbitrary." "Suam Monochordi divisionem esse mere arbitrariam." (*Idem*, p.246b.) And again: "Whereas you [Mersenne, Kepler] accept laws of harmony based on quantity and numbers, he ties his harmony to pure symbols." "Quamdiu vos quidem Harmonicas leges penes quantitatem, numerosque acceperitis: ipse vero Harmoniam suam alligaverit meris symbolismis." (*Idem*, p.227b.)

25    *Idem*, pp.231b, 233a.

26    "In Physica ... neminem fere videas ex ipsa natura, sed aut ex suis, aut ex aliorum insomniis philosophari. Cum res ipsas nemo inspiciat, immensa sunt tamen quae indigitantur de rebus, commentaria. Quidnam vero haec aliud quam commenta sint; cum mens humana, nisi experientia, et observatione regatur, sit ut bonae frugis sterilissima, sic fertilissima nugarum. Id tu eximie pervidisti qui vis aut experiri omnia, aut virorum fide dignorum experimentis solis fidere ... Legendus liber ipse naturae, si quidpiam certe addiscendum est ..." (*Idem*, p.266.)

27    Gassendi's claim that his Epicurean philosophy was a philosophy of progress needs to be carefully interpreted. Generally, Gassendi's notion of progress was of progress in understanding, not technological

progress. For Gassendi the natural philosopher was a contemplative and a spectator, exploring the effects of a creativity that was not his own. Thus Gassendi did not share the ideal of Francis Bacon of obtaining knowledge that will make humankind masters of nature. For Gassendi, the philosopher seeks *self*-mastery. Cf. P. Gassendi, *Opera omnia*, *I*, pp.1ff. In adhering to this idea of progress, Gassendi followed the tradition of medieval scholasticism; cf. F. Copleston: 1946-1975, *A history of philosophy*, 9 vols., Burns, Oates and Washbourne, London, *III*, pp.21, 357.

28  "De materiali principio, sive materia prima rerum", in P. Gassendi, *Opera omnia*, *I*, pp.229a-282b. This is the title given to the treatise in the *Syntagma* version written between 1649 and 1654. The *Syntagma* version is the 1637 version, MS Tours 709, Bk. XIII and Bk. XV, combined and expanded.

29  Lucretius, *De natura rerum*, (Loeb classical library edition), I, 635-950.

30  P. Gassendi, *Opera omnia*, *I*, pp.234a-237b; cf. MS Tours 709, ff.218v-228v. This section was much re-written for the *Syntagma* version.

31  *Idem, I*, p.241a-b; cf. MS Tours 709, ff.295v, 229rff.

32  *Idem, I*, p.244a; cf. MS Tours 709, ff.231v-232r.

33  *Idem, I*, pp.244b-247a; cf. MS Tours 709, ff.232v-233v.

34  "Sine qualitate, sine forma, sine specie, sine figura" *Idem, I*, pp.247b-256a; cf. MS Tours 709, ff.235r-243r.

35  According to Gassendi's account, all these philosophers had a theory of matter as devoid of all quality, *except*, in the case of some, *e.g.* Plato, the quality of shape. (Cf. Plato, *Timaeus* 53c-55c; also P. Gassendi, *Opera omnia*, pp.233a-b, 236a.)

36  P. Gassendi, *Opera omnia*, *I*, pp.256a-266a; cf. MS Tours 709, ff.166v-176r. Cf. Diogenes Laertius, *De clarorum philosophorum vitis, dogmatibus et apothegmatibus libri decem, X*, (G. Arrighetti (Ed.): 1973, *Epicuro opere*, G. Einaudi, Turin), 44.7-8.

37  Diogenes Laertius, *De clarorum philosophorum vitis*, 41.1-5.

38    "Plenam quandam, seu vacui expertem, solidamque adeo naturam; quippe quae non habeat qua ex parte aut quomodo fissuram admittat sicque dissolvatur." (P. Gassendi, *Opera omnia, I*, p.258b.)

39    Cf. MS Tours 709, f.167r.

40    "Adnotare autem lubet dici ατομον non ut vulgo putant (et quidem alioquin eruditi interpretantur) quod partibus careat, et magnitudine omni destituatur, sitque proinde aliud nihil quam punctum mathematicum." (P. Gassendi, *Opera omnia, I*, p.256b.)

41    Cf. *e.g.*, Plato, *Timaeus* 30c-d, 42a-d, 92.

42    For a study of this theory in the work of Paracelsus, van Helmont, Nicolas LèFevre and others, see D.R. Oldroyd: 1974, "Some neo-Platonic and Stoic influences on mineralogy in the sixteenth and seventeenth centuries", in *Ambix, 21*, pp.128-156; concerning the assumption in the writings of Agrippa, Pico, Reuchlin and Fludd, see S.K. Heninger, Jr.: 1977, *The Cosmographical Glass. Renaissance diagrams of the universe*, The Huntingdon Library, Pasadena, pp.81ff; for Paracelsus, van Helmont, LeFèvre, and for two other philosophers not so far mentioned, *viz.* Sir George Ripley and Jean d'Espagnet, see B.J.T. Dobbs: 1975, *The foundations of Newton's alchemy or 'The hunting of the greene lyon'*, Cambridge University Press, Cambridge, pp.35-39.

43    Cf., Dobbs, *The foundations of Newton's alchemy*, pp.39,193. Dobbs maintains that it was essential to the alchemists that the concept of matter be left vague, for in alchemy it was required that matter and spirit be interconvertible; only on that presumption could alchemical transmutations take place, Cf. Oldroyd's example of the claim of the alchemists to convert corporeal substances into spiritual by an application of heat; Oldroyd: 1974, p.149. There is little need to labour the point that matter as described by Gassendi provided no basis for spiritual alchemy.

44    Cf. Diogenes Laertius, *De clarorum philosophorum vitis*, 40.2; 41.3.

45    "Universum, ex Epicuro, duplici constare natura, corporea puta, et incorporea." (MS Tours 709, f.156r.)

46    Thus, "Liber decimus-tertius de atomis hoc est de natura corporea simplici" became "Liber decimus-tertius de atomis". (MS Tours 709, f.166v.)

47  "De inane, seu loco ..." (MS Tours 709, f.193r.)

48  *E.g.* MS Tours 709, f.193r; P. Gassendi, *Opera omnia, I,* p.185a.
    Gassendi's reference is to Sextus Empiricus, *Against the physicists*
    (Loeb classical library edition), II,2.

49  Gassendi explained the meaning of the term "nature" at the beginning
    of the *Pars physica* of the *Syntagma,* where he reproduced the
    essentials of his earlier explanation in MS Tours 709 (P. Gassendi,
    *Opera omnia, I,* p.125a-b; cf. MS Tours 709, f.147r). Gassendi's
    explanation of the term is quite Aristotelian (cf. Aristotle, *Physics* II,
    192b.7-40). Gassendi explained that the term "nature" translated
    " φύσις" which signified both something which brings to birth and
    something which is brought to birth. It thus refers to both a generative
    principle and something generated. Consequently it applies to all
    things which give rise to other things or which are given rise to.
    Finally, it applies to the totality of things that are and to the power of
    action that is in them, including the Divine force or nature that
    permeates, fosters and drives all things. (The last point of Gassendi's
    explanation was an addition to Aristotle's doctrine from his own
    voluntarist theology.)

50  "Liber decimus-quintus de principiis, seu elementis" ("seu materia
    rerum" having been crossed out and "seu elementis" having been put
    in its place). (MS Tours 709, f.215r.)

51  "C.1. Quatenus natura concreta materialibus principiis seu elementis
    indigeat." (MS Tours 709, f.215r.)

52  P. Gassendi, *Opera omnia, I,* pp.179a-184b. It is to be noted, also, that
    this description of space more closely resembles the Stoic doctrine of
    the void as described in Sextus Empiricus, *Outlines of Pyrrhonnism*
    (Loeb classical library edition), III, 124.

53  "De eadem iuxta Epicuram, Democritum, caeterosque adsertores
    atomorum." (MS Tours 709, ff.243v-246v.)

54  MS Tours 709, ff.206r,244v; cf. P. Gassendi, *Opera omnia, I,* p.281a.

55  Gassendi argued both that the Epicurean doctrine of atoms and the
    Aristotelian doctrine of prime matter, and that the Epicurean doctrine
    of modes and the Aristotelian doctrine of qualities and accidents, were
    equivalent. Cf. *supra,* Ch.3.

56    MS Tours 709, f.158r. Epicurus referred to the void as "intactile
      nature" (" ἀναφὴς φύσις "), D. Laertius, *De clarorum philosophorum
      vitis*, 40.2, 86.4), which also may be translated as "intactile substance".
      Gassendi interpreted Epicurus' text as having the full Aristotelian
      meaning when the term "nature"/"substance" was used.

57    "Durum quidem videri potest ipsum inane cum pertinere ad
      substantiam debeat, adpellari non modo ens, sed etiam ens per se
      existens; attamen ex infra dicendis tam de inani quam de tempore hoc
      non impossibile fiet. Illud est gravius, non quod substantia in
      corpoream et incorpoream dividatur, sed quod nomine incorporeae
      non intelligat Epicurus neque Naturam Divinam, neque naturam
      daemoniam, sive intelligentiarum, neque naturam animi." (MS Tours
      709, f.158r.)

58    Aristotle, *Physics* 211b.6-9, 212a.3-5.

59    P. Gassendi, *Opera omnia, I*, p.247a.

60    T. Campanella: 1620, *De sensu rerum et magia, libri quatuor* ...,
      Frankfurt, Bk. 1, ch. 12; cf. A. Fallico and H. Shapiro (Eds.): 1967,
      *Renaissance philosophy*, Vol. 1: *The Italian philosophers*, New York,
      pp.366-368; cf. also, E. Grant: 1981, *Much ado about nothing. Theories
      of space and vacuum from the Middle Ages to the Scientific
      Revolution*, Cambridge University Press, Cambridge, pp.194-199.

61    Cf. the sections added to the *Syntagma* version of Gassendi's treatise
      on space, especially pp.189a-191b; cf MS Tours 709, ff.202v-203r,
      204r, 206r-v.

62    T. Campanella, *De sensu rerum et magia* 1, 12.

63    F. Patrizi: 1587, *Philosophiae de rerum natura libri duo ... alter de
      spacio physico, alter de spacio mathematico*, Ferrara.

64    F. Patrizi: 1591, *Nova de universis philosophia in qua Aristotelica
      methodo, non per motum, sed per lucem et lumina, ad primam causam
      ascenditur, deinde propria Patricii methodo, tota in contemplationem
      venit divinitas; postremo methodo platonica, rerum universitas, a
      conditore Deo deducitur...*, Ferrara, f.65v, cols. 1-2.

65    "De hoc autem spatio, seu loco, cui trina dimensio, longitudo,
      profunditas competat, non alia [Patritius] tradit, quam quae ipsi de eo
      ratiocinati superius sumus." (*Idem, I*, p.246a.)

66 "Franciscus Patritius ... superiore saeculo ... novam, veram, integram (eius sunt verba) de universo conditurus philosophiam, comprobasse se illius pronunciata dixit ex divinis oraculis (intelligit autem non modo Mosaica, sed etiam, quae fuere Zoroastris, Trismegisti, Orphei, *etc*.) geometricis necessitatibus, philosophicis rationibus, clarissimis experimentis." (P. Gassendi, *Opera omnia I*, p.246a.)

67 *Idem, I*, pp.243b-247b.

68 "Dicunt ... Stoici nostri duo esse in rerum natura, ex quibus omnia fiunt, caussam, et materiam. Materia jacet iners, res ad omnia parata, cessatura si nemo movet. Caussa autem, id est ratio, materiam format, et quocumque vult, versat. Ex illa varia opera prodeunt. Esse ergo debet aliquid unde fiat, deinde a quo fiat. Hoc caussa est, illud materia. Omnis ars imitatio est naturae: itaque quod de universo dicebam huc transfer. Statua et materiam habuit quae pateretur, et artificem qui materiam daret faciem. Ergo in statua, materia aes fuit, caussa artifex. Eadem conditio rerum omnium est. Ex eo constant quod sit, et ex eo quod facit. Stoicis placet unam caussam esse id quod facit." (Seneca, *Ad Lucilium epistolae morales* (Loeb classical library edition), LXV, 2-3; MS Tours 709,f.247r; P. Gassendi, *Opera omnia*, *I*, p.229a.)

69 "De materiali principio, sive materia prima rerum." (P. Gassendi, *Opera omnia, I*, pp.229a-282b.)

70 "De principio efficiente, seu de causis rerum." (*Idem, I*, pp.283a-337b.)

71 "De causis, fortuna et fato." (MS Tours 709,f.247r.)

72 "De atomis." (*Idem*, ff.166v-192v.)

73 "De principiis, seu elementis." (*Idem*, ff.215r-246v.)

74 MS Tours 709, f.251v; cf. P. Gassendi, *Opera omnia, I*, pp.333b-334a. Gassendi represented the Stoics as having postulated corporeal or material causes, explaining that these causes were composed of a special - active - kind of matter (whereas Leucippus, Democritus and later, Epicurus made no distinction between matter as such and the efficient cause or principle). Gassendi described in this manner the Stoic doctrine that Air and Fire were active elements and the source of motion; cf. D. Laertius, *De clarorum philosophorum vitis, VII*, 156; Cicero, *De natura deorum* (Loeb classical library edition), II, 23-289. Concerning the doctrine of Leucippus and Democritus, cf. Aristotle,

*Metaphysics* 985b5-19. Concerning the doctrine of Epicurus, cf. D. Laertius, *De clarorum philosophorum vitis*, 43.4-10. Cf. also S. Samburksy: 1959, *Physics of the Stoics*, Routledge and Kegan Paul, London, Ch.1.

75 Cf. *supra*, Ch.3

76 "Superest pondus, seu gravitas, ex qua sequitur atomorum motus. Nomine autem gravitatis non est hoc loco intelligenda atomorum propensio in centrum, sive medium universi ... sed vis, seu impulsio naturae ex una parte universi in aliam absque ullo termino." (MS Tours 709, f.185r.)

77 He quoted Lucretius, *De rerum natura*, II, 64-65, 89-94, and then continued as follows: "Itaque censet Epicurus atomos omneis praeditas esse interna quaedam energia, seu vigore ingenito quo sese ipsas cieant, ac per inane ita compellant, ut nisi quid obstiterit, absque ullo fine moveantur." (MS Tours 709, f.185r.)

78 "... naturalis internaque facultas seu vis, qua per seipsam ciere, movereque potest atomus; seu mavis, quam ingenita, innata, nativa, inamissibilisque ad motum propensio, et ab intrinseco propulsio, atque impetus." (P. Gassendi, *Opera omnia*, *I*, p.273b.)

79 "Supponi potest atomos singulas accepisse a Deo creante ut quantulamcumque suam corpulentiam, magnitudinemve et figuram varietate ineffabili; sic et vim congruam sese movendi, ciendi, evolvendi, et consequenter sese extricandi, emergendi, prosiliendi, impingendi, retundendi, regrediendi." (*Idem, I*, p.280b.)

80 "Ut dicam vero id quod res est, non videtur materia nisi improprie dici caussa: neque enim proprie requisieris ex qua caussa facta sit statua." (MS Tours 709, f.248r; cf. P. Gassendi, *Opera omnia*, *I*, p.284a.)

81 "Et quamvis Epicurus posset materiam caussam dicere ob motum atomis coaevum, non tamen Aristoteles, qui materiam inertem facit." (MS Tours 709, f.248r; P. Gassendi, *Opera omnia*, *I*, p.284a.)

82 Aristotle, *Metaphysics* 985b.19, 1071b.31; *De caelo* 300b.8; *Physics* 254a.32.

83 Cf. W.K.C. Guthrie: 1962-1981, *A history of Greek philosophy*, 6 vols., Methuen, London, *II*, pp.396-399.

84    Gassendi wrote: "They [Leucippus and Democritus] did *not* neglect [to
      explain the principle of motion] but they only wanted to ensure that
      the efficient be not considered as distinct in substance from the
      material principle. It is to be noted ... that they considered atoms to be
      not at all inert and immobile, but to be, on the contrary, extremely
      active and mobile. And for this reason held them to be the first
      principle of motion. However, Epicurus expressed the doctrine more
      explicitly when he said that the property of atoms which Democritus
      did not name was in fact their weight, the source of their motion."
      "Enimvero illi [Leucippus et Democritus] non praetermiserunt, sed
      voluerint solum principium efficiens non distingui a materiali
      secundum substantiam. Notum quippe ... atomos ... habitas fuisse non
      inerteis ac immobileis, sed actuosissimas potius atque mobilissimas,
      adeo ut illas habuerint pro primo principio unde rerum motus.
      Epicurus autem rem magis expressit cum tacitam Democrito
      proprietatem atomorum pondus esse dixit, unde motus foret." (MS
      Tours 709, f.251v; cf. P. Gassendi, *Opera omnia, I*, p.333b.)

85    Lucretius, *De rerum natura*, II, 61-66, 83-85, 217-224.

86    "Quandam vim motus habebunt, a Democrito, impulsionis quam
      plagam ille appellat; a te, Epicure, gravitatis et ponderis." (Cicero, *De
      fato* (Loeb classical library edition), XX, 46.)

87    "Non modo numero, sed etiam substantia discretas" (MS Tours 709,
      f.251r).

88    MS Tours 709, f.2512v; P. Gassendi, *Opera omnia, I*. pp.333b-334a.
      Cf. Aristotle, *Metaphysics* 985b5-19; D. Laertius, *De clarorum
      philosophorum vitis*, 43.4-10.

89    "Quae sit physicarum caussarum substantia" (MS Tours 709, ff.250v-
      253r). Cf. R. Pintard: 1943, *La Mothe le Vayer, Gassendi - Guy Patin.*,
      Boivin, Paris, pp.38-39. Gassendi's very un-Aristotelian phrase "the
      *substance* of physical causes" shows the influence of Sextus Empiricus;
      cf. Sextus Empiricus, *Outlines of Pyrrhonism* (Loeb classical library
      edition), III, 13. However, Sextus Empiricus was not using the term
      "substance" in the strict Aristotelian sense in this passage.
      Consequently, Gassendi's attack on Aristotelian incorporeal causes was
      largely inspired by a misreading of Sextus Empiricus.

90    "Sequitur jam ut disquiramus quid philosophi de substantia harum
      caussarum senserint. De primum quidem non defuere qui incorporeas
      existimarint, quemadmodum Pythagoras ... [*Syntagma*: itemque Plato]
      unoque verbo quotquot voluerunt dari animam sive formam Mundi

cujus quae singulares rerum omnium sunt forma, particulae sint
[*Syntagma*: a quibus sit omnis efficacia in rebus]. Videtur quoque
sententia peripatetica esse, quatenus volunt formas esse actus quosdam
simplices rerum quos eosdem dicunt incorporeos ... " (MS Tours 709,
f,250v; cf. P. Gassendi, *Opera omnia, I*, p.333a-b.)

91   P. Gassendi, *Opera omnia, I*, pp.248a-250a, 285a, 334aff.

92   Gassendi suspended work on the *Syntagma* at this point. It was the
     year 1637, and he did not resume work until 1642. He gave as his
     reasons for the five-year interruption the death of Peiresc on 24th
     June 1637, his own illness, and the fact that he was too busy in that
     period to concentrate on his writing; cf. MS Tours 709, f.268r; cf. also
     a letter of Gassendi to Louis of Valois of 9.10.1641 in P. Gassendi,
     *Opera omnia, VI*, p.116. In fact he managed to complete a formidable
     volume of minor writings during the five-year period. He wrote a life
     of Peiresc, three of the four letters "On the apparent magnitude of the
     sun", the first two letters published as *De motu impresso a motore
     translato*, and his critique of the *Meditations* of Descartes. Thus his
     excuse that he was too busy to concentrate on his Epicurean project
     during those years would seem to have been well founded. O.R. Bloch
     has suggested that the suspension of work on the *Syntagma* is to be
     explained by the crisis in Gassendi's philosophical development that he
     experienced when he found his philosophy being dragged in the
     direction of materialism; cf. O.R. Bloch: 1971, *La philosophie de
     Gassendi*, pp.359-361; Since I dispute Bloch's interpretation, I see no
     reason not to accept Gassendi's own explanation of the five-year
     suspension of labour on the *Syntagma* project.

93   "Est autem concipienda praeterea intrinseca magis et substantialis
     forma, quae materiam appetitumque illius substantialem satiet,
     statuens cum illa compositum substantiale ac ens per se; adeo ut, cum
     materiam perficiat, dicatur ἐντέλεχεια , *perfectihabia*, itemque ἐνέργεια ,
     *actus*, quod materiam actuet seu informet; quod tribuat ipsi ut sit actu
     in certo entis genere; quod conferat composito vim agendi, sitque in eo
     radix proprietatum accidentiumque praecipuorum ipsius." (MS Tours
     709, f.235r; cf. P. Gassendi, *Opera omnia, I*, p.249a. Cf. Aristotle, *De
     anima* 412a.27ff; *De generatione animalium* 734a.30ff; *Metaphysica*
     1050a.23ff; *Physica* 257b.8ff.)

94   Cf. P. Gassendi, *Opera omnia, III*, p.125b.

95   *E.g.* Aristotle, *Physics* 193a30-b18; *Metaphysics* 12033a23 - 1034a.7,
     1035a.1-32, 1036a.26 - 1036b.32; *De partibus animalium* 640b.28,
     641a.25-32, cf. 663b.22; *De generatione animalium* 770b.16-17.

96   Aristotle, *Physics* 193a30-b18.

97   P. Gassendi, *Opera omnia, I*, p.249a-b; cf. MS Tours 709, f.235v.

98   P. Gassendi, *Opera omnia, I*, p.249b; cf. MS Tours 709, f.235v. R. Hooykaas has argued that the rejection of the theory of privation prepared the way for corpuscular theories; cf. R. Hooykaas: 1958, *Humanisme, science et réforme: Pierre de la Ramée (1515-1572)*, Leyden, p.44.

99   P. Gassendi: 1642, *De apparente magnitudine solis humilis et sublimis epistolae quatuor, in quibus complura physica opticaque problemata proponuntur et explicantur*, in P. Gassendi, *Opera omnia, III*, pp.422b-448a, espc. p.425b. The most significant of Gassendi's discussions of the Aristotelian forms in the later period are to be found in Bk. XVII of MS Tours 709 (on generation), and Bk. XIX of the same manuscript (on qualities) and in P. Gassendi, *Opera omnia, I*, pp.333a-337b, which is the extensively re-written version of Ch.3 of Bk XVI of MS Tours 709.

100  "It is quite out of the question to conceive of them [forms] in the way the Peripatetics do, as immaterial entities, for such entities are not even true entities, let alone being able to act and be causes." "Concipere illas profecto non licet, more Peripatetico, tanquam entitates experteis materiae, quae ne entitates quidem verae sunt, tantum abest ut agere, caussaeque esse valeant." (MS Tours 709, f.252r.) Cf. also P. Gassendi, *Opera omnia, I*, p.285a; this passage attacking the Aristotelian claim that forms are causes is almost entirely an addition to the *Syntagma* version. In MS Tours 709, ff.247r-248r Gassendi had been content to argue that forms were only improperly speaking causes, and that Aristotle had almost said as much; in the *Syntagma* version Gassendi attacked the Aristotelian doctrine explicitly on the false grounds that Aristotle claimed that forms were efficient causes.

101  P. Gassendi, *Opera omnia*, especially *I*, pp.466b-470b.

102  *Idem, I*, p.469a.

103  *Idem, I*, pp.469a-470b; cf. *I*, pp.231a, 466bff.

104  "Neque Aristoteles neque ipsi [the interpreters of Aristotle] propterea declarant unde haec forma seu actus sit ac vim agendi habeat ... Tametsi enim dicere soleant educi formam ex materia, id tamen

dicunt, quod captum fugiat, quatenus volunt formam esse veram aliquam entitatem distinctam a materia, et nihilominus non concedunt vel minimam particulam materiae transire in ipsam, atque adeo materiam quidpiam amittere, tametsi ex ea quidpiam educatur. Nam et quod aiunt formam educi ex potentia materiae, verba mera sunt. Quia si velint quidem eam sic educi ut sit tantum materiae modus quemadmodum figura statuae in quam aes aut lignum formatur, tum dicent quidem aliquid, sed forma erit mere passiva uti et materia cuius erit modus, nullatenus vero activum principium." (P. Gassendi, *Opera omnia*, *I*, p.335a.)

105 "... ex commistis et coalitis, et vi quadam omneis permanente contentis, veluti planta, animal." (P. Gassendi, *Opera omnia*, *I*, p.155b; cf. MS Tours 709, f.452r.)

106 "Plerique quidem, sed non omnes fatentur esse vim quandam per totum mundum sic diffusam, parteisque eius continentem, cuiusmodi in animali est anima; ut in nobis, membrisque nostris vis illa interna, qua vivimus, sentimus, imaginamur, movemur; et qua digressa dissolvimur, taleque nihil amplius praestamus." (P. Gassendi, *Opera omnia*, *I*, p.155b; cf. MS Tours 709, f.452r.)

107 Cf. Plato, *Timaeus* 34a-47e. This is the chief source for both Platonic and Pythagorean doctrine on the World Soul. Cf. also S.K. Heninger, Jr.: 1977, *The cosmographical glass*, pp.81-143.

108 P. Gassendi, *Opera omnia*, *I*, pp.155b, 157a; cf. MS Tours 709, ff.448r, 449v. Gassendi clearly misrepresented the position: there was considerable affinity between the doctrine of the World Soul of the new-Pythagoreans and neo-Platonists and that of the ancient Pythagoreans and Platonists. Furthermore, the World Soul doctrine was worked out in some detail by Plato (cf. *Timaeus* 34a-47e).

109 Cf. P. Gassendi, *Opera omnia*, *I*, p.155b.

110 "Arbitrabar nihil propterea derogari sacrae Fidei, quod et forma tantum quaedam a Deo dependens intelligeretur, et Anima diceretur esse sui generis, hoc est a tribus illis vulgatis, vegetativo, sensitivo ac rationali distincti, et nominatim spiritualis gratiae ac foelicitatis uti nostra humana est, esse incapax censeretur." (P. Gassendi, *Opera omnia*, *III*, p.236a.

111 "Vel Animam Mundi, vel Mentem, vel Deum, vel quidvis aliud." (MS Tours 709, f.235v.)

112 "Satis est enim quod tenuerint eandem prope rem quam nos profitemur." (MS Tours 709, f.253v.)

113 "Naturam ... divinam ubique adesse, quae in res omneis intime per sui essentiam, praesentiam, potentiamque sic illabatur, ut omnia conservet, coagat rebus omnibus, ipsa conditrix omnium rerum." (MS Tours 709, ff.253v-254r.)

114 "Neque obstat quod talem causam vel Deum, vel Mentem, vel Naturam, vel Necessitatem, vel Fatum, vel quidvis aliud dixerint, satis est enim quod tenuerint eandem prope rem quem nos profitemur." (P. Gassendi, *Opera omnia, I.* p.287b.)

115 "Vis illum [Deum] Fatum vocare? Non errabis; hic est ex quo suspensa sunt omnia, causa causarum. Vis illum Providentiam? Recte dices; est enim cuius consilio huic mundo providetur, ut inconcussus eat et actus suos explicet. Vis Naturam vocare? Non peccabis; est enim ex quo nata sunt omnia cuius spiritu vivimus, *etc.*" (Seneca, *Quaestiones naturales* (cf. Loeb classical library edition), II, 45.2.)

116 P. Gassendi, *Opera omnia, I*, p.155b; MS Tours 709, f.448r. The theory of an all-pervading heat was adopted by the Stoics. The following is a frequently quoted Stoic saying: "Nature is an artistically working fire, going on its way to create", (Diogenes Laertius, *De clarorum philosophorum vitis, VII*, 156.5.). Cf. S. Sambursky: 1959, *Physics of the Stoics*, Routledge and Kegan Paul, London, pp.3-4. Cf. the comprehensive article on the subject by Rosaleen Love: 1972, "Some sources of Herman Boerhaave's concept of fire", in *Ambix, 19*, pp.157-174. This passage concerning the alleged legitimate and illegitimate ways in which one might consider that the world had a soul reflects not only Gassendi's critique of the doctrine of the World Soul as expounded by Robert Fludd, but also a long history of philosophical discussion before that (cf. Richard C. Dales: 1980, "Medieval deanimation of the heavens", in *Journal of the history of ideas, 41*, pp.531-550).

117 P. Gassendi, *Opera omnia, I*, pp.158b-159a; MS Tours 709, ff.451v-452v.

118 P. Gassendi, *Opera omnia, II*, pp.169b-178b, especially pp.170b-171a.

119 "Quaeres forte quandonam fuerint ista semina in terra creata? ... at nobis dicendum posse perdurare a primo usque conditu rerum; fuisse enim a Deo effecta, et varie per terram ubicuique fuit commodius respersa cum iussit terram germinare, herbarumque et arborum species

omneis producere." (*Idem, II*, p.170b. Cf. D. Laertius, *De clarorum philosophorum vitis*, 38.9; 74.9-10.) In adopting the theory of "seeds" as presented by Epicurus, Gassendi eschewed the theories of the Stoic-Epicurean tradition which were underpinned by the World-Soul theory. Cf. D.R. Oldroyd: 1974, "Some neo-Platonic and Stoic influences on mineralogy in the sixteenth and seventeenth centuries", in *Ambix, 21*, pp.128-156.

120 *Genesis*, I, 11-12.

121 P. Gassendi, *Opera omnia, II*, p.170a-b.

122 This theory was not peculiar to Cabbalist doctrine.

123 "Nullam esse herbam aut plantam inferius cuius non sit stella in firmamento quae eam percutiat et dicat ei, cresce." (P. Gassendi, *Opera omnia, II*, p.170a.)

124 "Quippe opus quidem est calore solis quo terra stipata solvatur ipsaque seminum substantia discutiatur quadamtenus, sed calor huiuscemodi causa est solum extrinseca seu amovens impedimenta quae vim seminalem sive formatricem tenent irretitam, sopitam, inertem." (*Idem, II*, p.170b; cf. Aristotle, *De generatione animalium* 743a.35-36, and Theophrastus, *De causis plantarum* 1.5.5.)

125 P. Gassendi, *Opera omnia, II*, p.170b.

126 Cf. S.K. Heninger, *The gosmographical glass*, pp.81-143.

127 "Ita, quo lapides formentur, debet omnino praeter calorem aliudve agens extrinsecum esse interiorem quaedam vis quae conformationem moliatur et seminalis censeri possit." (P. Gassendi, *Opera omnia, II*, p.114a.)

128 *Idem, II*, pp.3a-b, 112a-143b. Cf. O.R. Bloch: 1971, *La philosophie de Gassendi. Nominalisme, matérialisme et métaphysique*, Martinus Nijhoff, The Hague, pp.261ff; Bloch considers that Gassendi was much influenced by Etienne de Clave in his treatment of the subject.

129 P. Gassendi, *Opera omnia, II*, p.113a-b.

130 P. Gassendi, *Opera omnia, I*, pp.713a-752b.

131 *Idem, II*, pp.113b-114a.

132 J. Kepler: 1611, *Strena seu de nive sexangula*, Frankfurt, (C. Hardie (Ed. and Transl.): 1966, J. Kepler, *The six-cornered snowflake*), Clarendon Press, Oxford.

133 "An rerum omnium naturalium ut peculiaria sunt semina ita peculiares figurae, atque adeo ut animalia, ut plantae, ut lapides, non-nisi certis delineantur formis, sic delineantur caeterae res seminum suorum necessitate? ... ut proinde possit nix quoque ratione illa sibi propria crescendo configurari." (P. Gassendi, *Opera omnia, II*, p.81a.)

134 *Idem, II*, p.81a.

135 Cf. the third letter *De proportione qua gravia decidentia accelerantur*, in P. Gassendi, *Opera omnia, III*, pp.625-650, espc. pp.630b-636a.

136 P. Gassendi, *Opera omnia, I*, pp.345b-346a; *II*, pp.122a-135b

137 P. Gassendi, *Opera omnia, II*, pp.128a-135b.

138 "Virtutem ... magnetis in ferrum emissam effluxum esse corporeum, constantemve ex corpusculis quae pro dispositione qua sunt corpusculorum ferri immutationem faciant." (*Idem, II*, p.129b.)

139 *Idem, II*, p.132a.

140 *Idem, II*, p.133a.

141 "Causaris deinde, me multa movere ut gravia non a propria natura, sed a Terra diffusis circumquaque corpusculis illecta, atque etiam illigata deorsum trahi persuadeam. Sed facio nimirum, Vir doctissime, ac religiossime, quod dum in pervestigatione causarum naturalium versor, nusquam non caligo mihi offundatur; atque idcirco tanquam incedens in densissimis tenebris nihil non palpitem, nihil non moveam, nullam non tentem semitam, si forte in aliquam speciem vel tenuissimae luculae emergam." (*Idem, III*, p.630b.)

142 "Difficultas praesertim est de caussis internis, quas qui investigant dicuntur non immerito scrutari arcana naturae." (MS Tours 709, f.248v; cf. P. Gassendi, *Opera omnia, I*, p.284a.)

143 Cf. Keith Hutchison: 1982, "What happened to occult qualities in the scientific revolution?" in *Isis, 73*, pp.233-252.

144 The results of my researches into Gassendi's attitude to "obscure" philosophy corroborate Brian Vickers' description of the opposition of

men of science in the seventeenth century to the "occult mentality"; cf. B. Vickers (Ed.): 1984, *Occult and scientific mentalities in the Renaissance*, Cambridge University Press, Cambridge, introduction and pp.95-163, "Analogy versus identity: the rejection of occult symbolism". I found Vicker's treatment especially helpful when I came to compose the next few paragraphs.

145 Robert Boyle: 1661, *The sceptical chymist*, (Everyman Library edition), p.23.

## Conclusion

1   P. Gassendi, *Opera omnia, III*, p.102.

2   E.J. Dijksterhuis: 1961, *The mechanization of the world picture*, Clarendon Press, Oxford, p.425. H. Kearney has presented a similar view, as follows: "His [Gassendi's] interest for contemporaries lay in his claim to have constructed a theory of atomism which could be reconciled with Christianity. He could claim to have baptised Democritus and Lucretius as Aquinas had baptised Aristotle." (H. Kearney: 1971, *Science and change, 1500-1700*, Weidenfeld and Nicolson, London, p.170.)

3   Cf. P. Gassendi, *Opera omnia, II.* p.425b; *III*, pp.101, 207b; *V*, p.171; *VI*, p.54a-b.

4   Gassendi wrote, for example: "Where religion prescribes a thing for our belief, it is rash, indeed it is madness, even to murmur in a way that contradicts." "Ubi religio praescripsit nobis aliquid, temeritas, imo furor est, in oppositum quidpiam mussitare." (P. Gassendi, *Opera omnia, V*, p.17a.)

5   Cf. H.O. Evennett: 1968, *The spirit of the Counter-Reformation*, Cambridge University Press, Cambridge, p.79.

6   Cf. Vatican Council II, "Decree on the training of Priests", par.15, in A. Flannery (Ed.): 1975, *Vatican Council II. The conciliar and post-conciliar documents*, Dominican Publications, Dublin, p.718; also "A note on the controversy about the place of St. Thomas in ecclesiastical studies", in H. Vorgrimler (Ed.): 1967-1969, *Commentary on the documents of Vatican II*, 5 vols., Burns and Oates, London, *II*, p.395.

7    Cf. *e.g.*, P. Hoenen S.J.: 1949, *Cosmologia*, fourth edition, Pontificia Universitas Gregoriana Press, Rome, pp.99-101, 107, 108, 155, 546, 547, 552. Such modern neo-scholastic manuals of philosophy for use in seminaries were very eclectic: they provided instruction on all important systems, doctrines and theories, sometimes presenting these latter as worthy of consideration or even acceptance, along with what was usually a much vulgarized version of Thomistic-Aristotelian philosophy.

# BIBLIOGRAPHY

## Works of Gassendi

Gassendi, P.: 1658, *Opera omnia*, 6 vols., Lyon (1964, Faksimile-Neudruck der Ausgabe von Lyon, F. Fromann, Stuttgart-Bad Cannstatt).

1624, *Exercitationum paradoxicarum adversus Aristoteleos libri septem. In quibus praecipua totius peripateticae doctrinae fundamenta excutiuntur: opiniones verae aut novae, aut ex vetustioribus obsoletae stabiliuntur. Authore Petro Gassendo ...*, P. Verderii, Grenoble.

1624, *Dissertations en forme de paradoxes contre les Aristotéliciens (Exercitationes paradoxicae adversus Aristoteleos)* (1959, Rochot, B., (Ed.), J. Vrin, Paris).

1630, *Epistolica exercitatio, in qua principia philosophiae Roberti Fluddi, medici, reteguntur, et ad recentes illius libros adversus R.P.F. Marinum Mersennum Ordinis Minimorum Sancti Francisci de Paula scriptos, respondetur*, S. Cramoisy, Paris.

1630, *Parhelia, sive soles quatuor qui circa verum apparuerunt Romae, die xx mensis martii anno 1629, et de eisdem Petri Gassendi ad Henricum Renerium epostola*, A. Vitray, Paris.

1632, *Mercurius in sole visus et Venus invisa Parisiis anno 1631 ... Epistolae duae, cum observatis quibusdam aliis*, S. Cramoisy, Paris.

1632-1633, *Lettres familiçres à Franèois Luillier pendant l'hiver 1632-1633* (1944, Rochot, B., (Ed.), J. Vrin, Paris).

1634, MS Carpentras 1832 (ff.205-259). (This manuscript contains three books of the logic and the first two chapters of the *Pars physica* of Gassendi's second version of his Epicurean philosophy. The manuscript is conserved in the Bibliothèque Inguimbertine in Carpentras, France.)

1636-1637, 1642, MS Tours 709 (ff.147-500). (This manuscript contains Bks. XII to XX of the *Pars physica* of Gassendi's second version of his Epicurean philosophy. The manuscript is conserved in the Municipal Library of Tours.)

1641, *Viri illustris Nicolai Claudii Fabricii de Peiresc Senatoris Aquisextiensis vita*, S. Cramoisy, Paris.

1642, MS Ashburnham 1239 (ff.501-575). (This manuscript contains Bk. XXI of the *Pars physica* of Gassendi's second and penultimate version of his Epicurean philosophy, the book which treated of God as Creator and Ruler of the universe. The manuscript is conserved in the Biblioteca Laurentiana, Florence.)

1642-1643, MS Tours 710 (ff.576-852). (This manuscript contains Bks. XXI to XXIV of the *Pars physica* of Gassendi's second and penultimate version of his Epicurean philosophy, the section which dealt with physical astronomy. The manuscript is conserved in the Municipal Library of Tours.)

1642, *De apparente magnitudine solis humilis et sublimis epistolae quatuor, in quibus complura physica opticaque problemata proponuntur et explicantur*, L. de Heuqueville, Paris.

1642, *De motu impresso a motore translato epistolae duae, in quibus aliquot praecipue, tum de motu universe, tum speciatim de motu terrae attributo, difficultates explicantur*, L. de Heuqueville, Paris.

1644, *Disquisitio metaphysica, seu dubitationes et instantiae adversus Renati Cartesii metaphysicam et responsa*, J. Blaeu, Amsterdam.

1644, *Disquisitio metaphysica, seu dubitationes et instantiae adversus Renati Cartesii metaphysicam et responsa. Recherches métaphysiques, ou doutes et instances contre la métaphysique de R. Descartes et ses reponses* (1962, Rochot, B. (Ed.), J. Vrin, Paris, 1962).

1644, MS Tours 707 (ff.853-1037). (This manuscript contains Bk. XXV of the *Pars physica* of Gassendi's second and penultimate version of his Epicurean philosophy, the section which dealt with "Earthly things" (*"De rebus terrenis"*). The manuscript is conserved in the Municipal Library of Tours.)

1645, MS Tours 708 (ff.1039-1577). (This manuscript contains the section of the *Pars physica* of Gassendi's Epicurean philosophy which was published in the *Syntagma* as the treatise on "Earthly living things, or animals" (Section 3, part 2). The manuscript is preserved in the Municipal Library of Tours.)

1645, *Oratio inauguralis habita in Regio Parisiensi Collegio, anno 1645, die novembris 23*, L. de Heuqueville, Paris.

1646, *De proportione qua gravia accidentia accelerantur epistolae tres, quibus ad totidem epistolas R.P. Cazrei ... respondetur*, L. de Heuqueville, Paris.

1647, *De vita et moribus Epicuri libri octo*, G. Barbier, Lyon.

1647, *Institutio astronomica iuxta hypotheseis tam veterum quam Copernici et Tychonis Brahei*, L. de Heuqueville, Paris.

1649, *Animadversiones in decimum librum Diogenis Laertii, qui est de vita, moribus, placitisque Epicuri*, G. Barbier, Lyon.

1649-1655, MS Tours 706 (pp.1-619). (This manuscript is a new version, published in the *Syntagma*, of MS Carpentras 1832, MS Tours 709, MS Ashburnham 1239 and MS Tours 710. The manuscript is conserved in the Municipal Library of Tours.)

1650, *Receuil de lettres des sieurs Morin ... et Gassend, en suite de l'apologie du sieur Gassend touchant la question "de motu impresso a motore translato" ... - Examen de la response du sieur Jean-Baptiste Morin, docteur en médicine et professeur de Roy aux mathématiques à Paris, à la lettre d'un faux amy de M. Gaultier ...*, A. Courbé, Paris.

1654, *Tychonis Brahei vita. (De vita et morte Tychonis Brahei oratio J. Jessendii.) Accessit N. Copernici, G. Peurbachii, et Joannis Regiomontani vita*, M. Dupuis, Paris.

1658, *Pierre Gassendi's Institutio logica (1658), a critical edition with translation and introduction* (1981, Jones, H. (Ed.), Van Gorcum, Assen).

1659, *The vanity of judiciary astrology, or divination by the stars. Lately written in Latin, by that great schollar and mathematician, the illustrious Petrus Gassendus, mathematical professor to the King of France. Translated into English by a Person of Quality*, H. Moseley, London.

- Fonds français, MS 12270. (This is a collection of Gassendi's correspondence and other manuscript material relating to Gassendi. The collection is conserved in the Bibliothèque Nationale, Paris.)

## Other primary sources

Alexandro, A. Ab: 1532, *Alexandri ab Alexandro ... Genialium dierum libri sex ...*, Paris.

Anon., *Fonds latin*, MS 11139 (seventeenth-century student note-book of scholastic philosophy conserved in the Bibliothèque Nationale, Paris).

Anon., *Fonds latin*, MS 11140 (follows MS 11139; seventeenth-century student note-book of scholastic philosophy conserved in the Bibliothèque Nationale, Paris).

Anon., *Fonds latin*, MS 11141 (seventeenth-century student note-book of scholastic philosophy conserved in the Bibliothèque Nationale, Paris).

Anon., *Fonds latin*, MS 11154, *Compendia philosophica* (seventeenth-century student note-book of scholastic philosophy conserved in the Bibliothèque Nationale, Paris).

Anon.: 1785, *Institutiones philosophicae, auctoritate D.D. Archiepiscopi Lugdunensis, ad usum scholarum suae diocesis editae*, Lyons.

Anon., MS Tours 715 (seventeenth-century student note-book of scholastic philosophy conserved in the Municipal Library, Tours).

Anon., MS Tours 718 (seventeenth-century student note-book of scholastic philosophy conserved in the Municipal Library, Tours).

Aquinas, T., *Summa theologiae* (1962-1980, Blackfriars edition, 60 vols., Eyre and Spottiswoode, London).

Aristotle, *The complete works of Aristotle* (1984, Barnes, J. (Ed.), the revised Oxford translation, 2 vols., Princeton University Press, Princeton).

Arnaudus, A.: 1609, *Ioci (Epistolae, etc.) ...*, J. Bramereau, Paris.

Augustinus, A., *De civitate Dei* (1955, Corpus Christianorum series latina, Brepols, Turnholt).

Beeckman, I.: 1604-1634, *Journal tenu par Isaac Beeckman de 1604 à 1634* (1939, de Waard, C., (Ed.), 4 vols., La Haye).

Bernier, F.: 1678, *Abregé de la philosophie de Gassendi*, 7 vols., Anisson et Posuel, Lyon.

Boyle, R.: 1661, *The sceptical chymist: or, chymico-physical doubts and paradoxes*, Crooke, London (Everyman library edition, J.M. Dent, London).

Bradwardine, T.: 1618, *De causa Dei contra Pelagium, et de virtute causarum, ad suosr Mertonenses, libri tres*, J. Billium, London.

Brahe, T., *Tychonis Brahe Dani opera omnia* (1913-1929).

Dreyer, I.L.E. (Ed.), 15 vols., Gyldendaliana, Copenhagen).

Bruno, G., *Opere* (1830, A. Wagner (Ed.), 2 vols., Weidmann, Lipsia).

Campanella, T.: 1620, *De sensu rerum et magia, libri quatuor* Frankfurt, 1620 (1967, Fallico, A., and Shapiro, H., (Eds.), *Renaissance philosophy*, Vol 1, *The Italian philosophers*, New York).

Casimir (Tolosate), P.: 1674, *Atomi peripateticae, sive tum veterum tum recentiorum atomistarum placita, ad neotericae Peripateticae scholae methodum redacta*, H. Martel, Biterris.

Cazrée, P. de: 1645, *Physica demonstratio, qua ratio, mensura, modus ac potentia accelerationis motus in naturali descensu gravium determinatur adversus nuper excogitatam a Galileo Galilei ... de eodem motu pseudoscientiam ...*, J Du Breuil, Paris.

Charleton, W.: 1654, *Physiologia Epicuro-Gassendo-Charltoniana: or, A fabrick of science natural, upon the hypothesis of atoms, founded by Epicurus, repaired by P. Gassendus, augmented by W. Charleton. Pt. 1.*, T. Heath, London.

Charron, P.: 1601, *De la sagesse livres trois*, S. Millanges, Bordeaux.

1606, *Traicté de sagesse, composée par Pierre Charron, Parisien*, D. Le Clerc, Paris.

Cicero, M.T., *Academica* (1933, Loeb classical library edition, Heinemann, London).

*De fato* (1942, Loeb classical library edition, 2 vols., Heinemann, London).

*De natura deorum* (1933, Loeb classical library edition, Heinemann, London).

*De oratore* (1942, Loeb classical library edition, 2 vols., Heinemann, London).

*De senectute* (1923, Loeb classical library edition, Heinemann, London).

Conimbricenses: 1601, *Problemata quae in Collegii Conimbricensis ... physicis commentariis enodantur ...*, Moguntiae.

1602, *Commentariorum Collegii Conimbricensis Societatis Jesu: in octo libros Physicorum Aristotelis Stagiritae,*

Denifle, H., and Chatelain, E. (Eds.): 1889-1897, *Chartularium Universitatis Parisiensis*, 4 vols., Delalain, Paris.

232 BIBLIOGRAPHY

Descartes, R., *Oeuvres de Descartes* (1897-1913: Adam, C., and Tannery, P., (Eds.), 12 vols., L. Cerf, Paris). *Oeuvres philosophiques* (1963-1967: Alquié, R. (Ed.), 2 vols., Garnier, Paris).

    1641, *Meditationes de prima philosophia, in qua Dei existentia et animae immortalitas demonstratur*, M. Soly, Paris.

    1664, *L'homme de René Descartes et un traitté de la formation du foetus du mesme auteur*, C. Angol, Paris.

    1979: *Le monde, ou Traitè de la lumiére* (M.S. Mahoney, Trans.), Abaris Books, Inc., New York.

Donalson, G., *Fonds latin 11143* (lecturer's notes for a seventeenth-century course in scholastic philosophy, conserved in the Bibliothèque Nationale, Paris).

Du Hamel, J.: 1705, *Philosophia universalis, sive commentarius in universam Aristotelis philosophiam ad usum scholarum comparatam*, 5 vols., C. Thiboust and P. Esclassan, Paris.

Du Hamel, J.-B.: 1669, *De consensu veteris et novae philosophiae libri duo*, Oxoniae.

    1684, *Philosophia vetus et nova ad usum scholae accommodata, editio tertia* ..., 2 vols., S. Michallet, Paris.

Du Laurens, A.: 1599, *Historia anatomica humani corporis et singularum eius partium multis controversiis et observationibus novis illustrata*, Frankfurt.

    1603, *Opera anatomica in quinque libros divisa*, Lyon, 1603.

Epicurus, *Opera* (1973, Arrighetti, G., (Ed.), *Epicuro opere*), G. Einaudi, Turin.

Filelfo, F.: 1512, *Francisci Philelphi epistolae breviores et elegantiores atque adolescentibus magis conducentes ex toto originario exemplari iam denuo transsumptae* ..., Tübingen.

Flannery, A. (Ed.): 1975, *Vatican Council II. The conciliar and post-conciliar documents*, Dominican Publications, Dublin.

Fludd, R.: 1629, *Sophiae cum moria certamen, in quo lapis Lydius a falso structore Fr Marino Mersenno ... reprobatus, celeberrima voluminis sui babylonici (in Genesim) figmente accurate examinat ....*

    1659, *Mosaicall philosophy, grounded upon the essentiall truth or eternal sapience. Written first in Latin, and afterwards thus rendred into English*, London.

Fontenelle, B. le Bovier de: 1686, *Entretiens sur la pluralité des mondes*, Paris.

Foscarini, P.: 1615, *Lettera del R. Padre Maestro Paolo Antonio Foscarini, Carmelitano, sopra l'opinione de' Pittagorici e del Copernico della mobilità della terra e stabilità del sole, e il nuovo Pittagorico sistema del mondo*, L. Scoriggio, Napoli.

Galen, *On the usefulness of the parts of the body*, περὶ χρέας μορίων, *De usu partium* (1968, May, M.T. (Trans.), 2 vols., Cornell University Press, New York).

Galilei, G., *Le opere di Galileo Galilei* (1890-1909, Edizione Nazionale sotto gli auspicii di sua Maestà il re d'Italia, 20 vols. in 21, G. Barbera, Florence).

*Discoveries and opinions of Galileo* (1957, Drake, S. (Ed.), Anchor, New York).

1610, *Siderius nuncius, magna ... spectacula pandens ... quae a Galileo Galileo ... sunt observata in lunae facie ... apprime vero in quatuor planetis circa Jovis stellam disparibus intervallis ... quos ... novissime author deprehendit primus atque medicea sidera nuncupandos decrevit*, T. Baglionum, Venice.

1613, *Istoria e dimostrazioni intorno alle macchie solari e loro accidenti comprese in tre lettere scritte all'illustrissimo signor Marco Velseri Linceo dal signor Galileo Galilei Linceo*, G. Mascardi, Rome.

*The controversy on the comets of 1618: Galileo Galilei, Horatio Grassi, Mario Guiducci, Johann Kepler* (1960, Drake, S., and O'Malley, C.D., (Trans.), University of Pennsylvania Press, Philadelphia).

1623, *Il saggiatore nel quale con bilancia esquisita e giusta si ponderano le cose contenute nella Libra astronomica e filosofica di Lotario Sarsi Sigesano scritto in forma di lettera ...*, G. Mascardi, Rome.

1632, *Dialogo di Galileo Galilei Linceo ... dove ne i congressi di quattro giornate si discorre sopra i due massimi sistemi del mondo Tolemaico, e Copernicano; proponendo indeterminatemente le ragioni filosofiche e naturali tanto per l'una, quanto per l'altra parte*, G.B. Landini, Florence, 1632.

1638, *Discorsi e dimostrazioni matematiche intorno a due nuove scienze attenenti alla mecanica e i movimenti locali*, Elseviri, Leiden.

Garasse, P.F.: 1625, *La somme théologique des véritez capitales de la réligion chrestienne*, S. Chappelet, Paris.

Gilbert, W.: 1600, *De magnete magneticisque corporibus et de magno magnete tellure physiologia nova*, P. Short, London.

Grant, E.: 1974, *A source book of medieval science*, Harvard University Press, Cambridge, Mass.

Grassi, O.: 1619, *De tribus cometis anni 1618 ... disputatio ... habita in Collegio Romano Societatis Jesu ab uno ex patribus ejusdem Societatis*, de Ducciis, Bologna.

Halliwell, J.O.: 1841, *A collection of letters illustrative of the progress of science in England from the reign of Queen Elizabeth to that of Charles the Second*, Historical Society of Science,

Heninger, S.K., Jr.: 1977, *The Cosmographical Glass. Renaissance diagrams of the universe*, The Huntingdon Library, Pasadena.

Herbert of Cherbury, Lord E.: 1624, *De veritate* (1937, Carré, M.H. (Trans.), *Edward, Lord Herbert of Cherbury, De veritate*, J.W. Arrowsmith, Bristol).

Hermes Trismegistus, *Hermetica. The ancient Greek and Latin writings which contain religious or philosophic teachings ascribed to Hermes Trismegistus* (1924-1936, Scott, W. (Ed.), 4 vols., Oxford.)

Hero of Alexandria, *The pneumatics of Hero of Alexandria*, (1851, Woodcroft, B., (Ed.), 1971 Facsimile Edition, Macdonald and Co., London).

Hoenen, P.: 1949, *Cosmologia*, fourth edition, P.U.G. Press, Rome.

Huet, P.D.: 1679, *Demonstratio Evangelica ad serenissimum Delphinum*, Paris.

Huet, P.D.: 1725, *The weakness of human understanding, by the late Mr. Huet, ancient Bishop of Avranche* (Combe, E., (Trans.)), de Varenne, London.

Kepler, J., *Gesammelte Werke* (1938-1959, W. von Dyck and M. Caspar (Eds.), Vols. 1-10, 13-18, C.H. Beck, München).

1604, *Ad Vitellionem paralipomena, quibus astronomiae pars optica traditur; potissimum de artificiosa observatione et aestimatione diametrorum deliquiorumque solis et lunae* ..., Marnium and Aubrii, Frankfurt.

1611, *Strena seu de nive sexangula*, Frankfurt (1966, Hardie, C. (Ed. and Trans.), *J. Kepler, The six-cornered snowflake*, Clarendon Press, Oxford).

1619, *Harmonices mundi libri V. Appendix habet comparationem hujus operis cum Harmonices Cl. Ptolemei libro III, cumque Roberti de Fluctibus dicti Flud ... speculationibus harmonicis, operi de Macrocosmo e microcosmo insertis*, G. Tampachius, Lincii Austriae.

1638, *Admonitio ad astronomos, rerumque coelestium studiosos, de raris mirisque anni 1631 phaenomenis Veneris puta et Mercurii in solem incursu, excepta ex ephemeride anni 1631 e certo authoris consilio huic praemissa* ..., G. Tampachius, Frankfurt.

Kircher, A.: 1631, *Ars magnesia, hoc est disquisitio ... de natura, viribus, et prodigiosis effectibus magnetis* ..., E.M. Zinck, Herbipoli.

Laertius, D., *De clarorum philosophorum vitis, dogmatibus et apophthegmatibus libri decem* (1973, G. Arrighetti (Ed.), *Epicuro opere*, G. Einaudi, Turin).

Liceti, F.: 1640-1650, *De quaesitis per epistolas a claris viris responsa*, Tibaldini and Schiratti, Bologna and Udina.

Locke, J.: 1694, *An essay concerning human understanding*, second edition (1924, Pringle-Pattison, A.S. (Ed.), Clarendon Press, Oxford).

Loyola, I., *The constitutions of the Society of Jesus* (1970, G.E. Ganss S.J. (Ed.), *Saint Ignatius of Loyola. The constitutions of the Society of Jesus*, Institute of Jesuit Sources, St. Louis.)

Lucretius, *De rerum natura* (1937, Loeb classical library edition, Heinemann, London).

*De rerum natura libri sex.* A.D. Lambino: 1563, ... utilibus commentariis illustrati, Parisiis.

Maignan, E.: 1673, *Cursus philosophicus, recognitus et auctior concinnatus ex notissimis cuique principiis, ac praesertim quoad res physicas instauratus ex lege naturae sensatis experimentis passim comprobata*, J. Grégoire, Lyon.

Malapertius, C.: 1633, *Austriaca sidera heliocyclia, astronomicis hypothesibus illigata, opera R.P. Caroli Malapertii* ..., Duaci.

Marolois, S.: 1628, *Oeuvres mathematicques ... traictant de la géométrie et fortification ... corrigées* ..., G.J. Caesius, Amsterdam.

Mersenne, M.: 1623, *Quaestiones celeberrimae in Genesim, cum accurata textus explicatione; in hoc volumine athei et deistae impugnantur, et Vulgata editio ab haereticorum calumniis vindicatur, Graecorum et Hebraeorum musica instauratur, Francisci Georgii Veneti cabalistica dogmata fuse refelluntur*, S. Cramoisy, Paris.

1624, *L'Impiété des déistes, athées, et libertins de ce temps, combattue et renversée de point en point par raisons tirées de la philosophie, et de la théologie* ..., 2 vols., P. Bilaine, Paris.

1625, *La vérité des sciences contre les septiques ou pyrrhoniens* ..., T. Du Bray, Paris.

1634, *Les préludes de l'harmonie universelle ou questions curieuses utiles aux predicateurs, aux theologiens, aux astrologues, aux medicins et aux philosophes*, H. Guénon, Paris.

*Correspondence du P. Marin Mersenne, Religieux Minime* (1945-1972, C. de Waard (Ed.), 12 vols., Centre National de la Recherche Scientifique, Paris).

Morin, J.-B.: 1631, *Famosi et antiqui problematis de telluris motu, vel quiete, hactenus optata solutio*, Paris.

1643, *Alae telluris fractae cum physica demonstratione, quod opinio copernicana de telluris motu sit falsa, et nove conceptu de oceani fluxu atque refluxu, adversus clarissimi viri Petri Gassendi libellum de motu impresso a motore translato* ..., Paris.

1650, *Dissertatio ... de atomis et vacuo contra P. Gassendi philosophiam Epicuream*, Paris.

Patrizi, F.: 1581, *Francisci Patricii discussionum Peripateticarum tomi IV. Quibus Aristotelicae philosophiae universa historia atque dogmata veterum placitis collata, eleganter et erudite declarantur*, Basileae.

1587, *Philosophiae de rerum natura libri duo ... alter de spacio physico, alter de spacio mathematico*, Ferrara.

1691, *Nova de universis philosophia in qua aristotelica methodo, non per motum, sed per lucem et lumina, ad primam causam ascenditur, deinde propria Patricii methodo, tota in contemplationem venit divinitas; postremo methodo platonica, rerum universitas, a conditore Deo deducitur*, Ferrara.

Peckham, J., *Perspectiva communis* (1970, Lindberg, D.C. (Ed.), *John Pecham and the science of optics: Perspectiva communis*, University of Wisconsin Press, Madison).

Peiresc, N.C.F. De, *Lettres de Peiresc* (1888-1898, Tamizey de Larroque, P. (Ed.), 7 vols., Paris).

Pereira, B.: 1579, *De communibus omnium rerum naturalium principiis et affectionibus libri quindecim qui plurimum conferunt, ad eos octo libros Aristotelis, qui de physico auditu inscribuntur, intelligendos* ..., T. Brumennium, Paris.

Pico della Mirandola, G.-F.: 1520, *Examen vanitatis doctrinae gentium, et veritatis Christianae disciplinae distinctum in libris sex, quorum tres omnem philosophorum sectam universim, reliqui Aristoteleam et Aristotelis armis particulatim impugnant, ubicumque autem Christiana et asseritur, et celebratur disciplina*, Mirandola.
    1572-1573, *Opera omnia Joannis Pici, Mirandulae Concordiaeque comitis* ..., 2 vols., Basileae.

Plato, *Timaeus* (1937, Cornford, F.M., *Plato's cosmology. The Timaeus of Plato*, Kegan Paul and Co., London).
    *Theaitetos* (1961, Everyman's library edition, J.M. Dent, London).

Plutarch, *Moralia: De Stoicorum repugnantiis* (1976, Loeb classical library edition, Heinemann, London).

Potherie, A. de la, *Mémoire touchant la naissance, vie et moeurs de P. Gassendi (revu par un membre de sa famille)*, Fonds français (Bibliothèque Nationale de Paris), MS 12270.

Ramus, P.: 1556, *Animadversionum Aristotelicarum libri XX, nunc demum ab authore recogniti et aucti*, A. Wechelum, Paris.

Rhodiginus, L.C.R.: 1542, *Lectionum antiquarum, libri XXX, recogniti ab auctore atque locupletati* ..., Frobenum, Basle.

Riccioli, G.-B.: 1651, *Almagestum novum astronomiam veterum novamque complectens*, V. Benatii, Bologna.

Saint-Paul, E. de: 1609, *Summa philosophiae quadripartita: de rebus dialecticis, moralibus, physicis et metaphysicis, authore Fr Eustachio a Sancto Paulo*, C. Chastellain, Paris.

Sarsi, L. (= Grassi, O.): 1619, *Libra astronomica ac philosophica, qua Galilei Galilei opiniones de cometis a Mario Guiducio in Florentina academia expositae, atque in lucem nuper editae, examinantur a Lothario Sarsio*, M. Naccarini, Perugia.

Scheiner, C.: 1630, *Rosa ursina, sive sol ex admirando facularum et macularum phaenomeno varius ... libris quatuor mobilis ostensus*, Bracciani.

Seneca, L.A., *Ad Lucilium epistulae morales* (1917-1925, Loeb classical library edition, 3 vols., Heinemann, London).
    *Naturales quaestiones* (1971-1972, Loeb classical library edition, 2 vols., London).

Sextus Empiricus, *Works* (1933-1949, Loeb classical library edition, 4 vols., Heinemann, London); *I, Outlines of Pyrrhonism. II, Against the logicians. III, Against the physicists. IV, Against the professors.*

1562, *Sexti philosophi Pyrrhoniarum hypotypwsewn [sic] ... interprete Henrico Stephano*, M. Juvenum, Paris.

1569, *Adversus mathematicos, Gentiano Herveto Aurelio interprete* ..., M. Juvenum, Paris.

Simplicius: (1540), *Commentaria in quatuor libros de celo Aristotelis Guillermo Morbeto interprete*, H. Scotum, Venice.

Soto, D.: 1582, *Super octo libros physicorum Aristotelis commentaria*, 3a editio, Terranova and Neyla, Salamanca.

Stellati, M.P.: 1552, *M. Palingerii stellati ... Zodiacus vitae, hoc est de hominis vita, studio ac moribus optime instituendis libri XII*, Basileae.

Theophrastus, *De causis plantarum* (1976, Loeb classical library edition, Heinemann, London).

Toledo, F. De: 1585, *Commentaria, una cum quaestionibus in octo libros Aristotelis "de Physica auscultatione"* ..., A. Mylii, Cologne.

Valerius, C.: 1568, *Ethicae, seu de moribus philosophiae brevis et perspicua descriptio, diligenter et ordine perfacili explicata* ..., T. Paganum, Lyon.

Vives, J.L., *Opera omnia* (1782, G. Majansio (Ed.), *Joannis Ludovici Vivis Valentini opera omnia*, 8 vols., B. Monfort, Valencia).

Volaterrani, R.: 1511, *Commentariorum urbanorum Raphaelis Volaterrani octo et triginta libri* ..., Paris.

### Secondary sources

Aaron, R.I.: 1937, *John Locke*, Oxford University Press, London.

Anscombe, G.E.M., and Geach, P.T.: 1973, *Three philosophers*, Basil Blackwell, Oxford.

Ariotti, P.: 1972, "Aspects of the conception and development of the pendulum in the seventeenth century", in *Archive for history of exact sciences*, 8, pp.329-410.

1972, "From the top to the foot of a mast on a moving ship", in *Annals of science*, 28, pp.191-203.

Barker, P. and Goldstein, B.R.: 1984, "Is seventeenth-century physics indebted to the Stoics?" in *Centaurus*, 27, pp.148-164.

Berr, H.: 1898, *An jure inter scepticos Gassendus numeratus fuerit*, Hachette, Paris.

Bloch, O.R.: 1966, "Gassendi critique de Descartes", in *Revue philosophique de la France et de l'Etranger*, 146, pp.217-236.

1971, *La philosophie de Gassendi. Nominalisme, matérialisme et métaphysique*, Archives internationales d'histoire des idées, 38), Martinus Nijhoff, La Haye.

1973, "Gassendi and the transition from the middle ages to the classical era", in *Yale French studies*, 49, pp.43-55.

Boas, M.: 1949, "Hero's *Pneumatica*. A study of its transmission and influence", in *Isis*, *40*, pp.38-48.

Boase, A.M.: 1935, *The fortunes of Montaigne. A history of the essays in France, 1580-1669*, Methuen, London.

Bougerel, J.: 1737, *Vie de Pierre Gassendi*, J. Vincent, Paris.

Bradbury, S., and Turner, G. L'E. (Eds.): 1967, *Historical aspects of microscopy*, Royal Microscopical Society, London.

Brett, G.S.: 1908, *The philosophy of Gassendi*, Macmillan and Co., London.

Brush, C.B. (Ed.): 1972, *The selected works of Pierre Gassendi*, Johnson Reprint Corporation, New York.

Busson, H.: 1933, *La pensée religieuse française de Charron à Pascal*, J. Vrin, Paris.

Canivez, A.: 1965, *Jules Lagneau professeur de philosophie. Essai sur la condition du professeur jusqu'à la fin du XIX siècle*. Tome I: *Les professeurs de philosophie d'autrefois*, Les Belles Lettres, Paris.

Charron, J.D.: 1960, *The "wisdom" of Pierre Charron. An original and orthodox code of morality*, University of North Carolina Press, Chapel Hill.

Chroust, A.H.: 1978, "Aristotle's doctrine of the uncreatedness and indestructibility of the universe", in *New scholasticism*, *52*, pp.268-279.

Clark, J.T.: 1963, "Pierre Gassendi and the physics of Galileo", in *Isis*, *54*, pp.352-370.

Coirault, G.: 1957, "Gassendi et non Locke créateur de la doctrine sensualiste moderne sur la génération des idées", in Rochot, B. (*et al.*): 1957, *Actes du Congrès du Tricentenaire de Pierre Gassendi (4-7 août, 1955)*, Digne, pp.69-94.

Copleston, F.: 1946-1975, *A history of philosophy*, 9 vols., Burns, Oates and Washbourne, London.

Crombie, A.C.: 1967, "The mechanistic hypothesis and the scientific study of vision: some optical ideas as a background to the invention of the microscope", in Bradbury, S., and Turner, G.L'E. (Eds.): 1967, *Historical aspects of microscopy*, Royal Microscopical Society, London.

    1975, "Marin Mersenne (1588-1648) and the seventeenth-century problem of scientific acceptability", in *Physis*, *17*, pp.186-204.

    1977, "Mathematics and Platonism in the sixteenth-century Italian universities and in Jesuit educational policy", in *ΠΡΙΣΜΑΤΑ*, *Festschrift für Willy Hartner*, Wiesbaden, pp.63-94.

Dales, R.C.: 1980, "Medieval deanimation of the heavens", in *Journal of the history of ideas*, *41*, pp.531-550.

Damrosch, Jr., L.: 1979, "Hobbes as reformation theologian: implications of the free-will controversy", in *Journal of the history of ideas*, *40*, pp.339-353.

Dear, P.: 1984, "Marin Mersenne and the probabilistic roots of 'mitigated scepticism'", in *Journal of the history of philosophy*, 22, pp.173-205.

Debus, A.G.: 1963, "Pierre Gassendi and his 'scientific expedition' of 1640", in *Archives internationales d'histoire des sciences*, 16, pp.129-142.

   1965,   *The English Paracelsians*, Oldbourne, London.

   1975,   "The chemical debates of the seventeenth century: the reaction of Robert Fludd and Jean Baptiste van Helmont", in Righini Bonelli, M.L., and Shea, W.R. (Eds.): 1975, *Reason, experiment and mysticism in the scientific revolution*, London, pp.19-47.

Detel, W.: 1978, *"Scientia rerum natura occultarum." Methodologische studien zur physik Pierre Gassendis*, de Gruyter, Berlin.

Dibon, P.: 1954, *La philosophie néerlandaise au siècle d'or*. Tome I, *L'enseignement philosophique dans les universités à l'époque précartésienne (1576-1650)*, L'Institut Français d'Amsterdam, Amsterdam.

Dick, S.J.: 1982, *Plurality of worlds: the origins of the extra-terrestrial life debate from Democritus to Kant*, Cambridge University Press, Cambridge.

Dijksterhuis, E.J.: 1961, *The mechanisation of the world picture*, Clarendon Press, Oxford.

Dobbs, B.J.T.: 1975, *The foundations of Newton's alchemy or 'The hunting of the greene Lyon'*, Cambridge University Press, Cambridge.

Donahue, W.H.: 1975, "The solid planetary spheres in post-Copernican natural philosophy", in R.S. Westman (Ed.): 1975, *The Copernican achievement*, University of California Press, Berkeley, pp.244-275.

   1981,   *The dissolution of the celestial spheres 1595-1650*, Arno Press, New York.

Dreyer, J.L.E.: 1890, *Tycho Brahe. A picture of scientific life and work in the sixteenth century* (1963, Dover Publications, New York).

Dugas, R.: 1958, *Mechanics in the seventeenth century. From the scholastic antecedents to classical thought*, (Jacquot, F., (Trans.)), Editions du Griffon, Neuchatel.

Duhem, P., *To save the phenomena. An essay on the idea of physical theory from Plato to Galileo*, (1969, Doland, E., and Maschler, C. (Trans.)), University of Chicago Press, Chicago. *The evolution of mechanics* (1980, Cole, M. ((Trans.), Maryland).

Evennett, H.O.: 1968, *The spirit of the Counter-Reformation*, Cambridge University Press, Cambridge.

Fellmann, E.A., "Fabri, Honoré", *Dictionary of scientific biography*, New York, 1970-1978, *IV*, pp.505-507.

Foster, M.B.: 1934, "The Christian doctrine of Creation and the rise of modern natural science", in *Mind*, 43, pp.446-468.

   1935,   "Christian theology and modern science of nature (I)", in *Mind*, 44, pp.439-466.

1936, "Christian theology and modern science of nature (II)", in *Mind*, *45*, pp.1-27.

Fusil, C.-A.: 1926, "Montaigne et Lucrèce", in *Revue du seizième siècle*, *13*, pp.265-281.

1928, "La renaissance de Lucrèce au XVIe siècle en France", in *Revue du seizième siècle*, *15*, pp.134-150.

Gabbey, A.: 1980, "Force and inertia in the seventeenth century: Descartes and Newton", in Gaukroger, S. (Ed.): 1980, *Descartes. Philosophy, mathematics and physics*, Harvester Press, Brighton, pp.230-320.

Gaukroger, S., (Ed.): 1980, *Descartes. Philosophy, mathematics and physics*, Harvester Press, Brighton.

Gay, P.: 1968, *Deism, an anthology*, Van Nostrand, Princeton.

Geymonat, L.: 1965, *Galileo Galilei. A biography and enquiry into his philosophy of science* (Drake, S., (Trans.)), McGraw-Hill, New York.

Godwin, J.: 1979, *Robert Fludd, Hermetic philosopher and surveyor of two worlds*, Thames and Hudson, London.

Granger, G.-G.: 1976, *La théorie aristotélicienne de la science*, Aubier Montaigne, Paris.

Grant, E.: 1969, "Medieval and seventeenth-century conceptions of an infinite void space beyond the cosmos", in *Isis*, *60*, pp.39-60.

1981, *Much ado about nothing. Theories of space and vacuum from the middle ages to the scientific revolution*, Cambridge University Press, Cambridge.

Gregory, T.: 1961, *Scetticismo ed empirismo. Studio su Gassendi*, Editori Laterza, Bari.

Gusdorf, G.: 1960, *Introduction aux sciences humaines. Essai critique sur leurs origines et leur développement*, Université de Strasbourg Press, Strasbourg.

Guthrie, W.K.C.: 1962-1981, *A history of Greek philosophy*, 6 vols., Methuen, London.

Hacking, I.: 1975, *The emergence of probability. A philosophical study of early ideas about probability, induction and statistical inference*, Cambridge University Press, London.

Hanson, N.R.: 1958, *Patterns of discovery*, Cambridge University Press, Cambridge.

Harré, R.: 1964, *Matter and method*, Macmillan, London.

Hess, G.: 1930, *Pierre Gassendi - Der französische Späthumanismus und das Problem von Wissen und Glauben*, W. Gronau, Leipzig.

Hoenen S.J., P.: 1949, *Cosmologia*, fourth edition, Pontificia Universitas Gregoriana Press, Rome.

Holland, A.J. (Ed.): 1985, *Philosophy, its history and historiography* (Royal Institute of Philosophy Conferences, Volume 1983), D. Reidel Publishing Co., Dordrecht.

Hooykaas, R.: 1958, *Humanisme, science et réforme: Pierre de la Ramée (1515-1572)*, E.J. Brill, Leyden.

Huffman, W.H., and Seelinger, R.A., Jr.: 1978, "Robert Fludd's 'Declaratio Brevis' to James I", in *Ambix*, *25*, pp.69-92.

Humbert, P.: 1931, "La première carte de la lune", in *Revue des questions scientifiques*, *100*, pp.193-204.

1934, "Un manuscrit inédit de Gassendi", in *Revue des questions scientifiques*, *106*, pp.5-11.

1936, *L'Oeuvre astronomique de Gassendi* (Actualités scientifiques et industrielles 378), Paris.

1940, "Une lettre inédit de Gassendi", in *Ciel et Terre*, *56*, pp.14-17.

1947, "Les observations astronomiques de Gassendi à Digne", in *Sciences*, *74*, pp.336-349.

1950, "A propos du passage de Mercure 1631", in *Revue d'histoire des sciences*, *3*, pp.27-31.

1952, *L'astronomie en France au 17e siècle*, Paris.

1953, *Philosophes et savants*, Paris.

Hutchison, K.: 1982, "What happened to occult qualities in the scientific revolution?" in *Isis*, *73*, pp.233-253.

Jardine, N.: 1982, "The significance of the Copernican orbs", in *Journal for the history of astronomy*, *13*, pp.168-194.

Jones, H.: 1981, *Pierre Gassendi. An intellectual biography*, B. De Graaf, Nieuwkoop.

1981, *Pierre Gassendi's Institutio logica (1658), a critical edition with translation and introduction*, Van Gorcum, Assen.

Kearney, H.: 1971, *Science and change, 1500-1700*, Weidenfeld and Nicolson, London.

Kiefl, F.X.: 1893, *Pierre Gassendis Erkenntnisstheorie* (Dissertation presented at the University of Fulda).

Kirk, G.S. and Raven, J.E.: 1957, *The presocratic philosophers. A critical history with a selection of texts*, Cambridge University Press, Cambridge.

Klaaren, E.M.: 1977, *Religious origins of modern science; belief in Creation in seventeenth-century thought*, Eerdmans, Grand Rapids.

Koyré, A.: 1939, *Etudes Galiléennes* (Actualités scientifiques et industrielles 852-854), 3 vols., Paris.

1957, *From the closed world to the infinite universe*, Johns Hopkins Press, Baltimore.

Kroll, R.W.: 1984, "The question of Locke's relation to Gassendi", in *Journal of the history of ideas*, *45*, pp.339-359.

Lakatos, I., and Musgrave, A.E. (Eds.): 1968, *Problems in the philosophy of science*, North-Holland Publishing Co., Amsterdam.

Langford, J.J.: 1966, *Galileo, science and the Church*, Desclee Co., New York.

Leclerc, I.: 1972, *The nature of physical existence*, Allen and Unwin, London.

Leff, G.: 1975, *William of Ockham. The metamorphosis of scholastic discourse*, Manchester University Press, Manchester.

Lenoble, R.: 1971, *Mersenne ou la naissance du mécanisme*, 2nd Edition, J. Vrin, Paris.

Lindberg, D.C.: 1976, *Theories of vision from Al-Kindi to Kepler*, University of Chicago Press, Chicago.

Love, R.: 1972, "Some sources of Herman Boerhaave's concept of fire", in *Ambix*, *19*, pp.157-174.

MacDonald Ross, G.: 1985, "Occultism and philosophy in the seventeenth century", in Holland, A.J.: 1985, *Philosophy, its history and historiography*, D. Reidel Publishing Co., Dordrecht, pp.95-115.

McGuire, J.E.: 1970, "Atoms and the 'analogy of nature'. Newton's third rule of philosophising", in *Studies in history and philosophy of science*, *1*, pp.3-58.

　　　　1972, "Boyle's conception of nature", in *Journal of the history of ideas*, *33*, pp.523-542.

　　　　1977: "Neoplatonism and active principles: Newton and the *Corpus Hermeticum*", in Westman, R.S. and McGuire, J.E.: 1977, *Hermeticism and the scientific revolution*, University of California Press, Los Angeles, pp.93-142.

Mandrou, R.: 1978, *From humanism to science 1480-1700*, Penguin, Harmondsworth.

Mansion, A.: 1946, *Introduction à la physique Aristotélicienne*, 2me edition, Institut Supérieur de Philosophie, Louvain.

Meyer, P.: 1833, "Les manuscrits du Connétable des Lesdiguières", in *Romania*, *12*, pp.336-342.

Mulligan, L.: 1984, "'Reason', 'right reason', and 'revelation' in mid-seventeenth-century England", in Vickers, B. (Ed.): 1984, *Occult and scientific mentalities in the Renaissance*, Cambridge University Press, Cambridge, pp.375-401.

Naess, A.: 1968, *Scepticism*, Routledge and Kegan Paul, London.

Norena, C.G.: 1970, *Juan Luis Vives*, Martinus Nijhoff, The Hague.

Oldroyd, D.R.: 1974, "Some neo-Platonic and Stoic influences on minerology in the sixteenth and seventeenth centuries", in *Ambix*, *21*, pp.128-156.

Osler, M.J.: 1979, "Descartes and Charleton on nature and God", in *Journal of the history of ideas*, *40*, pp.445-456.

　　　　1983, "Providence and Divine Will in Gassendi's views on scientific knowledge", in *Journal of the history of ideas*, *44*, pp.549-560.

　　　　1985, "Eternal truths and the laws of nature: the theological foundations of Descartes' philosophy of nature", in *Journal of the history of ideas*, *46*, pp.349-362.

Pav, P.: 1966, "Gassendi's statement of the principle of inertia", in *Isis*, *57*, pp.24-34.

Pendzig, P.: 1908, *Pierre Gassendis Metaphysik und ihr Verhältnis zur scholastischen Philosophie*, P. Hanstein, Bonn.

Pintard, R.: 1943, *Le libertinage érudit dans la première moitié du XVIIe siècle*, Boivin, Paris.

　　　1943, *La Mothe le Vayer, Gassendi - Guy Patin. Etudes de bibliographie et de critique suivie de textes inédits de Guy Patin*, Boivin, Paris.

　　　1948, "Modernisme, humanisme, libertinage - petite suite sur le 'cas Gassendi'", in *Revue d'histoire littéraire de la France, 48*, pp.1-52.

Popkin, R.H.: 1965, "The high road to Pyrrhonism", in *American philosophical quarterly, 2*, pp.18-32.

　　　1968, "Scepticism, theology and the scientific revolution in the seventeenth century", in Lakatos, I., and Musgrave, A.E., (Eds.): 1968, *Problems in the philosophy of science*, North-Holland Publishing Co., Amsterdam, pp.1-28.

　　　1968, *The history of scepticism from Erasmus to Descartes*, revised edition, Harper and Row, New York.

Rabb, T.K.: 1975, *The struggle for stability in early modern Europe*, Oxford University Press, New York.

Rattansi, P.M.: 1963, "Paracelsus and the Puritan Revolution", in *Ambix, 11*, pp.24-32.

Righini Bonelli, M.L., and Shea, W.R. (Eds.): 1975, *Reason, experiment and mysticism in the scientific revolution*, Macmillan, London.

Rist, J.M.: 1972, *Epicurus. An introduction*, Cambridge University Press, Cambridge.

Rochot, B.: 1944, *Les travaux de Gassendi sur Epicure et sur l'atomisme 1619-1658*, J. Vrin, Paris.

　　　1955, *et al., Pierre Gassendi 1592-1655, sa vie et son oeuvre*, Centre International de Synthèse, Paris.

　　　1955, "Beeckman, Gassendi et le principe d'inertie", in *Archives internationales d'histoire des sciences, 5*, pp.282-289.

　　　1955, "Gassendi et la 'logique' de Descartes", in *Revue philosophique de la France et de l'Etranger*, pp.300-308.

　　　1956, "Sur les notions de temps et d'espace chez quelques auteurs du XVIIe siècle, notamment Gassendi et Barrow", in *Revue d'histoire des sciences, 9*, pp.97-104.

　　　1957, "Gassendi et les mathématiques", in *Revue d'histoire des sciences, 10*, pp.69-78.

　　　1957, *et al., Actes du Congrès du Tricentenaire de Pierre Gassendi (4-7 août, 1955)*, Digne.

　　　1964, "Gassendi et l'expérience", in *Mélanges Alexandre Koyré*, 2 vols., Paris, *II*, pp.411-422.

Rosen, E.: 1984, "Kepler's attitude towards astrology and mysticism", in Vickers, B. (Ed.): 1984, *Occult and scientific mentalities in the*

*Renaissance*, Cambridge University Press, Cambridge, 1984, pp.253-272.

1985, "Dissolution of the solid celestial spheres", in *Journal of the history of ideas*, *46*, pp.13-31.

Rossi, P.: 1975, "Hermeticism, rationality and the scientific revolution", in Righini Bonelli, M.L., and Shea, W.R. (Eds.):1975, *Reason, experiment and mysticism in the scientific revolution*, Macmillan, London, pp.247-273.

Sambursky, S.: 1959, *Physics of the stoics*, Routledge and Kegan Paul, London.

Sarasohn, L.T.: 1982, "The ethical and political philosophy of Pierre Gassendi", in *Journal of the history of philosophy*, *20*, pp.239-260.

1985, "Motion and morality: Pierre Gassendi, Thomas Hobbes and the mechanical world-view", in *Journal of the history of ideas*, *46*, pp.363-379.

Schaffer, S.: 1985, "Occultism and reason", in Holland, A.J.: 1985, *Philosophy, its history and historiography*, D. Reidel Publishing Co., Dordrecht, pp.117-143.

Schiffman, Z.S.: 1984, "Montaigne and the rise of skepticism in Early Modern Europe", in *Journal of the history of ideas*, *45*, pp.499-516.

Schmitt, C.B.: 1964, "Who read Gianfrancesco Pico della Mirandola?" in *Studies in the Renaissance*, *11*, pp.105-132.

1967, *Gianfrancesco Pico della Mirandola (1469-1533) and his critique of Aristotle*, Martinus Nijhoff, The Hague.

1972, *Cicero scepticus: a study of the 'Academica' in the Renaissance*, Martinus Nijhoff, The Hague.

1973, "Towards a reassessment of Renaissance Aristotelianism", in *History of science*, *11*, pp.159-193.

1978, "Reappraisals of Renaissance science", in *History of science*, *16*, pp.200-214.

Schuster, J.A.: 1977, *Descartes and the scientific revolution 1618-1634. An interpretation* (Ph.D. dissertation presented to the faculty of Princeton University).

1980, "Descartes' *Mathesis universalis*: 1619-1628", in Gaukroger, S. (Ed.): 1980, *Descartes. Philosophy, mathematics and physics*, Harvester Press, Brighton, pp.41-96.

Shea, W.R.: 1972, *Galileo's intellectual revolution*, Macmillan Press, London.

Sortais, G.: 1922, *La philosophie moderne depuis Bacon jusqu'à Leibniz*, P. Lethielleux, Paris.

Spink, J.S.: 1960, *French free-thought from Gassendi to Voltaire*, Athlone Press, London.

Stanley, T.: 1655-1662, *The history of philosophy*, 4 vols., H. Moseley and T. Dring, London.

Straker, S.M.: 1970, *Kepler's optics. A study in the development of seventeenth-century natural philosophy* (Ph.D. dissertation presented to the University of Indiana).

Strowski, F.: 1906, *Montaigne*, F. Alcan, Paris.

Tack, R.: 1974, *Untersuchungen zum philosophie und wissenschaftsbegriff bei Pierre Gassendi (1592-1655)*, A. Hain, Meisenheim am Glan.

Thomas, P.-F.: 1889, *La philosophie de Gassendi*, F. Alcan, Paris.

Vickers, B. (Ed.): 1984, *Occult and scientific mentalities in the Renaissance*, Cambridge University Press, Cambridge.

Villey, P. de: 1908, *Les sources de l'évolution des essais de Montaigne*, Fondation Thiers, Paris.

Vorgrimler, H. (Ed.): 1967-1969, *Commentary on the documents of Vatican II*, 5 vols., Burns and Oates, London.

Walker, D.P.: 1972, *The ancient theology: studies in Christian Platonism from the fifteenth to the eighteenth century*, London.

1975, *Spiritual and demonic magic; from Ficino to Campanella*, University of Notre Dame Press, Notre Dame.

Westfall, R.S.: 1962, "The foundations of Newton's philosophy of nature", in *British journal of the history of science*, I, pp.171-182.

1980, *Never at rest: a biography of Isaac Newton*, Cambridge University Press, Cambridge.

Westman, R.S. (Ed.): 1975, *The Copernican achievement*, University of California Press, Berkeley.

1977, and McGuire, J.E., *Hermeticism and the scientific revolution*, University of California Press, Los Angeles.

1984, "Nature, art, and psyche: Jung, Pauli, and the Kepler-Fludd polemic", in Vickers, B. (Ed.): 1984, *Occult and scientific mentalities in the Renaissance*, Cambridge University Press, Cambridge, pp.177-229.

Yates, F.A.: 1964, *Giordano Bruno and the Hermetic tradition*, Routledge and Kegan Paul, London.

1972, *The Rosicrucian enlightenment*, Routledge and Kegan Paul, London.

# INDEX

# SYNTHESE HISTORICAL LIBRARY

Texts and Studies in the History of Logic and Philosophy

*Editors:*

N. KRETZMANN (Cornell University)
G. NUCHELMANS (University of Leyden)

1. M. T. Beonio-Brocchieri Fumagalli, *The Logic of Abelard* (transl. from the Italian). 1969.
2. Gottfried Wilhelm Leibniz, *Philosophical Papers and Letters*. A selection translated and edited, with an introduction, by Leroy E. Loemker. 1969.
3. Ernst Mally, *Logische Schriften* (ed. by Karl Wolf and Paul Weingartner). 1971.
4. Lewis White Beck (ed.), *Proceedings of the Third International Kant Congress*. 1972.
5. Bernard Bolzano, *Theory of Science* (ed. by Jan Berg). 1973.
6. J. M. E. Moravcsik (ed.), *Patterns in Plato's Thought*. 1973.
7. Nabil Shehaby, *The Propositional Logic of Avicenna: A Translation from al-Shifa: al-Qiyas*, with Introduction, Commentary and Glossary. 1973.
8. Desmond Paul Henry, *Commentary on De Grammatico: The Historical-Logical Dimensions of a Dialogue of St. Anselm's*. 1974.
9. John Corcoran, *Ancient Logic and Its Modern Interpretations*. 1974.
10. E. M. Barth, *The Logic of the Articles in Traditional Philosophy*. 1974.
11. Jaakko Hintikka, *Knowledge and the Known. Historical Perspectives in Epistemology*. 1974.
12. E. J. Ashworth, *Language and Logic in the Post-Medieval Period*. 1974.
13. Aristotle, *The Nicomachean Ethics* (transl. with Commentaries and Glossary by Hypocrates G. Apostle). 1975.
14. R. M. Dancy, *Sense and Contradiction: A Study in Aristotle*. 1975.
15. Wilbur Richard Knorr, *The Evolution of the Euclidean Elements. A Study of the Theory of Incommensurable Magnitudes and Its Significance for Early Greek Geometry*. 1975.
16. Augustine, *De Dialectica* (transl. with Introduction and Notes by B. Darrell Jackson). 1975.
17. Arpád Szabó, *The Beginnings of Greek Mathematics*. 1978.
18. Rita Guerlac, *Juan Luis Vives Against the Pseudodialecticians. A Humanist Attack on Medieval Logic*. Texts, with translation, introduction and notes. 1979.
19. Paul Vincent Spade (ed.), *Peter of Ailly: Concepts and Insolubles. An Annotated Translation*. 1980.
20. Simo Knuuttila (ed.), *Reforging the Great Chain of Being*. 1981.
21. Jill Vance Buroker, *Space and Incongruence*. 1981.
22. E. P. Bos, *Marsilius of Inghen*. 1983.
23. Willem Remmelt de Jong, *The Semantics of John Stuart Mill*. 1982.
24. René Descartes, *Principles of Philosophy*. 1983.
25. Tamar Rudavsky (ed.), *Divine Onmiscience and Onmipotence in Medieval Philosophy*. 1985.
26. William Heytesbury, *On Maxima and Minima*. Chapter 5 of *Rules of Solving Sophismata*. Translation. 1984.
27. Peter King, *Jean Burridan's Logic*. The Treatise on Supposition. The Treatise on Consequences. 1985.
28. Simo Knuuttila and Jaakko Hintikka (eds.), *The Logic of Being*. 1986.